SCIENCE IN THE SE OF EMPIRE

Joseph Banks, the British State and the Uses of Science in the Age of Revolution

JOHN GASCOIGNE

CAMBRIDGE
UNIVERSITY PRESS

CAMBRIDGE UNIVERSITY PRESS
Cambridge, New York, Melbourne, Madrid, Cape Town, Singapore,
São Paulo, Delhi, Dubai, Tokyo, Mexico City

Cambridge University Press
477 Williamstown Road, Port Melbourne, VIC 3207, Australia

Published in the United States of America by Cambridge University Press, New York

www.cambridge.org
Information on this title: www.cambridge.org/9780521181365

© Cambridge University Press 1998

First published 1998
First paperback edition 2010

A catalogue record for this publication is available from the British Library

National Library of Australia Cataloguing in Publication data

Gascoigne, John, 1951–   .
Science in the service of empire: Joseph Banks, the
British state and the uses of science in the age of
revolution.
Bibliography.
Includes index.
ISBN 0 521 55069 6.
1. Banks, Joseph, Sir, 1743–1820. 2. Science and state –
Great Britain – History. 3. Great Britain – Politics and
government – 1760–1820. I. Title.
500.941

ISBN 978-0-521-55069-7 Hardback
ISBN 978-0-521-18136-5 Paperback

Contents

1006463983

Illustrations

Acknowledgements

My thanks to those who have helped me in my long association with Joseph Banks have already been largely recorded in my earlier work, *Joseph Banks and the English Enlightenment*. As Banks well knew, the advancement of knowledge requires patrons and material support of the kind which I received from the Australian Research Council and the University of New South Wales. It also depends on academic fellowship – hence my gratitude to the many scholars with whom I have shared my interests and particularly to Patricia Fara and Marie Peters and two anonymous readers for their detailed comments on drafts of this volume (though, of course, only I can be held responsible for the final product).

I am also grateful to Robin Derricourt and Phillipa McGuinness at Cambridge University Press for their interest in and support for this long-running project. As with the previous volume, the accuracy and appearance of the text owes much to the close scrutiny of Jean Cooney and the index is the outcome of the meticulous labours of Alan Walker. Like Banks I have greatly benefited from the unsung labours of librarians: hence my thanks to the many institutions listed in the list of abbreviations (pp. 225–6). Access to copies of some of the more out-of-the-way of Banks's farflung manuscripts was made possible by Mr Harold Carter, former director of the Banks Archive Project at the British Museum of Natural History, whose work, along with that of the late Warren Dawson, has done much to remedy the late nineteenth-century scattering of Banks's papers.

My scholarly career owes much to the influence of my father whose death in 1994 is one of the reasons for the belated appearance of this volume and whose life is one of the reasons that it appears at all. To my wife, Kate, and my children, Robert and Catherine, whose lives have for so long been overshadowed by Sir Joseph, I express my warm appreciation for their tolerant companionship during my long journey in his company.

Brief chronology of the life of Sir Joseph Banks

1743 Birth
1752 Begins at Harrow
1756 Moves to Eton
1760 Matriculates at Christ Church, Oxford
1761 Inherits Revesby estates on the death of his father
1766 Expedition to Newfoundland and Labrador
      Elected FRS
1768 Sails on the *Endeavour* expedition
1771 Return of the *Endeavour* expedition
1772 Withdraws from the *Resolution* expedition
      Voyage to Iceland
1773 Takes over informal direction of the Royal Botanic Gardens, Kew
1774 Joins the Council of the Royal Society
1778 Elected President of the Royal Society
1779 Marriage to Dorothea Hugessen
      Evidence in favour of a convict settlement at Botany Bay before
      the Bunbury Committee of the House of Commons
1785 Evidence in favour of a convict settlement at Botany Bay before
      the Beauchamp Committee of the House of Commons
1787 First consulted by the Privy Council Committee for Trade
1788 Arrival of the First Fleet, Botany Bay
      Helps found the Association for Promoting the Discovery
      of the Interior Parts of Africa
1797 Made Privy Councillor as member of the Privy Council
      Committee for Trade and Plantations and Committee
      for Coinage
1801 Supervises the equipping of the *Investigator* expedition under
      Flinders
1809 Last attendance at the Privy Council Committee for Trade and
      Plantations
1810 Secures an Order in Council granting Iceland neutrality
1815 His Soho Square house attacked during the Corn Law riots
1820 Death

For my son, Robert

Introduction

For good and ill the institution of the State has proved to be the West's most tangible and potent contribution to the way in which humanity has ordered (or disordered) its affairs. Throughout much of late medieval and early modern Western Europe the feudal order, based on localised power owing often nominal allegiance to the international institutions of Pope or Empire, was gradually subverted by the centralising energies of monarchies based on the dynastic principle. As the scale and cost of war increased so, too, the need for more effective modes of raising taxes and exercising effective control over the country's resources increased, prompting the development of larger and more effective bureaucracies.

In the eighteenth and early nineteenth centuries the conflict between the two major European superpowers, Britain and France, prompted both countries to jettison engrained traditions in the quest for greater efficiency in the struggle with its rival. Both countries had to tolerate the growth of larger bureaucracies which inevitably posed a challenge to the traditional forms of localised political power. While in France the Revolution led to a wholesale reordering of the nation's institutions (building in many cases on more partial reforms begun under the Old Regime), in Britain change was more gradual and hence more disguised. But, as Brewer has shown, the machinery of the British State was re-shaped by the needs of war as the collection of excise taxes grew in scale and efficiency over the course of the eighteenth century.[1] In the late eighteenth and early nineteenth centuries the bureaucracy more generally was gradually brought more firmly under the control of the State as it grappled with the problems caused by defeat in the War of American Independence and the titanic struggle with revolutionary France. One major aspect of this more assertive role of the late eighteenth-century British State was a growing insistence on keeping track of public finance – the changing climate of opinion being reflected in the remark of George Rose, Pitt the Younger's close political adviser, in 1799 that 'There has been no period in the history of this country in which so much anxiety has been shewn to inform the public fully and clearly of the true state of its finances, as in the last twelve or fourteen years'.[2]

In the development of that seminal institution, the State, the late eighteenth and early nineteenth centuries – the period of the three revolutions, American, French and Industrial – is therefore of particular importance. It was in this period that the dynastic State gradually gave way to one shored up by more 'rational' institutions and practices which were based less on the demands of tradition and hierarchy and more on the need to exercise effective control over the workings of government. The term 'State' itself which to Elizabeth I had been a suspect word smacking of Dutch republicanism[3] gained greater currency and acceptance as the conduct of government was more and more distinguished from the personal rule of the monarch. The conservative Blackstone defined the State uncontentiously and approvingly as 'a collective body, composed of a multitude of individuals united for their safety and convenience, and intending to act together as one man'.[4] It was a definition which, in good Lockean fashion, emphasised the contractual character of the State, underlining the obligations of the governors to the governed, but it also drew attention to the way in which the State required unity, something which could be corrosive of traditional, more localised sources of power. It was a definition of the State which is not inconsistent with such modern sociological descriptions of that institution as 'a sovereign territorial group' or a body 'distinguished from all other associations by its exclusive investment with the final power of coercion'.[5]

With the growing consciousness of the power of the eighteenth-century State went an awareness of the increasing significance of government. As Paine caustically put it in his *Rights of Man:* 'Almost everything appertaining to the circumstances of a nation, has been absorbed and confounded under the general and mysterious word government'.[6] The terms 'State' and 'government' were (and are) closely linked but can be distinguished since, as the sociologist Ballard defines it, government can be regarded as the 'mechanism through which the state acts'.[7] It was a mechanism which, as Innes has stressed, was available not only to the executive of the State which was principally concerned with strategic and military ends but also to parliament. For, over the course of the eighteenth century, parliament grew more active in its attempts to prompt government to address domestic concerns ranging from Poor Law reform to the reordering of systems of weights and measures.[8]

Despite the frequently reiterated complaints about the growth of government in the late eighteenth and early nineteenth-century, the British State was generally successful (unlike its French rival) in maintaining the loyalties and taxes of its citizens. As Langford has stressed, this owes much to the ability of the traditional landowning governing elite to persuade the growing number of those dependent on commerce that the State, with its respect for property of all kinds, was acting in their interests.[9] It also reflects the growth of a patriotic ideology based on a shared history and religion which, as Wilson and Colley have argued, helped sustain British stability in the aftermath of the American debacle and in its long struggle with France.[10] Nonetheless, those in power recognised the uneasy tension between the British public and the demands of the State. The aftermath of the American War brought with it an attempt to prune some of the more luxuriant growth in public officials and a programme of reform which did help restore public confidence in the efficacy of the State. Though such a reform movement did begin to take root in the often Byzantine structures of government with their strange mixture of the modern and the deeply traditional,[11] the attempt to roll back the frontiers of the State had only partial success in an age which demanded governmental action on an increasing number of fronts. Moreover, the coming of the wars with revolutionary France brought with it a clear justification for the growth of state power. With the end of those wars, however, the cry was once more for 'cheap government' – a demand which, as Harling has recently emphasised, was to a large extent achieved as the expensive military establishment was largely dismantled.[12]

Such an engrained suspicion of central government meant that the British State was denied the resources to deal adequately with the demands placed on it in an age shaped by political and economic revolution. The result was that government officials were often dependent on expert advice from outside the formal bureaucratic apparatus – a movement that gathered pace in the aftermath of the American War as Pitt sought guidance for his programme of national reconstruction.[13] Richard Price assisted with the mathematical expertise required to devise Pitt's Sinking Fund of 1786,[14] while John Palmer aided Pitt in reorganising the Post Office. Sir John Sinclair advised government on the establishment and running of the part-public part-private Board of Agriculture in 1793, Jeremy Bentham gave advice (which to his chagrin was rarely heeded) on penal issues and John Rickman largely organised the preparation of the first census of 1801 before he became a civil servant. Such expert advice was, to modern eyes, often scientific in character with Price and Rickman providing mathematical information or Sinclair agricultural, though the boundaries between science and 'useful knowledge' more generally in the eighteenth century were often very indistinct. What is significant, however, is the increasing interest of late eighteenth-century government in receiving such expert advice.

By contrast, the scientifically-informed 'projectors' whom Stewart describes in the early eighteenth century rarely had such access to the power of the State.[15] It was an indication of the increasing scope and efficiency of the British State that it could acknowledge the need for such expert advice even if the long-engrained suspicion of central government prevented it from appointing its own paid in-house advisers.

While most such expert advisers were consulted on specific issues at a specific period, Joseph Banks – the focus of this study – was drawn into

the workings of government on a continuing basis since he could provide on-going advice to government on a wide range of issues connected
with both science and imperial concerns – the two areas frequently being
intertwined. It is the thesis of this book, then, that his involvement with
government illustrates the more general growth of the concerns and
expertise of the British State as it struggled to deal with the upheavals
unleashed by the American, French and Industrial Revolutions. But the
fact that the British State was so dependent on Banks for advice on issues
which impinged on matters linked with science or, to a lesser extent, with
the expansion of empire also indicates the limitations of a State which
lacked its own officials to deal with such matters.

The responsibilities and aspirations of the State were, then, often
greater than its own formal bureaucratic resources. However, this
deficiency was lessened by a social order based on an oligarchy which
linked the formal institutions of the State with a range of other bodies
including Banks's power base, the Royal Society. Such ties between the
inner workings of government and the larger world of English elite
society are evident in Banks's ability to win over influential figures
holding ministerial office thus creating a conduit to government. For in
a State which still retained many traditional characteristics the exercise of
influence was closely linked with patronage. This helps to explain the
topography of Banks's influence within government with a strong base
at the Privy Council Committee for Trade and Plantations and the
Committee for Coinage, a lesser presence in the Home Office, the
Colonial Office and the Admiralty and a fairly fleeting role at the Board
of Ordnance, the Excise Office and the War Office. Weak political connections or the influence of rivals meant that in some areas of government he played a minor part even in institutions so obviously linked
with the conduct of science as the Board of Longitude or the Royal
Greenwich Observatory. For all his energy and ability Banks as an outside
adviser could only partly shape the institutions of a slowly modernising
British State to his own ends.

Banks's relations with the British State in its formative period during the
age of revolution form, then, the connecting thread through the
different sections of this book. Chapter One traces the changes ushered
in to the workings of the State by the shock of defeat in the American
War and links this with the emergence of Banks as the unofficial adviser
to government on matters scientific or, as one of his contemporaries
facetiously put it in 1791, Banks's elevation to the position of 'His
Majesty's Ministre des affaires philosophiques'.[16] This latter theme is
developed further in Chapter Two which traces the changing relations
between the Royal Society and the British State, while Chapter Three
traces the patronage networks and political connections which made it
possible for Banks to exercise his influence within government. Banks's
view of the proper role of the State in promoting agricultural improve-

ment and national self-sufficiency at home and abroad is the subject of Chapter Four and Chapter Five looks at the institutional mechanisms through which such goals were achieved. The need to deal in detail with many of the projects Banks pursued with the support of government is lessened since they have already been recounted by Mackay. For this study has underlined Banks's significance as an adviser to government by demonstrating the way in which he promoted measures intended to turn such achievements as Cook's exploration of the Pacific to British economic advantage.[17]

Banks's ethic of service to government – which owed much to his strong identification of the interests of the British State with his own class – the British gentry – was also balanced by an acknowledgement that science had an international as well as a national dimension, the tension between these two loyalties being the subject of Chapter Six. Finally, Chapter Seven considers Banks's role as an adviser on specifically imperial issues, an area which the British State more readily absorbed into its inner workings with the creation of the Colonial Office than it did Banks's role as an adviser on scientific matters – an issue not explicitly addressed in the mechanisms of government until the twentieth century.

Banks's career *qua* government adviser, then, highlights the transition from the informal methods of patronage and connection natural to the unreformed, oligarchic constitution to the beginnings of a bureaucratic order based on career civil servants whose first loyalty was supposed to be to an impersonal State. Similarly, my earlier book, *Joseph Banks and the English Enlightenment. Useful knowledge and polite culture* (Cambridge, 1994), attempted to show how in the scientific realm Banks's life marks the passage from the wide but unsystematic intellectual sympathies of the gentlemanly *virtuoso* or collector to something closer to a disciplinary specialist. Not that Banks altogether welcomed such a transformation for it was also part of the argument of that work that he saw the polite and useful scientific culture which was sustained by the Royal Society under his presidency being challenged by the growth of specialist scientific societies in the early nineteenth century.

Similarly, in the political realm Banks generally took a hostile view of developments which might weaken the traditional dominance of the landed classes over the conduct of government. Scientific specialisation and administrative efficiency were goals which he admired in the abstract but he found it difficult to accept the cost their attainment might mean in the weakening of the gentlemanly culture with its clublike connections which was his natural *milieu*. The aim of both this and the previous work has been, therefore, to place Banks in the context of the larger development of the age – whether it be the Enlightenment in its distinctively English guise or the growth of the British State – and to illustrate the extent to which Banks's wide girth embodied some of its more significant features.

CHAPTER ONE

An Expanding State

THE BEGINNINGS OF ADMINISTRATIVE REFORM

When the House of Commons passed the motion moved by John Dunning in 1780 that 'the influence of the crown has increased, is increasing and ought to be diminished'[1] he was testifying both to the increasing distrust of the power of the executive and the ineluctable growth of government. For all the free-born Englishman's hostility towards centralised government as a brake on freedom, the British State was growing in size and competence. Under the spur of increasing military competition with its ancient enemy, France, the British State grew ever more expert at prising taxes out of a reluctant population. Indeed, it was more successful at doing so than its Bourbon competitors, despite the continuing checks on the power of centralised government posed both by the forms of constitutional monarchy and of a continuing attachment – wherever possible – to local rather than centralised government. The maintenance of such traditions of constraint on the power of the British State may in fact have helped to reconcile the privileged members of society to taxes which they could regard as in some ways having been imposed with at least some measure of their consent.[2] By contrast, the French practice of buying off the privileged by granting tax exemptions proved expensive both in forgone taxes and in ill-will from those not similarly indulged.

It was the needs of war that chiefly fuelled the growth of the State, an historical reality pithily expressed in Tilly's remark that 'War made the state, and the state made war'[3] – a maxim borne out by Mann's graph of British state expenditure from 1695 to 1820 (Figure 1).[4]

The growth in the number of government office-holders during the period of the French Revolutionary wars also underlines the same point

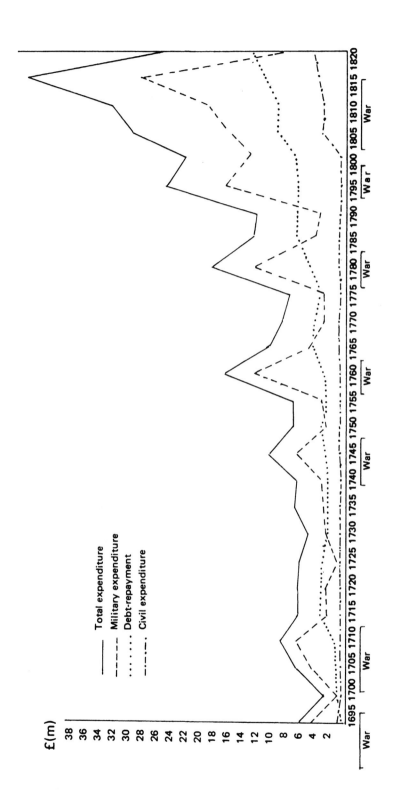

£(m)

Total expenditure
Military expenditure
Debt-repayment
Civil expenditure

British State expenditure 1695–1820 (at constant prices: 1690–9 = 100)

as the government establishment went from 16,267 in 1797 to 20,221 in 1805 and thence to 22,931 in 1810 and 24,598 in 1815; by contrast, after the end of the war in 1815 there was a slight decline, with the figure for 1819 being 24,414 and that for 1827 22, 912.[5]

But, as the machinery of centralised government grew under the stimulus of war, it also served other, lesser functions. The mercantilist attitude to trade which prevailed for most of the century, despite Adam Smith's fulminations, naturally linked the conduct of government policy with the advance of Britain's commercial interests. In a world where trade was frequently regarded as the continuation of war by other means, it was only to be expected that the British government's determination to promote its self-sufficiency and to weaken the economic power of its rivals should impinge directly on the conduct of commerce. And, as government turned its attention to the advancement of trade, so too it was also inevitably drawn into the issue of how best the practical fruits of science could be used to advance national interests. This is a theme with which this work will be chiefly concerned, focusing as it does on Sir Joseph Banks, the British government's de facto scientific adviser in an age when customary certainties were being challenged by political revolution, whether that of the American or the French, and when the traditional pattern of society and the economy was beginning to be transformed by the Industrial Revolution.

In considering the work of Banks in attempting to link the advancement of science with the cumbersome machinery of the British State it is important to bear in mind that Banks was operating in a period when the British State was undergoing some renewal and revitalisation. The hitherto largely unknown experience of defeat in foreign war did, as Baker emphasises,[6] contribute to an undermining of British self-confidence in their own institutions as the spectre of defeat in the American War became ever more real. A bureaucracy that could not provide the means to defeat the untrained forces of the early American republic was plainly in need of an overhaul – a process that began, appropriately, in 1780, the same year as Dunning's motion. Consequently, the suspicion of 'placemen', which had been a staple of opposition rhetoric since the Glorious Revolution, now began to take concrete political form. At the demand of Edmund Burke and his fellow 'economical reformers' – those who sought to reduce the number of government posts, partly to spare the taxpayer but, more importantly, to provide less opportunity for government patronage – Lord North established in 1780 a commission to examine 'the public accounts of the kingdoms'. The inclusion in the full title of this commission of the phrase 'to report what balances are in the hands of accountants which may be applied to the public service'[7] pointed towards one of the fundamental problems with which the commissioners had to grapple and which bedevilled so much of the bureaucracy: that official posts were in fact often largely under the control of private individuals who were barely answerable to government – in some cases passing on such offices as hereditary fiefdoms.[8] Moreover, as the terms of the commission also suggested, such officials often maintained themselves by an array of charges which strengthened both their independence and the outrage of the public.

As so often, an initial enquiry showed the need for further enquiries and in 1785 another commission was established which again grappled with the problem of wresting back effective state control over what were meant to be public offices. Thus the 1785 commission was directed 'to inquire into the fees, gratuities, perquisites, and emoluments which are or lately have been received in the several public offices to be therein mentioned'. As the evidence such enquiries generated mounted, the pressure for reform increased – though, of course, the results were often meagre as the entrenched traditions of patronage and 'Old Corruption' were only slowly replaced by notions of a professional bureaucracy aloof from the political arena.[9]

Nonetheless, the reforming impetus thus generated from 1780 did do something to transform the character of the British State from the 1780s. To some extent at least, government officials became in fact civil servants answerable to the State. One straw in this growing wind was the exclusion in 1782 of government contractors and revenue officials from parliament – an indication that at least the notion of an apolitical civil service was starting to take root, even if the reality often fell far short of this ideal.[10] Another major step in this transformation was the insistence from 1782 that all fees for Treasury officials be abolished and that they be paid directly by the State in the form of a salary; the insistence that government posts were no longer to be considered as private fiefdoms was also reflected in the attempts from 1782 onwards to abolish the use of deputies.[11] The year 1782 also saw some spring-cleaning of government sinecures: Burke's Civil List Act of that year abolished some 134 offices and Pitt maintained the assault on sinecures while Chancellor of the Exchequer, from 1782–3 abolishing another 144.[12]

Paralleling such changes was the monarchy's increasing distancing of itself from day-to-day politics, both because of the damage to royal prestige caused by the American War and because of George III's worsening medical condition. Moreover, one aspect of the financial reforms was increasing parliamentary control over the Civil List and hence a weakening of the Crown's independent patronage.[13] As the king moved more to the periphery of the political cock-pit so, too, public officials were less likely to conceive of themselves as serving an individual king or an individual minister who owed his position to royal favour, but rather gradually transferred their loyalty to an impersonal State or Crown. As Parris writes: 'The departure of the Crown and the civil service from the political arena began about 1780 ... As the monarchy rose above party, so the civil service settled below party. Constitutional bureaucracy was the counterpart of constitutional monarchy'.[14]

Pitt continued to maintain some of the momentum of administrative reform that had been begun by Lord North in 1780 and had been accelerated in 1782 by both the administration of the Marquis of

Rockingham and Lord Shelburne. His own elevation to the post of Prime Minister in December 1783 was an indication of the changing tenor of the times since he owed his position primarily to his abilities as an administrator rather than to any particular favour of the king. Though Pitt was enough of a political realist not to push the reforming vessel too vigorously, his own example as an efficient and incorruptible administrator helped to create higher expectations which were strengthened by a number of reforms over key areas of the civil service. In 1785 he created a treasury commission of audit to oversee that most basic of government functions: the supervision of its finances. In the same year the functions of the Tax Office were to some extent rationalised, while supernumerary posts in the revenue services were steadily pruned with 440 places being abolished between 1784 and 1793.[15] The continuing insistence on the need for government officials to be directly responsible to government scrutiny was reflected in Pitt's abolition in 1782 (while serving as Chancellor of the Exchequer) of the practice of the Treasurer of the Navy having personal control over its accounts together with the requirement that such moneys should be lodged in the Bank of England and be balanced annually.

THE CHARACTER OF LATE EIGHTEENTH-CENTURY GOVERNMENT

These moves, together with other attempts by Pitt to rationalise the collection and administration of state finances (including the moneys paid to the monarchy under the terms of the Civil List), were all instances of a more generalised attempt to create a more efficient governmental apparatus which would be more directly responsive to the demands of the executive. The needs of war and the growth of the State were, in the late eighteenth century, increasingly shaping the complex and often unco-ordinated set of administrative arrangements which had developed over the centuries into something which more and more resembled a 'government'.

Such a government was, as Atkinson puts it, 'an institution which is pervasive through time and space, which is permanent from day to day, which has headquarters but no necessary boundaries, and which is executive rather than representative'.[16] So long as officialdom had been largely responsible to itself, or had been perceived as part of the personal retinue of the politicians of the day or even of the King, it was difficult to conceive of an impersonal State which remained though officials might come and go. The increasing efficiency of the revenue services, and especially the excise service, had, over the course of the century, done something to generate some notion of a government which transcended the individual interests of its officials.[17] But such a sense of an impersonal State was vitiated by the personal loyalties that the ubiquitous use of patronage created. The notion of service to the State was further weakened by the ability of many officers to turn such posts into personal fiefdoms by drawing their income from fees and perquisites rather than a state-imposed salary and by the use of deputies who were answerable to their principals rather than the State they were supposed to serve.

Consequently, however partial and inadequate were the reforms that began in 1780 and were continued by Pitt, they did do something to transform British officialdom into state servants serving institutions which were instruments of government. For a government should be, as Bentham had defined it in his *Introduction to the Principles of Morals and Legislation* (1776), 'the total assemblage of the persons by whom the several political operations ... came to be performed'.[18] Such a government was also one that relied less in the traditional manner on the advice and partnership of local interests which were linked to the centre by the ties of blood and common membership of the landed class. The growth of the machinery of centralised government also meant, then, the gradual replacement of an aristocratic and gentry ethos with that of the bureaucratic expert who owed his position to seniority – or perhaps even merit – rather than to birth and connection. As Eastwood writes: 'Gradually central government exchanged a partnership with the localities for a partnership with experts'.[19]

The need for such a 'government' became ever more evident in the 1780s and 1790s as Britain faced the problems that followed in the wake of the American and French Revolutions and, less evidently, but, in the long term, more momentously, those generated by the Industrial Revolution. Defeat in the American War meant reconstructing Britain's diplomatic alliances and re-organising its pattern of trade now that the captive market of the American colonies had been lost. As the full extent and explosive potential of the French Revolution became ever more evident, Britain needed a governmental apparatus capable of generating unparalleled sums of money and of co-ordinating its armed forces on a scale not hitherto contemplated. That Britain was largely successful in doing so is testimony to the effectiveness of the reform movement which had, since 1780, done much to re-shape the apparatus of government to make it a more effective instrument of state policy.

Ironically, though the reforming tide had been largely generated by the zeal for economic reform, the British State was to widen rather than to contract its domain. Though many offices were abolished, the need for government action over a wider and wider range of activities became obvious – thus making the gulf between the theoretical reach of the State and the practical limitations posed by a shortage of bureaucratic manpower ever more evident. Tasks once left to bodies which were not formally a part of the State came to be regarded as part of the responsibilities of government. One striking example of this was the way in which chartered companies – and above all the mighty East India Company – came more and more directly under the purview of the State. Hence the establishment in 1784 of the Board of Control charged with the responsibility for overseeing the East India Company, a board which gradually integrated the Company into the overall fabric of government.[20] Though the Board of Trade was abolished in 1782, in the high tide of 'economical reform', the need for the State to become more closely involved in promoting and overseeing the country's commerce became increasingly apparent prompting its virtual re-establishment through the back door by the setting up of a Committee for Trade and the Plantations of the Privy Council in 1784. This was followed in 1786 by its elevation to a department of state with the creation of the position that came to be known as the President of the Committee for Trade. It was a bureaucratic resurrection that underlined the inexorable growth of the State.

The activities of the Committee for Trade closely meshed with the scientific concerns of Banks as the symbiosis between the growth of commerce and the exploitation of science – and particularly the imperial uses of botany – became more evident. The involvement of Banks points to another symptom of the increasing significance of the State: the expanding need for expert advisers. The activities of the Committee for Trade, which relied more and more on statistics and the forms of 'political arithmetic' more generally, also indicate the growing sophistication of the State's activities as the range and complexity of its activities expanded to meet the manifold problems of the late eighteenth century.[21]

The Committee for Trade filled another bureaucratic vacuum by becoming ever more involved in dealing with the problems posed by imperial expansion in the wake of the catastrophic defeat of the American War as the loss of much of the first British Empire was made good by the acquisition of new territories. The mounting imperial responsibilities of the Committee for Trade were yet another instance of the growth of the British State and the tardiness of the bureaucratic response to such growth. For imperial matters were not accorded a department of their own until 1801 with the establishment of a Secretary of State for War and the Colonies. Since the choice of territories in the second British Empire was largely dictated by their utility in advancing British trading interests, the Committee for Trade became a central agency in directing Britain's imperial affairs. Here, too, Banks was to play a key role as his unofficial role as governmental scientific adviser was expanded to embrace the field of imperial affairs – especially those that impinged on areas, like Australia, which he had visited.

It was against the backdrop of such changes in the character and activities of the British State, then, that Joseph Banks was to integrate scientific policy into the fabric of government. In the period which coincided with Banks's election to the position of President of the Royal Society in 1778 and his steady advance towards the centres of government power, the administrative machinery of the British State was being gradually re-shaped to make it a more effective instrument of government policy, one that was less subject to the alarums and excursions that accompanied the rise and fall of politicians or the vagaries of the royal

John Russell's portrait of Banks around the time he became President of the Royal Society at the age of thirty-five.
(By courtesy of the Knatchbull Collection, photograph Courtauld Institute of Art)

will. This applied particularly in relation to the State's expanding role in promoting Britain's economic life – an area which closely impinged on Banks's activities in promoting the use of science for the benefit of the nation and, where possible, to accomplish the Baconian goal of working for 'the relief of man's estate'. As a broad-acred member of a landed oligarchy Banks had access to those who held the levers of power and, as a born administrator, he also had a natural affinity with the officials who served them – officials who were increasingly determined to make the creaky apparatus of government work more effectively to advance Britain's interests at home and abroad. Though the administrative machinery of the late eighteenth- and early nineteenth-century British State was still insufficiently developed to provide any formal or systematic state direction for scientific activity, Banks was able to impress some of his goals, both scientific and imperial, on the workings of the late Hanoverian State.

Contemporaries were aware that Banks was carving out for himself the novel position of a de facto science adviser to the British government. Well before Banks's position as an expert adviser to government was recognised by the conferral of the title of Privy Councillor in 1797, the need for scientific advice and Banks's utility in providing it was becoming evident. In 1785, for example, Banks was, as he himself wrote, 'applied to by Government' to recommend a botanist to accompany Commodore Thomson's expedition to Southwest Africa[22] – an expedition prompted by the search for a suitable penal settlement which ultimately led to British colonisation of Australia. Banks himself encouraged the development of such a role, expressing in 1787 the hope to William Eden, Lord Auckland, that if, while in Paris negotiating a trade treaty, 'you have any business in the Philosophical Way you will make me your Commissioner'.[23] Appropriately, it was Auckland who, a few years later, christened Banks 'His Majesty's Ministre des affaires philosophiques'[24] (minister of philosophical, that is scientific, affairs) – an acknowledgement of Banks's position as the government's unofficial science adviser. A similar tribute to Banks's role in linking science with the affairs of government came in 1794 from a correspondent wishing for information on the disposal of the post of 'King's Telegrapher' in a letter which described Banks as 'the very centre of Science in General'.[25]

It was Banks's great ability to draw together the different threads which linked government with the conduct of science. In doing so, he lacked the bureaucratic convenience of working through a single department of government. Instead, he had to co-ordinate a diverse range of government agencies, or bodies associated with government, which offered some scope – however circumscribed – for fostering the discovery or dissemination of what the eighteenth century called 'useful knowledge'. Moreover, despite the often roundabout methods and channels by which Banks had to work, he had sufficient social and political standing to stamp some degree of consistency and order on what we might, with Dupree,[26] anachronistically call the British government's science policy. The growth of the British State and its administrative machinery in the late eighteenth century, then, provided the setting for a merging of public policy and the uses of science. How Banks utilised his position as President of the Royal Society to foster such a closer union will form the subject of the next chapter.

CHAPTER TWO

The Royal Society and the Emergence of Science as an Instrument of State Policy

FROM BACON TO BANKS: THE BEGINNINGS OF A BRITISH 'SCIENCE POLICY'

To appreciate both the extent and importance of Banks's work in coupling together the affairs of science and government it is instructive to survey briefly the way in which, over the course of the previous two centuries, such a potentially fruitful marriage had never been properly consummated. In particular, this chapter will focus on the nature and extent of the Royal Society's involvement with government from its foundation in 1660 – both because the Society was so closely associated with Banks, its President from 1778 to 1820, and because it, as the nation's foremost scientific institution, was the natural base on which a union between science and government might be built.

Some conception of the benefits which might accrue from such a union had been outlined with great eloquence by the Royal Society's spiritual father, Francis Bacon, early in the seventeenth century. In his *New Organon* (1620) he had summed up the profoundly important political dimension of the infant scientific involvement with his maxim that 'Human knowledge and human power meet in one'.[1] If science, as Bacon urged, were to be used 'for the relief of man's estate' then this could only be achieved if such knowledge was put to use by those who controlled society. As Rossi has argued, Bacon's conception of science involved a break with the view that it was the preserve of a coterie of Faustian magi, for, to Bacon, science, to be both effective and ethically-based, should be collaborative and direct its activities towards the common good.[2] But, if science were to be collaborative and directed towards the public good, it required patrons to support such an enterprise and to exploit its fruits. Such patronage might, to some extent, be supplied by the Church or the aristocracy but, if Bacon's vision of a society released from unending toil and misery by science were to be properly implemented, it required the active support of government. In his proposals for the reform of natural philosophy, as in his proposals for the reform of the law, Bacon, as Martin has argued, hoped to promote royal control.[3]

Appropriately, then, Bacon dedicated both his *Advancement of Learning* (1626) and the *New Organon* – his two most eloquent statements of his views on the transforming power of science – to the government in the. person of James I. Moreover, the second book of the *Advancement of Learning* was prefaced by a long disquisition on the importance of royal patronage of learning. But Bacon had little success in enlisting the support of the political establishment of his own day. James I, who was well versed in scholastic learning, found Bacon's whole conception of an ever-expanding frontier of knowledge incomprehensible: 'It is like the peace of God', he remarked, 'that passeth all understanding'.[4]

Portrait of Sir Francis Bacon by John Vanderbank, ?1731, copy.
(By courtesy of the National Portrait Gallery, London)

Perhaps the Stuarts' indifference to Bacon's work arose from more than simple incomprehension. Bacon's vision of a society transformed by science was likely to be corrosive of the established political and societal order since change in one area of society might well lead to agitation for change elsewhere. As Webster has shown,[5] when the crust of tradition was broken during the Interregnum, the possibility of realising some aspects of Bacon's vision became more real. During this period a number of those, like Samuel Hartlib, who saw themselves as Bacon's disciples began to attempt to involve government in prospects for utilising science for the relief of 'man's estate'. Though political life during the Interregnum was too unsettled for such activities to make a lasting impact on government, the work of Hartlib and his allies did help to strengthen in the minds of the Royal Society's founders an admiration for Bacon and a commitment to using the Society for the dissemination of socially useful knowledge.

Despite its links with the King, however, the Royal Society had little success in enlisting the support of the government of Restoration England for such goals. By its nature the Restoration – the attempt which, on the whole, was largely and remarkably successful, to restore the traditional order in Church and State – was resistant to fundamental change. Charles II showed little inclination to act as a patron of science since what money he could prise out of a reluctant parliament was used to support the traditional system of maintaining political order by means of an elaborate court and fluctuating system of spoils designed to keep at bay potentially dangerous aristocrats. Moreover, if government – which, in the Baconian scheme of things, was necessarily science's chief patron – were to form a fruitful marriage with science there needed to be a willingness to promote new administrative forms which would allow the promotion and exploitation of the new science. But the government administration of the Restoration, writes J. R. Jones, 'had a reactionary character since it involved the replacement of a salaried, professional bureaucracy by a very various collection of office-holders appointed through favour and connection, with little or no regard to their capacity and skill'.[6]

The informal links between the Royal Society and government were strong – politicians, courtiers, diplomats, sinecurists and government officials made up 23 per cent of the Society's membership between 1660 and 1685 – but until the King and his ministers developed a system of administration which could actively promote what expertise the Royal Society had to offer such connections bore little fruit.[7]

One partial exception to this generally bleak bureaucratic picture was the administration of the armed forces and, in particular, the Admiralty[8] – a connection on which Banks was later to build. Under Samuel Pepys, the Secretary of the Admiralty from 1673–9 and 1684–8, this department established administrative procedures which (at least by the standards of the day) were considered effective enough to ensure its survival as a permanent department in its own right. Pepys, who was made a Fellow of the Royal Society in 1665 and later served as its President (1684–6), also played a part – along with another representative of the armed forces bureaucracy, Sir Jonas Moore, Surveyor-General of the Ordnance (FRS 1674)[9] – in persuading Charles to establish two scientific institutions relevant to the needs of the Navy: the Royal Observatory (founded 1675) which was intended to supply astronomical charts suitable for navigation and the Royal Mathematical School (1673), or Christ's Hospital, the primary purpose of which was to produce scientifically trained recruits for the Navy. Predictably, both remained woefully underfunded and only barely survived.

In the face of general government indifference, then, some of the projects which the founders of the Royal Society had hoped to promote in order to realise something of Bacon's vision faded into oblivion. Plans of acting in conjunction with government as a patent office were never realised and the Society's attempt to stimulate industry by compiling a history of trades achieved little.[10] As the Royal Society became dependent on its gentlemen members for its finances so, too, it necessarily increasingly reflected the interests and culture of the virtuosi. Its activities, then, were shaped more by those for whom the advancement of learning was regarded as a means of collecting diverting and amusing specimens – whether scientific in the modern sense or antiquarian – than by the sort of programmatic and socially influential enterprise that Bacon had hoped to promote. For, while the virtuosi may have been quite content to see their findings utilised for practical ends, this was an unintended consequence rather than the goal of their activities.[11]

Ironically, Bacon's hopes of promoting a partnership between science and government had greater success across the Channel at the courts of Louis XIV and, to a lesser extent, those other European monarchs who modelled their style of government – and their patronage of learning – on the Sun King. Such absolutist (or, at least, would-be absolutist) regimes came closer than England to developing the necessary financial and administrative structures to promote state-directed scientific research. In contrast to the government of Restoration England, too, French absolutism, at least in its early phases, did involve something of a break with traditions such as the ancient powers of the aristocracy. It therefore provided an appropriate climate for new forms of government action such as those involved in harnessing scientific expertise. The French absolutist model continued to set the tone for the association between science and government throughout the eighteenth century not only in France but throughout Europe generally. As McClellan writes: 'Science and the state were allies in the progressive fights against tradition, cultural inertia, and gross stupidity'.[12] Of course, the activities of the Académie des Sciences reflected the goals of a regime preoccupied with dynastic and military glory but they also performed roles which were closer to the Baconian vision such as the dissemination of new forms of technology. Thus the Académie eventually undertook some of the tasks which the Royal Society had vainly hoped to fulfil, such as the examination of patents and the compilation of a history of trades.[13]

The nearest that England came to the development of a centralising, bureaucratic monarchy along French lines was in the brief and stormy

Visit by King Louis XIV and Colbert to the French Academy. (Frontispiece of C. Perrault, *Mémoires pour servir à l'histoire naturelle des animaux*, 1671). (By courtesy of Cambridge University Library)

reign of James II, a period when, significantly, government began to display rather more interest in the activities of the Royal Society. But James II's unpopularity and his eventual overthrow in the Glorious Revolution further strengthened that opposition towards consolidation of the power of the central government which had already been so marked a feature of the Restoration period. True, the challenge of the wars with Louis XIV did lead to some bureaucratic and, more particularly, financial initiatives. However, for much of the eighteenth century the engrained opposition to any expansion in the role of the central government acted as a brake on any developments likely to promote an alliance between science and the State.[14]

Occasionally the government of the day would look to a President of the Royal Society for scientific advice. Newton, for example, assisted parliament when, in 1714, it established the Board of Longitude as a result of a petition from a group of London merchants and captains.[15] The Board relied chiefly on the honorary services of its members but it had at its disposal the power to grant substantial rewards for inventions which assisted in 'the discovery of Longitude at Sea' and over the 114 years of the Board's existence some £101,000 was expended in this way.[16] Characteristically, then, the English State promoted work on this project, which was so vital for its naval and commercial goals, by the indirect means of issuing prizes to those individuals who developed inventions on their own initiative rather than directing such investigations through state-funded collaborative activity in the manner of the Académie des Sciences. Apart from this episode, the only other notable instance of a President of the Royal Society being consulted by a government in his scientific capacity before the reign of George III was the work of Lord Macclesfield in helping to prepare the bill for the introduction into England of the Gregorian calendar in 1751.

By the time of George III, however, the increasing competition with France, both in war and in trade, was beginning to lead to an overhaul of the traditional machinery of government. As we have seen, such a process began to gain momentum after British complacency was rudely shaken by the novel experience of defeat when, in 1783, the Treaty of Versailles brought to an end the War of American Independence. The period following the American War was one when attitudes to the role of central government began to change. Defeat, largely as a result of government bungling, underlined the need for an effective system of centralised administration, despite all the traditional, engrained opposition to central as opposed to local government. Defeat also provided a climate of opinion conducive to reform and revitalisation of administrative practice – something which was to be promoted by William Pitt the Younger, whose long political ascendancy began at the end of 1783.

This widening of the traditionally circumscribed activities of the British State was to be carried further as a result of the need to cope with the challenges posed by the French Revolutionary wars. Moreover, though the English were to pride themselves on having a night-watchman-State which left economic affairs to the energies of its individual citizens, the economic changes to which we give the name 'the Industrial Revolution', also began to make greater demands on government – especially in an age when mercantilist assumptions still largely prevailed and when the conduct of war and of foreign trade were still close cousins.

This increase in the scope and sophistication of government administrative activity from the 1780s helped to provide the institutional matrix within which scientific considerations at last began to impinge on the concerns of the British State – a belated and very partial realisation of Bacon's conception of science being at the service of society. But it is an indication of what was, by later standards, the still undeveloped state of British government that such scientific issues lacked a natural administrative base, apart from the informal links with government and the Royal Society which developed apace during the reign of George III, particularly after Banks's election as President in 1778. Consequently, the promotion of governmental patronage of science in the age of the three-fold revolutions – American, French and Industrial – was chiefly the task, not of a member of the government or the embryonic civil service, but rather of Sir Joseph Banks, an independent landowner, whose only formal governmental office (and that belatedly conferred) was the honorary one of Privy Councillor from 1797 until his death in 1820.

The wealthy offspring of a relatively *nouveau* Lincolnshire landed family, Banks shared with many of his fellow gentry the tastes of a virtuoso. Like other virtuosi he liked to collect curiosities whether they were from the natural world – such as botanical or zoological specimens – or from the world of humankind in the form of archaeological or antiquarian items. However, Banks shared with many of his fellow landowners not only some of their virtuoso amusements but also their sense that, as a privileged class, they had a responsibility to undertake public office. Early in his career Banks decided – despite considerable local, and also probably family, pressure to the contrary – not to stand as an MP but instead to devote himself to what, in 1788, he described to Lord Hawkesbury as 'the Scientific Service of the Public'.[17]

For, like Bacon, Banks grasped the political importance of science: that it needed patronage – especially by government – to achieve the enormous potential it offered for accomplishing some of the goals of government. In a moment of unintended profundity William Harvey had said of Bacon that he wrote philosophy like a Lord Chancellor[18] – a comment that inadvertently underlined Bacon's recognition of the important political role which science could play. Similarly, it could be said of Banks that his conception of science was that of a Privy Councillor or a senior civil servant: one which looked to science to serve the needs of government and which, although it left some role for what we would call 'pure' science (or what Banks called the 'ornamental sciences', which he contrasted with the 'useful' sciences),[19] did not place a high priority on promoting scientific research in fields which had no obvious application.

Though Banks shared with Bacon an appreciation of science's political importance, the humanitarian goals of Bacon – while not altogether absent – were rather less evident in Banks's work. For Banks, science was to be used not so much for 'the relief of man's estate' as for the advancement of Britain's national interests – a difference that partly reflects the increasing intensity of national rivalries (particularly between Britain and France) over the course of the eighteenth century. Perhaps, too, this was the inevitable cost of translating Bacon's lofty vision into the realm of practical politics: if governments were to be persuaded of the political significance of science, they were also likely to become aware of the advantages to be derived from denying their rivals the same scientific or technological expertise. As President of the Royal Society during the French Wars Banks did defy some nationalistic critics by continuing to cultivate scientific interchange with the Académie des Sciences and its post-revolutionary successor, the Institut National. But, in Banks's mind, this did not involve any breach of his own strongly nationalistic and anti-revolutionary principles – for his aim, as Dupree points out,[20] was to gain scientific advantages for Britain by means of a calculated exchange of information and service.

Banks's rise to become the unofficial minister for science[21] was at first gradual, though it began to gather momentum from 1784 after Pitt was endorsed as Prime Minister in a general election and began to preside over the re-organisation of Britain's creaky machinery of government following the humiliation of defeat in the American War. By late 1784, too, Banks was less distracted by the internal dissensions which had divided the Royal Society over the course of the previous year.[22] The roundabout way in which Banks's unofficial, but nonetheless widely recognised, position of importance in government affairs was achieved reflects the growing complexity and sophistication of British government as it gradually re-shaped its system of administration to cope with the problems posed by the Age of Revolution.

THE ROYAL SOCIETY AS A SOURCE OF ADVICE
TO GOVERNMENT

When Banks first became a public figure in 1771, after his return from the first of Cook's great voyages, virtually the only agency which could provide government with scientific advice was the Royal Society. Though the British government had traditionally not found much need to trouble the Royal Society, this situation was beginning to change by the time that Banks became a member of the Society's Council in 1772. The rivalry of the French and, to a lesser extent, the Dutch and the Spanish, had prompted Britain to involve itself more actively in exploration and this national rivalry had also helped to stimulate a growing awareness of the scientific advantages to be derived from these expeditions. Such scientific information was valued firstly for its potential commercial and strategic advantages but it was also seen as a means of enhancing national prestige – scientific and geographical achievement being another arena in which the national rivalries of the age could find expression. Both these motives are reflected in the opening paragraph of Cook's 'secret' instructions for the *Endeavour* voyage which assert that 'the making Discoverys of Countries hitherto unknown ... will redound greatly to the Honour of this Nation as a Maritime Power, as well as to the Dignity of the Crown of Great Britain, and may tend greatly to the advancement of the Trade and Navigation thereof'.[23]

The *Endeavour*'s voyage – which was prompted chiefly by the British Crown's determination to play a conspicuous part in the multinational observation of the transit of Venus of 1768 – was also an indication of the extent to which national honour was linked with the advancement of astronomy, the oldest and most prestigious of the physical sciences. In his successful bid to persuade the Crown of the importance of Britain mounting an expedition for the observation of the earlier transit of Venus in 1760, the Earl of Macclesfield (then President of the Royal Society) had argued that the motives on which such an expedition should be based were 'the Improvement of Astronomy and the Honour of this Nation'. Moreover, he continued, if Britain did not play its part this 'might afford too, just ground to Foreigners for reproaching this Nation' particularly since the French King was actively involved. Similar arguments helped persuade the Crown to part with £4,000 to aid the expedition of 1768.[24]

Significantly it was the Royal Society which was entrusted with the disposal of the royal grants for both expeditions for the observation of the transit of Venus – an indication of the way in which the Royal Society was beginning to be drawn more closely into the workings of government as the British State began to concern itself more with matters of science. Another example of the same process was the way in which, from 1773, the Royal Society was involved in advising government on the design of lightning conductors to protect royal ordnance depots.[25] The Society's recommendation in 1775 for pointed, rather than rounded, conductors resulted in the royal displeasure since pointed conductors had as their most influential advocate the rebellious Benjamin Franklin. The royal displeasure was further heightened by the remark of Sir John Pringle, Banks's predecessor as President of the Royal Society and a warm advocate of the pointed conductors, that, 'Sire, I cannot reverse the laws and operations of nature'.[26]

After Banks became President of the Royal Society in 1778 the Society was to be involved in an increasing range of activities associated with government, an early recognition of which was a state grant for more extensive accommodations for the Society in 1780.[27] From 1783 to 1787, for example, Banks supervised the expenditure of a royal grant of £3,000 towards the cost of an official geodetic survey of England.[28] Again, as with

the transits of Venus, the stimulus for this project was largely determination to match French royal support for astronomy. For the survey
grew out of a proposal by the director of the French royal observatory
for ascertaining, with a degree of accuracy appropriate for astronomical
calculation, the relative positions of the two royal observatories at Paris
and Greenwich. The French proposal was transmitted via the British
Foreign Secretary to Banks as President of the Royal Society and it was
he who watched over the planning of the project. He also selected its
director, William Roy, a fellow of the Royal Society who had been closely
identified with Banks since he sided with him in the internal dissensions
of 1783–4.[29] In his paper delivered to the Royal Society describing the
early stages of the project, Roy was politic enough to strengthen the ties
with the State by emphasising not only the scientific advantages of the
project but also the fact that it was 'of great public utility, as affording the
surest foundation for almost every kind of internal improvement in time
of peace and the best means of forming judicious plans of defence,
against the invasions of an enemy in time of war'.[30]

The project involved collaboration between the Royal Society and two
separate arms of government: the Army, which provided most of the
manpower for clearing the ground, and the Master-General of Ordnance
(a separate department from the Army until the late nineteenth
century), who provided the more skilled engineers (including William
Roy). The success of Roy's triangulations led to an expansion in the
activities of the Ordnance department to the conducting of ordnance
surveys – though this was an area of government where Banks's writ did
not run, it being largely dominated by 'mathematical practitioners'
opposed to the Royal Society and its gentlemanly ethos.[31] This mapping
branch of the Ordnance department was, in turn, later, in 1832, to give
birth to the Geological Survey[32] – a series of transformations which
indicate both the growing scale of government in the late eighteenth and
early nineteenth centuries and the way in which government was
ineluctably being drawn into the scientific domain in this period.

As President of the Royal Society, Banks also served on special
committees of enquiry requiring scientific expertise such as that which
was convened in 1814 at the behest of the Home Secretary, to examine
the safety of the Gas Light Company's reservoir.[33] Predictably, after the
bonds created by the Royal Society's work on lightning conductors and
the Paris–Greenwich triangulation project, the Board of Ordnance
frequently called on the Royal Society for scientific advice. In 1783 Banks
was asked to investigate the inflammatory possibilities of a new mineral
substance and in 1801 to comment on 'the best covering for the floors of
Powder Works in Magazines to prevent the bad effect of friction'. Banks's
and the Royal Society's knowledge of entomology was invoked in 1803 to
determine 'the best mode of preserving Flannel for Cartridges'.[34] Such
links between the Royal Society and the agencies of government began
to multiply as the business of government became more complex and
impinged more on the realm of science.

The meeting room of the Royal Society in Somerset House, where Banks sat as President.
(By permission of the President and Council of the Royal Society)

Banks was also called upon by other departments of government requiring specialised scientific expertise. Thus in 1791 the Excise Office commissioned Banks to ascertain 'the just proportion of duty to be paid by any kind of spirituous liquor'.[35] Nor would it approve a new hydrometer for measuring the specific gravity of spirits without Banks's approval. For, in 1794, it requested Banks's aid in designing experiments to determine the proof point of various liquors. In 1797 the Office also applied to Banks for advice on the scientific-cum-political issue of persuading the Treasury to part with £200 as a reward for a Mr Gilpin's tables of specific gravity.[36] Similarly, in 1809, the Victualling Office (a branch of the Navy) requested him, in his capacity as President of the Royal Society, to comment on the effectiveness of some newly-invented iron water storage vessels for use at sea. Banks reassured the office that he and his colleagues at the Royal Society saw no increased danger from lightning as a result of such vessels though he doubted their superiority to the traditional casks. He concluded by assuring the Victualling Office that he positively welcomed such an association being 'always . . . ready if you have occasion to apply to me to procure for you the opinions of which my Friends of the Royal Society as are best acquainted with the subjects on which you have need of information'.[37]

The association between the Royal Society and scientific exploration which had enabled Banks to take part in the *Endeavour* voyage was to be further strengthened under Banks's presidency. Cook's third great Pacific voyage of 1776 to 1779, which had as its goal the discovery of the Northwest Passage, was, for example, largely initiated by the Royal Society.[38] Banks himself was to be closely involved in providing scientific advice and in recruiting scientific personnel for most of the major exploratory voyages of the period.

How far he directly involved the Royal Society is unclear though one can assume he commonly sought out the advice of Royal Society colleagues. Certainly he did so when he drew up for the Admiralty a list of appropriate instruments for the expedition in 1818 to the Arctic. The Admiralty, moreover, had sufficient faith in the expertise of Banks and the Royal Society to accept all their recommendations.[39] More fundamentally, it was the Royal Society itself, at Banks's instigation, which suggested to the government the utility of such an expedition to the Arctic. Characteristically, Banks combined the hopes of scientific discovery with the lure of commercial advantage urging the Admiralty to

The *Racehorse* and the *Carcass* under the command of the Hon. Constantine Phipps, off Spitzbergen, 10 August 1773. Drawing by John Cleveley Jun., engraving by Pierre Canot, 1774. (From C. J. Phipps, *A voyage towards the North Pole*, 1774)
(By courtesy of Cambridge University Library)

consider 'that discoveries may now be made ... not only interesting
to the advancement of Science but also to the future intercourse of
Distant Nations'. Banks also invoked the precedent of the expedition
of his friend, Lord Mulgrave, towards the North Pole in 1773 – an
expedition which had also been prompted by the Royal Society.[40]

The government looked to the Royal Society, too, for advice on more
general issues of policy such as the issue of weights and measures which
had been intermittently considered by government since the mid-
eighteenth century. At the direct command of the Home Secretary, Lord
Sidmouth,[41] the aged Banks chaired a committee from 1817 to 1819 to
review Britain's system of weights and measures, a body principally made
up of Banks's close associates within the Society: Davies Gilbert, William
Hyde Wollaston, Thomas Young and Henry Kater. The subject was well
suited to one with Banks's cast of mind. Both as a disciple of Linnaeus
and as a born administrator Banks valued classificatory order and, as a
landowner, was well aware of the muddle that different, locally-based
systems of weights and measures could cause.[42] In terms of scientific and
Enlightenment values the most obvious alternative was to adopt the
French metric system and, at times, Banks and the Royal Society appeared to lean towards it or, at least, towards some system that was
constructed along similar lines. In 1802 he wrote to a French correspondent that

> the Royal Society are well aware of the great importance of an universal measure &
> perfectly ready to adopt such a one whether it is discovered in France in England or
> elsewhere on Condition however that the Principles on which it is Founded are simple
> & sufficiently correct to allow it in case of need to be reconstructed with rigorous
> exactitude in every part of the Globe.[43]

But the metric system, for all its simplicity, was besmirched by its close
association with the French Revolution – which largely explains why
Banks turned against it, despite his earlier enthusiastic advocacy of the
decimal system when it came to coinage.[44] A few months after the
previous letter he expressed his dismay at the way in which the French
had 'fatigued & disgusted the rest of Europe' with 'the new arrangements of weights & measures of time and scientific language'. He therefore thought 'there never was a worse time than the present to propose
an hypothetical improvement which is evidently imperfect to the
voluntary choice of the Public'.[45] Gallophobia probably also accounts for
the Royal Society Committee decision not to adopt the French standard
based on a quadrant of the circumference of the earth – particularly as
the quadrant taken as a standard ran through French territory – but
rather one derived from the amplitude of a swinging pendulum.[46]
Predictably, in the final report, Banks and his fellow committee members
urged that, as far as possible, the traditional system be retained, though
with provision for proper nationwide standards. Such a system, the
report asserted, was 'more convenient for practical purposes than the
decimal scale.'[47] This report, in turn, served as the basis for the imperial

system of weights and measures which was introduced in 1824.[48] It was a measure which indicated the increasing role of central government as local measurements lost their legal status.[49]

As President of the Royal Society, too, Banks held ex officio appointments at the Board of Longitude and the Royal Greenwich Observatory – both government instrumentalities established primarily to aid navigation. Their links with government were further strengthened by their close association with the Admiralty and, in the case of the Royal Observatory, with the Board of Ordnance which met the cost of the Observatory's equipment after the Royal Society had approved such purchases.[50] From 1765 the post of Astronomer Royal was held by the redoubtable Nevil Maskelyne who was to be one of Banks's opponents in the disputes within the Royal Society in 1783–4 between those who termed themselves 'men of science' as against the 'macaronis'[51] – Banks's virtuoso-inclined followers. Though Banks was active in the affairs of both the Royal Observatory and the Board of Longitude, frequently in opposition to Maskelyne, the latter's will generally prevailed, thanks to the support of the professors of astronomy from Oxford and Cambridge who were also ex officio members of the Board.[52] Nonetheless, important ties with the Royal Society remained – the Royal Observatory, for example, was still subject to periodic official visitations from the Royal Society (as it had been since 1710)[53] and it continued the practice, introduced in 1767, of having its reports published by the Royal Society.

When Maskelyne died in 1811, Banks controlled the appointment of his successor – Spencer Perceval, the then Prime Minister, assuring Banks that the post would not be given to anyone who did not have his 'perfect approbation'.[54] The appointment of Banks's protégé, John Pond, as Maskelyne's successor, then, drew both the Royal Observatory and the Board of Longitude more fully into the orbit of Banks and the Royal Society. Banks's sway over the Royal Observatory was further strengthened by an alliance with the Admiralty which took the view, as a resolution of the Council of the Royal Society put it in 1816, that the Board of Admiralty had 'a deeper interest in the Welfare of the Royal Observatory than either of the two other departments of the public Service' (the Treasury and the Board of Ordnance) which had hitherto been involved in its workings. Moreover, the resolution continued, the Admiralty was 'better enabled to estimate the value of the discoveries made there'.[55] Banks's alliance with the Admiralty also helped to smooth the passage in 1818 of an act with the aim, as Banks put it, of 'modifying the Board of Longitude and making it more Effective',[56] something which Banks had vainly been attempting to achieve since at least 1805.

The extent of Royal Society dominance entailed in the new act is evidenced in the fact that three Fellows of the Society – Young, Wollaston and Kater (all closely associated with Banks) – were given stipendiary positions. The Society was also permitted to appoint three unpaid members to the Board. The association with the Admiralty was reinforced by the fact that the commissioners of the Board of Longitude were intended, as Banks's warm admirer, Sir John Barrow, the second secretary of the Admiralty, put it, 'to be a kind of Council to the Admiralty on scientific subjects'.[57] Thus in yet another area Banks's influence helped to strengthen the links between the Royal Society and the workings of the State; the Royal Observatory and Board of Longitude being of particular significance because of their growing association with that all-important agency of government: the Admiralty.

THE ROYAL SOCIETY'S RELATIONS WITH THE STATE

The activities of the Royal Society under Banks's presidency indicate, then, the growing need for scientific advice in a period when the British State was having to expand its activities to cope with the challenges posed by increasing foreign rivalry and rapid economic growth. But the fact that some of this advice was provided by a body such as the Royal Society – which received only very occasional grants from the central government and which proudly proclaimed that, unlike its French counterpart, it was not an arm of the State – indicates the often indirect methods by which the British State had to work in this period. The long British tradition of hostility to centralisation and of distrust of bureaucracy – both because of its expense and because of the opportunity it provided for the exercise of royal and ministerial patronage – meant that many of the tasks that in other States were performed by state bureaucracies were in Britain the province of institutions only loosely connected with the workings of central government. What helped to provide some measure of cohesion for a system of government which worked by such informal methods was the fact that most positions of power from local government upwards were held by members of the landed class bound together by ties of family, education and (at least in the late eighteenth century) a remarkable degree of consensus about basic political values.

Thus, although the Royal Society was not formally a part of government, it nonetheless performed some of the tasks of government thanks to the close ties that existed between Banks and the inner circles of government. In this sense, then, the Royal Society can be regarded as part of that network of institutions which collectively made up the British State. As McClellan suggests, the relations between the Royal Society and the English government did not differ completely from those between the Continental scientific academies and their absolutist governments – rather the character of 'English government itself was different. It depended on a loose, de facto co-ordination among many bodies, in theory separate but in fact linked together by a ruling class'.[58]

The self-image of the Royal Society in the eighteenth century was, of course, otherwise, reflecting a more generalised British chauvinism about the superiority of their institutions in preserving the liberties of free-born Britons – in contrast to the despotism of their Continental counterparts. It is a view clearly reflected in Banks's letter to a German

correspondent of 1785 which waxed eloquent on the distinction between the Royal Society and the Académies of Paris and Berlin. 'Both of
these academies', he wrote with confident British pride in both the prior
institution and superior functioning of the Royal Society,

> appear to have been instituted in Imitation of ours as nearly as the policy of the
> respective governments would allow: they are associations of learned men collected
> together by their respective monarchs, constantly calld upon to answer such Questions
> as their Governments think proper to put to them & held to the necessity of answering
> them whatever they might be by Pensions granted at the will of the Monarch.

By contrast, continued Banks,

> we are a set of Free Englishmen, elected by each other & supported at our own
> expence without accepting any pension or other emolument which can in any point of
> view subject us to receive orders or directions from any department of Government be
> it ever so high ... we have uniformly resisted when our Government have calld upon
> us for decisions.[59]

But when one looks at the actual practice of Banks and the Royal
Society the gulf between the Royal Society and the Continental academies appears much less unbridgeable. True, there was the fundamental
distinction that members of the Royal Society did not receive a salary in
contrast to their counterparts in France and elsewhere in Europe. But
neither did the members of the gentry and aristocracy who very largely
ran the British State both at the level of local and of central government
in contrast, again, with their counterparts in Europe who were much
more likely to be paid officials. Public service, as Banks was well aware,
was something that was expected of a landed gentleman as a return for
his social position and the economic security that went with it. As his
warm admirer, Sir Everard Home, wrote of him: he considered 'that the
services of every man of independent fortune were to be always ready
when his country required them, and should be given free of all
reward'.[60] Unpaid services by the Royal Society and its members to the
State were akin to the unremunerated tasks performed by a JP or an MP.
Both reflected the character of a polity dominated by a landowning
oligarchy which was willing to offer unpaid service in return for
involvement in the processes of government and preservation of what it
conceived of as its liberties.

Nor, despite Banks's disparaging remarks about Continental acad-
emicians being obliged 'to answer such Questions as their Government
think proper to put to them', was the Royal Society markedly different in
being available to provide scientific advice when called upon to do so.
On the contrary, Banks was only too willing to cement the ties between
the Royal Society and government by fielding such enquiries. As late as
1818, two years before his death, he actively welcomed the Society's
involvement in two government commissions – one on weights and
measures and the other on forged bank notes – despite personal doubts
about their effectiveness since 'I did not think it advisable to Refuse my

assistance when calld upon by government'. Banks immediately added, with a comment that underlines his belief in the importance of the Royal Society involving itself with government, that 'I fancy that the Royal Society is Rising in the Public Estimation'.[61]

Indeed, Banks's complaint was generally not that the Royal Society was at the beck and call of the State but rather that the government, because of its financial parsimony and reluctance to value expert advice, took too little account of the Royal Society and science in general. Thus he complained to Lord Liverpool of Pitt's neglect of science and bemoaned the Treasury's scanty support in matters related to science. It was a complaint echoed by his close Royal Society colleague, Richard Kirwan, who welcomed his appointment in 1797 as a Privy Councillor as an overdue mark of respect for science itself. For, wrote Kirwan: 'Science in its present abject state required that Government, & particularly good Kings, sh[oul]d shew that they held it a good Title for constitutional distinction.'[62]

And, for all his encomiums on the liberty of the Royal Society, Banks looked with some jealousy on the financial support and official recognition which some Continental academies received. A letter by Banks of around 1781 urging on government the need for larger quarters for the Royal Society contrasted English parsimony in support of science with relative Continental opulence:

> the Academies of the Nations who are our Rivals in Sciences are cherished by their respective Governments at an expence which to their Lordships may ... appear incredible. The Royal Academy of Sciences at Paris have Elegant & spacious apartments ... & Berlin & Petersburg & c the Flourishing Academies are in like manner maintained at Considerable expence.[63]

One strong reason for providing government with assistance was that it gave the Royal Society greater leverage in prising funds out of a reluctant State. In 1822, two years after Banks's death, the Council of the Royal Society attempted to use such an argument to persuade the Treasury to provide additional accommodation for the Society. Thus it argued that 'various matters of great national importance as well as those which more exclusively belong to the general interests of Science are frequently brought before them'.[64]

The association between the Royal Society and the British State which Banks did much to strengthen was, then, marked by the same reliance on voluntary public service and the use of informal contacts that characterised so many other branches of the workings of government. The Royal Society was linked by numerous ties of friendship and class solidarity with the inner core of government and hence was available to provide advice as required without the need for an institutionalised bureaucracy. It was, indeed, a role that the Royal Society continued to fulfil in British society into the twentieth century. Even by 1915, writes Alter, 'the Royal Society had not yet fully given up its function as an unofficial advisory board for the government'.[65]

But for all the flexibility that such a relationship provided the lack of a more permanent and secure partnership between the Royal Society and the State meant that the Society had to tolerate scanty financial assistance and considerable fluctuations in political support for science. It was a situation that contrasted with France where government was taking an increasing interest in science and beginning to draw it into its bureaucratic processes.[66] This was most obviously true at the level of the relations between the Académie des Sciences and its post-revolutionary equivalent, the Institut National, but it also applied to much of the bureaucratic machinery of government where scientific concerns were institutionalised into the more general formulation of policy.[67] In Britain a relatively smaller and less professionalised bureaucracy impeded such a transformation but it was Banks's achievement at least to set such a process in train. That this task fell to an unpaid landed gentleman with only a rather tenuous formal connection with the apparatus of government underlines again some of the important differences between the functioning of the French and British States.

Banks's official position as President of the Royal Society, then, provided him with an official platform on which to build closer ties between science and government. However, Banks was to take this union further by developing links with particular bureaucratic departments and by involving himself actively in their workings. Despite such close links with government, Banks's self-image was that of one who remained chastely aloof from the hurly-burly of party machinations in return for being allowed to exercise some scientific influence. As he primly wrote to a French correspondent: 'The ministers of my Government sometimes allow me to influence their final decisions in matters of science; but it is an implied Compact between them and me that I am never to intermeddle with their opinions'.[68]

But, while it was true that Banks generally avoided the more overt manifestations of party politics, bureaucratic influence was, necessarily, purchased by political alliances. It is the purpose of the next chapter, then, to examine how such alliances were formed and how it was that Banks was able to build on his work as President of the Royal Society in order to construct a wider scientific edifice which encompassed the inner workings of the British State.

CHAPTER THREE

The Levers of Power

THE SANDWICH CONNECTION

Banks's rise to the position which Lord Auckland humorously referred to as 'Ministre des affaires philosophiques',[1] the de facto minister of science, required political alliances – alliances which could transform his aspirations for science into the common coin of government business. Such alliances drew Banks into the administrative workings of a State which was expanding its activities and reponsibilities, if not the bureaucratic structures needed to cope with such business adequately. Indeed, Banks's increasing involvement in the affairs of government was an indication of the underdeveloped nature of its administrative machinery as Banks – a landed gentleman of independent means – was more and more pressed into service in roles which in a later age were to be the province of professional civil servants. In this chapter, then, we turn to the question of how Banks amassed the political capital which he was able to invest so profitably in integrating science with the mechanisms of government.

How, then, did Banks, the offspring of a wealthy but relatively *nouveau* Lincolnshire landed family come to assume the position of the trusted adviser of the King and many of his chief ministers? Sheer ability and industry and, as time went on, proven competence played a major role once Banks had established himself within the inner recesses of government. But there still remains the question of how Banks first came to royal and governmental notice as someone who could provide expert advice on a range of scientific and imperial issues, something which the British State had increasing need as its tradition-bound bureaucratic apparatus struggled to keep pace with the problems generated by the American, French and Industrial Revolutions.

In an age when the fabric of political life was woven from patron-client relations, any consideration of Banks's political allegiances must begin by an examination of his early patrons of whom the most significant was John Montagu, the fourth Earl of Sandwich. Banks appears to have been first drawn to Sandwich by the simple accident that they were near neighbours when Banks was living at his mother's house on the Thames at Chelsea; both, moreover, were keen anglers.[2] Their friendship was strengthened by their joint participation in the pleasures of the world of the elite *demi-monde*, and the amiable relations they enjoyed with each other's mistresses. We find, for example, Banks in 1775 asking Sandwich to pass on 'my best respects to Miss Ray [Sandwich's mistress] & a thousand thanks to her for being my Friend'.[3] Banks and Sandwich were both clubbable and gregarious in nature for though, *qua* politician, Sandwich inspired fierce hatreds, he was plainly an agreeable companion. The linguist, William Jones, whose politics were quite opposed to those of Sandwich nonetheless wrote of him that he was 'a wonderfully pleasant man in society; he is quite what the French call *aimable*, and possesses to a high degree the art of putting all around him at their

John Montagu, fourth Earl of Sandwich. Canvas after John Zoffany c.1763.
(By courtesy of the National Portrait Gallery, London)

ease'.[4] Sandwich, then, was very much at home in the clubbable world of the London learned societies – something which further strengthened his friendship with Banks, since both were members of the Royal Society and the Society of Dilettanti.

In a world where political power depended on the good will of patrons Banks's friendship with Sandwich helped to open many governmental doors. This was particularly true of the Admiralty with which Sandwich's political career was closely associated since he served as first Lord of the Admiralty for three terms: from 1748 to 1751, from April to September 1763 and, most significantly, from 1771 to 1782. Under his politically astute management the British Navy was to increase in size and competence[5] – a transformation which reflects the more general growth of the machinery of the late eighteenth-century British State. It was Sandwich who appears to have cleared the way for Banks's participation in the *Niger* expedition to Labrador and Newfoundland in 1766 and, more momentously, the great *Endeavour* voyage of 1768 to 1771.[6] In doing so Sandwich helped to forge that tradition of combining scientific enquiry with naval exploration which, in the nineteenth century, was to produce such epoch-making voyages as those of the *Beagle*, the *Rattlesnake* and the *Challenger*. As one of Banks's obituarists wrote of Sandwich: 'This nobleman patronised all Mr. Banks's plans, supported him in all his schemes for the advancement of his favourite study, and finally enabled him to carry his measures into execution'.[7]

Such an encomium does, however, overlook the fact that Sandwich's support for Banks's scientific voyaging fell short of allowing Banks to re-order Cook's second great voyage (on the *Resolution*) to accommodate his greatly expanded scientific entourage. Such an attempt for a civilian to take control of a naval expedition was too much for the Admiralty to swallow and Sandwich, for all his friendship for Banks and sympathy for his scientific objectives, ultimately put his public duty before his private affections. Hence his blistering description of Banks's actions in a letter which Sandwich had prepared if Banks should attempt to make the matter one of public controversy:

> Mr. Banks seems throughout to consider the Ship as fitted out wholly for his use; the whole undertaking to depend on him and his People; and himself as the Director and Conductor of the whole; for which he is not qualified, and if granted to him would have been the greatest Disgrace that could be put on His Majesty's Naval Officers.[8]

Nonetheless, Sandwich remained committed to the marriage between science and naval exploration, writing to the Prime Minister, Lord North, to urge him to include that prickly polymath, Johann Reinhold Forster, on the expedition.[9] Ironically, it appears to have been Sandwich who first encouraged Banks to contemplate a second major voyage – something to which Banks reproachfully alluded in his letter to Sandwich announcing his withdrawal from the expedition:

When it was first proposd to me by your Lordship to go to the South Seas again if his Majesty should think proper to send ships to perfect the discoveries that had been begun in the last voyage, I Joyfully Embracd a proposal of all others the best suited to my dispositions and pursuits.[10]

And, despite the *Resolution* debacle, Sandwich continued to urge Banks to apply himself to the cause of scientific exploration. Thus he encouraged Banks to consider alternative voyages, writing that he hoped 'that for the advantage of the curious part of Mankind, your zeal for distant voyages wil not yet cease' – although he did add that 'I would advise you in order to insure that success to fit out a ship yourself; that and only that can give you the absolute command of the whole Expedition'.[11] It may well have been Sandwich, too, in his capacity as the major power-broker within the East India Company,[12] who lay behind what Banks referred to as 'several overtures from the East India Company who seemd inclind to send me on the same kind of voyage next spring'[13] – a scheme which never eventuated.

The friendship between Banks and Sandwich survived the contretemps over the *Resolution* and the two men continued to work together to promote the cause of exploration and science in general, thus establishing Banks's credentials as the government's chief adviser on matters to do with exploration.[14] Thus Sandwich looked to Banks for scientific advice on some of the outcomes of Cook's second voyage deferring, in a letter to the King, to his opinion that the 'seed of the remarkable flax plant in New Zealand' should be planted as soon as possible. Sandwich also enthusiastically joined with Banks in welcoming the Tahitian visitor, Omai, who returned with Cook and was introduced to the King with Banks acting as interpreter.[15] When the botanist, John Ellis, attempted to interest the British government in the imperial uses of the Tahitian breadfruit it was naturally to Sandwich, as a patron of exploration, that he turned. His pamphlet on the subject was therefore dedicated to Sandwich in acknowledgement for 'the zeal, my Lord, with which you have seconded his Majesty's intentions, to promote the honour and the happiness of his subjects, in the late important enterprises for disovery'.[16] Appropriately, it was Banks who was largely to bring this project to fruition.

Within the micro-politics of the Royal Society, too, Sandwich was a loyal ally to Banks. A letter to Sandwich from his client, Charles Burney, which speaks of his 'canvassing for Mr.Banks' among his acquaintances within the Royal Society indicates that Sandwich used his well-honed skills as a political manager on Banks's behalf to help him to secure the presidency.[17] Significantly, too, it was Sandwich who, in December 1778, arranged for Banks to be presented to George III following Banks's election as President of the Royal Society.[18] A few days later the records of the Society of Dilettanti indicate that the relations between the two men exhibited their customary bonhomie: 'Ld Sandwich and Mr. Banks having calld this respectable society by the disrespectful name of

Club were fin[e]d a bumper each which they drank with all proper humility'.[19]

Banks's friendship with Sandwich naturally made him a target for those seeking to enlist the support of the Admiralty. Hence Jeremy Bentham's advice to his brother, Samuel, a naval architect, that he should suggest to Banks's old travelling companion, Dr James Lind, that 'it might be in Banks's power to be of service to me, by means of the interest he has with Ld Sandwich'.[20] Later that same year, another of Banks's travelling companions, James Matra, looked to Banks to 'renew Your influence with Ld Sandwich in my behalf'.[21] But, as Banks recognised, his influence with Sandwich was limited by the fact that Banks had deliberately eschewed involvement in party politics and hence could not repay Sandwich in the political currency basic to the unreformed constitution. As Banks wrote to Sandwich when requesting that he appoint a friend to a government position:

> I am thoroughly sensible that I have no claim of any kind either in present or future to be of use in any political line therefore depending only on private intimacy I cannot expect to be preferrd to those who can be useful in both capacities.[22]

Nonetheless, Sandwich continued to act upon Banks's behalf when an opportunity arose to advance his scientific interests. He probably also helped to cement the friendship between Banks and the King from which so much of Banks's political influence derived. Sandwich, as Cook's patron, kept Banks closely informed of the progress of Cook's third voyage for, as Banks later wrote to Cook's biographer, at that time the two men 'livd in habits of great intimacy'.[23] Following the return of the *Resolution* in 1780 from Cook's ill-fated third voyage, Sandwich deferred to Banks in dismissing one of its gardeners and in making arrangements for the publication of the journals commenting that 'your advice will be of great use to me in the conduct of this matter'.[24] This association carried on the long-standing co-operation between the two men in promoting the dissemination of Cook's findings. Indeed, it was Sandwich who had arranged for Hawkesworth to write his account of Cook's first voyage which depended heavily on Banks's journal. Hence Hawkesworth's thanks to Sandwich for 'your Lordship's powerfull Influence with Mr. Banks for the use of his Journal'.[25]

After Sandwich's fall from office in March 1782 as one of the scapegoats for the defeat in the disastrous American War, the friendship between the two men continued; inevitably, however, Banks, by then an established figure at court, no longer looked to Sandwich as a political patron. Sandwich and Banks continued to work together on preparing an edition of Cook's journals from the third voyage but the once-influential Sandwich had now to be cautious in his dealings with government. As he wrote to Banks in September 1782 about arrangements for the printer: 'all my feelings in these minute parts of the business are to give as little umbrage as possible to those who have authority in their hands'.[26]

Before this political eclipse, however, Sandwich appears to have served not only to promote Banks's connection with the great and powerful from the King downwards, but also in making the political establishment more sympathetic to the goals of scientific exploration with which Banks became so closely associated. It was Sandwich who, as Kippis – Cook's first biographer – wrote, was 'the great patron of our navigator and the principal mover in his mighty undertakings'.[27] It was while Sandwich was first Lord of the Admiralty, too, that Constantine Phipps, a mutual friend of Banks and Sandwich, undertook his exploration of the Arctic region in the *Racecourse* expedition of 1773. Sandwich's assistance in promoting this expedition resulted in a vote of thanks from the Council of the Royal Society 'for his great readiness in promoting all matters of science recommended to him on the part of the Council; and particularly for his Lordship's assistance respecting the late expedition to explore the circumpolar regions'.[28]

Appropriately, Sandwich was also among those active in exploring the possibility of new settlements to serve British imperial interests – an indication of the way in which the late eighteenth-century British State was expanding its domain abroad as well as at home. Sandwich was involved in the discussions about a proposed settlement at Madagascar.[29] When this plan was scuttled because it infringed on the trading interests of the East India Company, Sandwich appears to have joined Banks and Mulgrave together with Sir George Young[30] and James Matra in proposing a settlement at Botany Bay.[31] Such schemes for the expansion of empire also took the more traditional forms of support for military conquest – Sandwich being an early patron of Clive and one of the major voices in the East India Company when it was consolidating its hold on the subcontinent at the expense of the French.[32]

Sandwich's strong commitment to the defence of the imperial gains made by Britain in the Seven Years War and his belief that the Empire could act as a source of revenue and hence power for Britain came out clearly in the strategy he urged during the War of American Independence. Hence he argued for making the defence and, if possible, the expansion of British power in the West Indies – the economic jewel in the imperial crown – a primary goal of British naval strategy. It was a strategy in which he had the support of the King who wrote to him in 1779 that 'if we lose our Sugar Islands it will be impossible to raise Money to continue the War and then no Peace can be obtained but such a one as He that gave one to Europe in 1763 never can subscribe to'.[33] It was a strategy that ultimately proved successful with Admiral Rodney's great victory at the Battle of the Saintes in February 1782 establishing British naval supremacy in the Caribbean.[34] However, the fruits of his strategy came too late for Sandwich who by then had been driven from office.

Sandwich's imperial designs were also reflected in the plans advanced by his close associate, the virtuoso, Daines Barrington. Thus Barrington wrote to Sandwich in 1779 suggesting that:

if we should soon get possession of any of the French sugar islands the white
inhabitants should be removed and the island delivered up to the Negroes with whom
we might afterwards form an alliance.[35]

It was appropriate that Barrington turned to Sandwich in 1774 in order
to promote further exploration of the Arctic by Sandwich's client,
Constantine Phipps, in order to benefit both science and, more spec-
ulatively, British trade routes.[36] This commitment to an expansion of
empire, both by scientific exploration and the use of force, which
Sandwich did so much to promote, left its mark on Banks's outlook. It
also coloured the Admiralty culture in which Banks had to operate so
that voyages of discovery were generally linked in some way to the
struggle with France for world dominance.

The link between Banks and Sandwich was strengthened by the fact
that both were close friends with Phipps (from 1775 Lord Mulgrave),
a contemporary of Banks at Eton. In the manner of the British
Establishment Banks's friendship with this old Eton chum helped open
many political doors since Phipps's long and varied political career
embraced service on the Admiralty Board (1772–82), the Privy Council
(from 1784), the Privy Council Committee for Trade (1784–6) and the
Board of Control (1784–91). Banks played an active role in promoting
Phipps's early political career using his influence both as a Lincolnshire
landowner and as a client of Sandwich on his behalf. Banks was closely
involved in the political manoeuvring that accompanied Mulgrave's
entry into parliament and subsequent shifts of allegiance – so much so
that it suggests that Banks as a young man was not as averse to party
politics as he later became. Indeed, he may even have flirted with the
idea of a political career before such notions were eradicated by his
election as President of the Royal Society in 1778 – for Banks regarded
this post as incompatible with parliamentary politics.

When Phipps (Mulgrave) stood as MP for Lincoln City in 1768 Banks
intervened promptly sending orders to his steward to support Phipps by
canvassing local freemen and sending them to the poll.[37] Such an intervention, the steward informed Banks, proved decisive: 'Your Interest was
of vast service to Mr. Phipps, and without it he must inevitably have lost
his Election'.[38] Phipps was appropriately grateful expressing to Banks his
'most sincere thanks for your assistance'.[39] Banks's support no doubt
chiefly derived from personal friendship rather than a strong commitment to Phipps's political views. Nonetheless, Phipps's description of
himself at the time of the election as being a supporter of the
government 'as far as I could consistently with the Feelings of an honest,
and the Character of an independent Man'[40] probably mirrored Banks's
own. After becoming an MP, however, Phipps came to ally himself with
the opposition and the cause of reform. This was to contrast con-
spicuously with his later reputation as a supporter of the government and
an opponent of parliamentary reform.[41]

For, from 1774, Phipps's opposition sympathies began to wane as he
was drawn more and more into the political orbit of Sandwich – a

Constantine Phipps, first Lord Mulgrave. (From H. B.
Wheatley (ed.), *Historical and posthumous memoirs of Sir
N. W. Wraxall*, III, facing p. 400)
(By courtesy of Cambridge University Library)

transformation which may have owed something to Sandwich's support
for his Arctic exploration of 1773. In February 1774 Horace Walpole
expressed his surprise that in the debate on the Navy estimates 'it was
remarkable ... that Captain Phipps, generally an opponent, made a high
panegyric on Lord Sandwich'.[42] But Phipps still remained wary and even
contemptuous of Sandwich's skills as a borough-monger. In September
1774 he described Sandwich to Banks's scientific lieutenant, Charles
Blagden,[43] as 'an excellent county Canvasser & equal to the Management
of a small Borough both [of] which are conducted by the same means[:]
the finding out which will serve i.e. corrupt a few'. One of the chief
figures attempting to push Mulgrave more securely into the political
arms of Sandwich was Banks. In the same letter to Blagden Mulgrave
refers to meeting him at Sandwich's seat at Hinchingbrook where his
behaviour 'was like what I have always experienced from Him on every
Occasion in the Course of a long & uninterrupted Friendship'.[44]

When Phipps failed to be elected in late 1774 the pressure to align
himself with Sandwich increased, with Banks acting as the go-between.
In August 1775 we find Banks writing to Sandwich while a guest at the

house of Lord Mulgrave (as Phipps became after his father's death in that same year), reporting that 'he has by no means engagd himself in the way your Lordship thought he had when I last had the honour of conversing with you upon the subject'.[45] But within a few weeks Banks had better news and could report to Sandwich that 'I am sure he is well inclind to Government & particularly loud in his applauses of the present measures pursued in american affairs' and that 'in most other points also he speaks favourably of Government'.[46] And, soon afterwards, Banks was able to write that I 'am much rejoic'd to hear of the determinations he [Mulgrave] has taken with regard to your Lordship' and offering 'if it was thought proper [to] Canvass for him & pay the expences of the election'.[47]

Mulgrave's relations with Sandwich later became rather strained when he declined to support the Fox-North coalition (April–December 1783) with the result that Mulgrave moved from the seat of Huntingdon (which was in the gift of Sandwich) to Newark in 1784. Banks vainly attempted to interest Mulgrave in the seat of Boston, an offer which he declined leaving Banks feeling 'injurd' and disillusioned with local politics – so much so, indeed, that he declared 'in matters of election I shall never more interfere'.[48] Thereafter, Mulgrave resumed his more customary role as a member of the government by providing early and enthusiastic support for Pitt. The Prime Minister promptly rewarded Mulgrave for his support by appointing him to the lucrative post of Paymaster General in 1784[49] – a post he held until promoted from the Irish to the English peerage (and hence to the House of Lords) in 1791, a year before his death.

Banks's long-standing connection with Mulgrave was of lasting political benefit, particularly since Mulgrave shared many of Banks's views about the way in which Britain could use scientific exploration to advance its commercial and strategic interests. For, like his former patron, Sandwich, Mulgrave was to be among the architects of the expansion of the British Empire which the growth in the powers and competence of the late eighteenth-century British State made possible. The early friendship between Mulgrave and Banks had been cemented by their partnership on the *Niger* expedition to Newfoundland and Labrador in 1768. Banks had also been closely involved in Mulgrave's expedition to the Arctic Circle in 1773. Thus in his account of this voyage Mulgrave acknowledged Banks's aid in providing 'very full instruction in the branch of natural history'.[50] Among the various Banksian ventures for which Mulgrave provided political support were the expeditions to the northwest coast of North America from 1785[51] and the *Bounty* breadfruit expedition – for Mulgrave was among those to whom Banks addressed his proposal of March 1787, arguing that sending out a vessel 'for sole purpose of bringing breadfruit to West Indies is more likely to be successful than that of dispatching one of the transports from Botany Bay'.[52] Mulgrave also appears to have been involved in the early discussions about a settlement at Botany Bay.[53]

Two years before his death in 1792 Mulgrave paid testimony to their long and fruitful association. After assuring Banks of his support for a position for one of his clients he added that 'we are, I believe the oldest friends to each other, & I can with truth assure you that the length has only added to the proofs of the value of such a friendship in my estimation'.[54] After Mulgrave's death, Banks's connection with the family continued to pay political dividends. For Constantine's younger brother, Henry Phipps (who inherited the title of Lord Mulgrave), another loyal supporter of Pitt, served as Secretary of State for Foreign Affairs from 1805 to 1806 and as first Lord of the Admiralty from 1807 to 1810. It was to him, for example, that Banks appealed in 1808 when attempting to gain promotion for his protégé, the explorer, Matthew Flinders.[55] Banks also sought his good offices in gaining government support for Bligh after he was forcibly deposed as Governor of New South Wales in 1808.[56]

As well as his help in enabling Banks to gain access to the inner recesses of the workings of government, Mulgrave also provided Banks with help on the smaller political stage of the Royal Society. In 1773 he joined the Council of the Royal Society along with Banks and, no doubt, played an active role in ensuring Banks's election as President in 1778. During the internecine battles within the Royal Society in 1784 Mulgrave was one of Banks's most loyal lieutenants. In a note on the dispute Banks, for example, recorded the way in which Mulgrave attempted to silence Horsley by moving a motion against those who 'interupt the business of the ordinary meetings with vexatious or frivolous motions'.[57]

COURT CONNECTIONS

Banks's associations with Sandwich and Mulgrave – both known sup-porters of the government's controversial American policy – may well have played a part in helping to ensure royal favour for Banks's election as President of the Royal Society. Banks's predecessor, Sir John Pringle, was said to have resigned because he had 'excited much disgust by indecent expressions of regard to the cause of the lately revolted colonies of North America'. Though Banks himself appears to have said little publicly on the American crisis, according to his critics he 'was no sooner seated in the President's chair than he began to manifest his dislike of Americans and American philosophy'.[58] When, years later in 1814, Banks joined in the controversy over whether Americans still retained rights as British subjects – a position which Banks vehemently rejected – his language and style of argument certainly indicated that he had no sympathy for the American colonists. 'Every American who levied War against his natural Sovereign', he wrote, 'or who accepted the protections of the Government establishd by those who did Levy such War, is guilty either of High Treason or of Misprision of that Crime'. Britain's acknowledgment of American independence Banks viewed rather quixotically as a 'Sentence' for such infidelity, for it amounted to 'a declaration that Americans are no longer Subjects to Great Britain'.[59]

The very fact that Banks was well regarded at court throughout the period of the American War is itself an indication of his pro-government sympathies. Banks's friendship with the King began after he was feted by London society following his return from the *Endeavour* expedition in 1771. The King's enthusiasm for agriculture and improvement further strengthened the association and led to Banks's appointment as de facto director of the Royal Gardens at Kew in 1773. Banks's basic conservatism and his determination to avoid identifying himself with any particular party further endeared him to a king who regarded himself as above the ruck of party politicians. As Lord Brougham wrote:

> Sir Joseph's political principles, too, those of a high tory, were much to the Monarch's liking; and a country gentleman who never troubled himself with Parliamentary life, nor ever desired to rise above the rank he was born to, was sure to find a friend in His Majesty.[60]

By the early 1780s Banks's links with the court were further consolidated by the King's enthusiastic involvement in the plan to introduce Spanish merino sheep in England, with Kew Gardens as their testing-ground. In his diary for 1781 the royal equerry recorded how George III responded with alacrity to the suggestion that Banks might be involved in the project: 'Sir Joseph Banks is just the Man. Tell him from Me that I thank Him, & that his assistance will be most welcome'.[61]

One tangible indication of royal goodwill both for Banks and for the scientific estate he represented was Banks's success in 1782 in obtaining for the astronomer, William Herschel, a position at the private royal observatory at Kent (and thus a quite separate position to that of the official Astronomer Royal).[62] In responding to Herschel's effusive thanks, Banks re-directed his gratitude to the King with a loyal tribute to the royal largesse as a patron of the sciences: 'was every Kingdom blessed with a Sovereign as capable of distinguishing & as ready to reward merit as ours is Philosophy would indeed be a Fashionable study'.[63] For Banks's admiration for George III owed much to the fact that he saw the King as providing hitherto unparalleled royal support for science – a sentiment that recurs in both his public and private correspondence. As President of the Royal Society, Banks predictably heaped praise on the royal bounty to science – in a speech in 1781, for example, he spoke of the way in which George III had outdone 'eminently ... the most extensive Ideas of Liberality' of previous patrons of the Royal Society.[64] But Banks also echoed such views in private sharing with the virtuoso, William Hamilton, for example, his fear of the consequences for the Society of the onset of the royal illness in 1788: 'where', he wrote, 'she [the Royal Society] will get so good a Patron as the Last I confess I do not even hope'.[65]

The friendship between Banks and George III survived the onset of the King's long illness. Indeed, Banks was among those whom he

King George III, portrait by Thomas Gainsborough.
(The Royal Collection © 1997 Her Majesty Queen Elizabeth II)

particularly requested to see while being treated in 1789.[66] After the King recovered Banks continued to act as his intermediary with the world of science and agricultural improvement. In 1799, for example, Arthur Young followed an agricultural excursion with the King by returning 'my best thanks for having spoken to his Majesty in my behalf'. He also asked Banks to enquire whether the King would permit an article on the royal farming practices to be published in the *Annals of Agriculture*.[67] Later that same year the King commended Banks on his 'very able report' about the Royal Flock.[68]

Banks's favour with the King was also strengthened by the fact that George III turned to botany and, after the onset of his mental illness, to pottering around Kew Gardens as a form of therapy. As Banks remarked in 1802: 'Since the King has Forborne the violent Exercise which usd to Contribute so much to his majesties amusement he has taken more & more interest in the Botanic Garden'.[69] The royal interest in botany helped smooth the way for a number of Banks's scientific enterprises. In April 1803, for example, Banks could report to the East India Company that the King looked with favour on the proposed expedition to China (which included a gardener) as something which would bring 'Reel advantage to this Country & her Colonies, as well as much improvement to the Science of Botany & to the Botanic Gardens at Kew, which are now a favorite Object of recreation to the whole of the Royal Family'.[70]

Such interests also appear to have lessened the damage done to Banks's standing at Court by Banks's enthusiastic and public acceptance of membership of the French Institut National in March 1802 – something which led to scalding criticism in Cobbett's *Weekly Political Register* by the anonymous 'Misogallus'. It was a controversy which reportedly 'had the effect of cooling the regard previously entertained for him at Windsor'.[71] But, despite this indiscretion, Banks continued in his role as the King's adviser on scientific matters. When, in August 1803, it was proposed to dedicate to George III an abridgment of the *Philosophical Transactions*, Banks was requested to broach the matter with the King 'it being known that in matters of science, no person has so much weight with his Majesty as yourself'.[72] Banks's rapport with the King on such scientific matters rested on a strong personal respect, the King in his view being 'the most virtuous prince that ever wielded a sceptre';[73] by contrast, he described the future George IV (accurately enough) as 'a Profligate Prince'.[74]

Ironically, however, Banks penned this tribute to George III a few weeks before the two men were largely to part company as a result of the increasingly erratic behaviour of the King brought on by his illness. Royal displeasure over Banks's disposal of some members of the royal flock of merinos resulted in Banks unburdening himself thus to his old friend, the King's equerry:

We have both Observed for some years past that H.M. mind is more irritable & Less placable than it usd to be & since this change has taken place I do not recollect an instance of any one of whom so hard a thing has been said as he has said to me being restord to Confidential favor[. I]t will be far better for me to be dismissd than to Remain under sufference only[.] I feel a personal friendship for the King & if it is Returnd as it usd to be I can never forego it but Coldness from a friend tho a king I can not support.[75]

Banks still continued to have some contact with the court – in September 1817, for example, he entertained the Queen and the Princess Royal at his country retreat at Spring Grove[76] – but after 1805 his role as a courtier had largely finished. By this time, however, the favour of an increasingly erratic king was of less and less significance politically. Banks's earlier rapport with George III had helped to bring him to notice as a man who could obtain a hearing in official circles for the needs of science and scientists. By 1805 Banks's reputation as an unofficial scientific adviser to government was too securely established to be weakened by the petulance of an ill and aging monarch.

BANKS AS A POLITICAL INDEPENDENT

Banks's long and, for the most part, close association with the King was consistent with his own conception of his role in public life as the servant of the King and his administration rather than as someone allied with any particular party or faction. As Banks became more involved in public affairs so, too, his determination to avoid compromising himself politically increased. For a man with Banks's talents and fortune such a refusal to follow the obvious path to the House of Commons and possible ministerial office was a considerable departure from the normal expectations of his class. Some sense of the sacrifice involved surfaces in his plea to the East India Company for consideration of his views on the botanical gardens at Calcutta on the grounds that his devotion to sciences had meant forgoing the chance of 'Parliamentary consequence & possibly of high office'.[77]

As a young man, in the period before he became President of the Royal Society – an office he regarded as being incompatible with party politics – there are hints that he flirted with the idea of a political career. Such a career would have been sanctioned by family tradition, for his father, grandfather and great-grandfathers had been MPs.[78] We have seen already that around 1775 he was actively involved in persuading Mulgrave to align himself politically with Sandwich. A note by his devoted sister from around the same period further suggests that at least the possibility of Banks entering politics had been discussed in the family circle. To a prayer urging God's blessing 'should He ever become a Senator' she added the aside: 'My Brother has never yet been in Parliament (or attempted it) from a motive highly honest & Praiseworthy: not thinking it right to undertake so great a trust, without he had determined to give up his time in a proper attendance on the Duties of it'.[79] At this stage of his life, in the years before he was elected President of the Royal Society in 1778 and married in 1779, Banks appears to have been casting about for a clear role – a restlessness reflected in a later autobiographical sketch of 1782 in which he wrote that 'On my return from Iceland [1772], I livd in no particular station till . . . I was elected President of the Royal Society'.[80]

If the presidency of the Royal Society had not become his perhaps he might well have considered more seriously taking the obvious choice for one of his station and talents and embarking on a parliamentary career – particularly since a parliamentary seat within Lincolnshire was his for the asking. He was offered and declined the seat of Boston in 1777, 1782 and 1784.[81] But, in Banks's mind, true devotion to science and, particularly, to the office of President of the Royal Society precluded party politics. As early as April 1768, while in the full flush of enthusiasm for the preparations for the *Endeavour* voyage, Banks appears to have enunciated this view to the naturalist Dru Drury. For Drury reported to Peter Pallas (his indefatigable Continental correspondent on matters connected with natural history) that 'Mr Banks has judgement enough to prevent his engaging in Affairs of State & consequently detaching himself from all Parties has more leisure to pursue his darling Study'.[82] More publicly, Banks proclaimed his political neutrality on accepting the presidency of the Royal Society in December 1778. 'My time hitherto free from the Shackles of Politics', he asserted, 'shall be chearfully devoted to your service'.[83]

Thereafter Banks continued to emphasise his aloofness from the ruck of party politicians – though, as we shall see, this did not prevent his playing a role behind the scenes in defence of the landed interest. This enabled Banks to remain on good terms with some scientific figures who may well have been alienated by a public demonstration of Banks's stance on the major political issues of the day. Despite his lack of sympathy for the American colonists, for example, he maintained a cordial correspondence with Franklin. In August 1782, when Britain was reluctantly having to accept that it had been defeated by the Americans, he confided to Franklin that 'I have never entered the doors of the House of Commons & I will tell you that I have escaped a Million of unpleasant hours & preserved no small proportion of Friends of both parties by that fortunate conduct'.[84] Banks regarded such an apolitical stance as increasing his usefulness not only as a patron of science but also in advancing his schemes that depended on the apparatus of government. Hence, in February 1789, at a time when the British political establishment had been divided by the Regency crisis provoked by George III's first onset of madness, he declared his unwillingness to take office lest it mar his ability to aid the infant colony of New South Wales: 'I could not take office and do my duty to the colony. My successor would naturally oppose my wishes. I prefer, therefore, to be friendly with both sides'.[85]

By distancing himself from the political fray Banks could also discourage unwanted clients who, in a system permeated by patronage, naturally looked to anyone such as Banks, with a wide acquaintance among the major political figures of the day, for advancement. The attempt by a distant relative to enlist Banks's influence on his behalf was met with the discouraging response that 'I never shall possess Parliamentary interest the only key which shall open the Trunk in which ministers of England lock up their good things'.[86] A relative of an old school friend received much shorter shrift when, four years later, he endeavoured to persuade Banks to obtain a government post for him:

> I hold no such place myself & never have nor do I mean to receive a Salary from Government. My independence of action & opinion I value beyond any thing that can be given to me and as I am not or ever have been in Parliament I have not even a Vote which I can give to a Minister.[87]

Banks was, indeed, too politically astute to squander his influence with those who held power by aligning himself too closely with the passing parade of the party faithful or by making a nuisance of himself by seeking too many favours for importunate clients. His role as a trusted adviser to government and as a confidant to the King rested on the assumption that his advice would not be coloured by party political considerations. Hence his reponse to the French scientist-explorer, Pierre Dupont de Nemours, in 1798 that he could help him only in scientific matters and not in political ones, since his majesty's ministers consulted him on scientific questions so long as he did not meddle in politics.[88]

Maintaining such a degree of political aloofness required a degree of vigilance and nice judgement on Banks's behalf. Honours or positions could only be accepted when they did not carry with them the price of political obligation. Thus Banks declined the Order of the Bath in 1794, an honour he coveted greatly, since he was then serving as the High Sheriff of Lincolnshire. For, since he was then involved in promoting Pitt's plans to deal with the emergencies of war – plans which had been challenged by the parliamentary opposition – to accept the honour might be considered a political reward. This he feared (as he explained to the Home Secretary, Henry Dundas) would diminish 'my Pretentions to the Character of an independent Landowner'. If this should happen, Banks warned, his ability to gain the trust of his scientific friends would diminish and so, too, would 'that assistance whatever it may be that Government has consistently receivd from active & not unsuccessful exertions on my part to do them service'.[89] By the following year, however, Banks was sufficiently removed from the political stage to accept the honour, particularly as it was seen as being conferred at the instigation of the King himself, thus 'coming in a direct Course from the pure Fountain of honor without any portion of Ministerial Contamination'.[90]

Banks's contemptuous reference to 'Ministerial Contamination' and his aloofness from party politics are indicative of a rather less than whole-hearted enthusiasm for the workings of constitutional monarchy. Banks was too loyal an Englishman and too strong a believer in the enlightened credentials of the eighteenth-century British constitution not to regard it as superior to other forms of polity. His travel advice to

James Gillray, 'The Great South Sea Caterpillar, Transform'd into a Bath Butterfly' (c.1795). A satire on the investiture of Banks with the Order of the Bath on 1 July 1795. (From M. D. George, *Political and personal satire*, VII, p. 218 no. 8718) (By courtesy of the British Museum, Dept of Prints)

the young Henry Brougham in 1799, for example, included an endorsement – albeit of a rather qualified variety – of the British constitution. 'Every little Court of Germany, however', he wrote,

> gives the opportunity of Studying the Misuse of Sovereign power, & the Consequent misery of the Lower Classes ... which can scarce fail of making a Briton devoted to the Constitution of his own Countrey, after having Compard it with others, if he will give himself the trouble of computing the actual proportion of human happiness drawn from different modes of government.[91]

But Banks looked upon the actual working of the British constitution with some distaste telling Blagden in 1783, for example, to spare him all but the most important political news while he was in the country for 'I care not for & never wish to hear the grating of any but the Large wheels of that cumbrous machine'.[92] The defeat of the landed interest in the House of Commons in 1788 over the issue of the export of wool prompted Banks to discourse on the drawbacks of a parliamentary system since, he argued,

> the great advantages we draw from a free government are almost necessarily accompanied by great evils. A representative assembly can inflict injustices ... a whole parliament can establish and have executed laws so oppressive in their nature that an absolute monarch would never dare to propose the like without running the risk of seeing himself totter on his throne.[93]

At times, Banks, the faithful servant of his own king, hinted at a certain admiration for absolute monarchies – provided that they were guided by enlightened principles. Like the French *philosophes*, he regarded Catherine II of Russia as such a model of applied enlightenment, describing her as 'an Empress who has proved herself a continual friend to humanity ... [with] her prudent & wise administration of a system calculated by her to insure the prosperity of her dominions & the happiness of her people'.[94]

Though Banks was loud in his denunciations of Napoleon as the mortal enemy of Britain, his enthusiasm for his role as patron of the sciences suggests a certain sympathy for more autocratic forms of government as a way of cutting through the muddle and confusion inseparable from parliamentary systems. Like Napoleon, Banks was a man who liked to get things done and his sympathies were with the executive rather than the legislative divisions of government – hence his remark to Hawkesbury that he always stood ready 'to do anything I might be thought capable of by the executive government of the country'.[95] Moreover, as he grew older Banks came to regard the constitution as having got out of balance with parliament having subverted some of the traditional prerogatives of the King and his ministers. As he wrote in 1814:

> the house of Commons [is] far more nice than wise in the over rigid adherence to their Rules made in times when prerogative was a Formidable Enemy to Privilege, in

these times when Privilege is so much more than a match for Prerogative & indeed
when like Bonaparte she is stripd of all her Terrors it is Ridiculous to oppress the
subject under pretence of being afraid of a Phantom.[96]

Such an ambivalent attitude to constitutional monarchy was not un-
common within the scientific community. Hunter has pointed to the
sympathy that some of the early Royal Society scientists had for 'strong
government' in the Restoration period.[97] Stuart attempts to bypass parliament and institute forms of government closer to French absolutism
seemed to offer more hope of implementing scientific schemes. Moreover, absolutism of the French variety seemed a much more active patron
of science than British constitutional monarchy. Nor had the situation
changed vastly by Banks's day: English scientists of the period still
continued to compare the relative largesse of the French State (both
in its monarchical and republican forms) with the much more parsimonious practice of the British government.

PITTITE POLITICS AND THE LINCOLNSHIRE
CONNECTION

But for all Banks's distaste for the realities of parliamentary government
and his attempts to maintain an Olympian detachment from the ebb and
flow of political life, the fact remained that Banks needed political
support to implement his plans for placing science at the service of the
British government. And so, however discreetly, Banks needed the aid of
patrons and power-brokers. In particular, as Banks began to become
involved in the workings of government from the mid-1780s, he needed
the aid of William Pitt, the Prime Minister from the end of 1783 until his
death in 1806 (apart from a period out of office from 1801 to 1804
occasioned by George III's aversion to Pitt's plans for Catholic emanci-
pation). For it was Pitt who was to do most to re-mould Britain's
traditional forms of government to accommodate the changing realities
of the late eighteenth century – changes which flowed from the expansion of the British State in response to the problems posed by an age
of political and economic revolution.

Pitt stood for many of the things which Banks valued: efficiency,
probity, and a determination to rebuild Britain's pride and place in the
world after the shattering defeat in the War of American Independence
and to maintain them during the titanic struggle with France from 1793.
Like Banks, too, Pitt saw himself first and foremost as the King's servant
and was reluctant to identify himself with any particular party grouping.
Nonetheless, Banks was frequently critical of Pitt, particularly as he grew
older. Banks's waning enthusiasm for Pitt largely reflected the views of
Charles Jenkinson, Lord Hawkesbury, his chief ally in affairs of state. For,
as he faded from active political life (particularly after he became Earl of
Liverpool in 1796), Liverpool reported to Banks regularly on the slights

he received from Pitt's servants. Nor, presumably, had he altogether forgotten or forgiven Pitt's early reluctance to be closely associated with him as the alleged secret adviser to the King.[98] The eclipse of Liverpool also meant that Banks himself was pushed more to the margins of political life. Moreover, the multifarious demands on Pitt produced by the war meant that Pitt had less time for the imperial and commercial schemes which had been the political lifeblood of both Liverpool and Banks.

When Pitt first swept the country in the election of 1784, offering new direction and hope after the miseries of defeat and national humiliation, Banks appears to have welcomed his advent. At the Boston election of 1784 Banks supported the candidacy of his old friend, Mulgrave, a close and early ally of Pitt. When Mulgrave withdrew Banks offered his support to 'any friend of Mr. Pitts [who] choses to come forth'.[99] As a loyal friend of the King, Banks naturally sided with Pitt's position in the Regency crisis of 1788 – which was precipitated by the first onset of the King's illness – of limiting as much as possible the power granted to the Prince Regent, a position actively opposed by the Prince's allies among the opposition Foxite Whigs. At the height of the crisis Banks confided to a French correspondent that 'at this moment even I am occupied in Politics as the singular & unexpected situation of this Countrey makes it necessary every one should be'.[100] Moreover, Banks's initiative of 1789 in summoning a county meeting in Lincolnshire to send an address of congratulation on the King's recovery (and, with it, the elimination of plans for a Regency council) had a partisan character which was underlined by the conspicuous non-attendance of some of Lincolnshire's more prominent Whigs.[101]

As Sheriff of Lincolnshire in 1794 Banks co-operated closely with Pitt and his political lieutenant, George Rose, in accepting the position and in instituting the proposed measures for the militia and preparation for war and possible invasion.[102] A by-election for the county seat in September 1794 left Banks in the awkward situation of having to balance his abiding wish 'to keep the Peace of our vast County'[103] by avoiding contested elections with his support for Pitt's government – a government which, as he had told Dundas earlier that year, 'has consistently receivd from active & not unsuccessful exertions in my part to do them Service ever since Mr Pits system of Prudence honesty & clear handedness has been adopted'.[104] Happily, Banks's dilemma was overcome by the withdrawal of Sir Gilbert Heathcote, the candidate favoured by Pitt, and an uncontested election proceeded.[105] Banks took a similar position at the general election of 1796, once again favouring an uncontested election to preserve 'the Peace of the County'. However, if this did not come to pass he promised his support to the Pittite Heathcote who, wrote Banks,

> I think most likely to support the measures of the present administration, the conduct of which has hitherto given me so much more satisfaction than that of the opposition as induces me to think it a duty to give them support when it is in my power.[106]

Again, gentlemanly consensus prevailed: Heathcote was elected un-opposed after one of the former sitting members withdrew. Overall, then, until the end of the century Banks viewed Pitt's administration in a reasonably favourable spirit and, from a discreet distance, supported it in his capacity as a Lincolnshire power-broker.

When Banks most actively intervened in the political arena as a defender of the landed interest there were few direct clashes with Pitt himself. Though Pitt's administration was less sympathetic than Banks wished to the landowners' position in such controversies as the debate over the export of wool in the 1780s and the revision of the Corn Laws in the 1790s this did not prompt Banks to regard Pitt with hostility. In his comments on the bill dealing with the export of wool Banks even went so far as to praise Pitt for his 'fair and honest conduct' in telling those who framed an earlier and particularly draconian version of the bill that its 'regulations were inadmissible'.[107]

Banks's formal elevation to the dignity of a Privy Councillor in 1797 meant a deeper immersion in the affairs of government. It also meant a deeper sense of frustration at Pitt's lack of attention towards what Banks considered important. A letter to Liverpool on the workings of the gold standard in June 1798 included a muted complaint (in the third person) about Pitt's dilatory habits: 'Sir Joseph cannot help feeling regret at the delay which originates with Mr Pitt but concludes it unavoidable'.[108] Liverpool amply shared his sense of frustration, having complained earlier that year to Banks that meetings of the Privy Council Committee for Coin were subverted by members 'interrupt[ing] the Course of Business . . . & Mr.Pitt unfortunately sets the Example'.[109] Exasperation at having to deal with a man as busy and distracted as Pitt was compounded by Banks's and Hawkesbury's distaste for Pitt's political lieutenant, George Rose, about whose 'abominable' conduct Banks complained to Boulton in December 1799.[110]

Such slights made Banks wonder if the Privy Council was deliberately being allowed to wane in its significance while the influence of the per-manent bureaucratic officials waxed – particularly that of the Treasury officials with whom Banks, in his capacity as an adviser on the nation's coinage, frequently crossed swords. Hence his bitter complaint to Liverpool that since the Whig Cabinet came to power (presumably a reference to the formation of a coalition of the Duke of Portland and his Whig followers with Pitt in 1794) the Privy Council 'has been wantonly trampled upon', especially by the Treasury clerks.[111]

Banks's annoyance with Pitt was further heightened by Pitt's lack of interest in matters scientific. To what appears to have been an enquiry from Liverpool about the possibility of the Royal Society making a presentation to Pitt on the occasion of his resignation from office in February 1801, Banks replied that the Royal Society was unlikely to respond with unanimous approval. Pitt, he wrote, 'has so uniformly neglected science' that members of the Society would not be well disposed to 'any thing in which he has a concern'.[112] In a letter to his

faithful steward, Parkinson, Banks could give freer vent to his accumulated displeasure at what he considered was Pitt's lack of order and
system – qualities that the methodical Banks valued highly. He would
'not be uneasy' at the change of ministry, he wrote after Pitt's resignation
in February 1801, for though Pitt's 'talents for oratory are certainly very
great ... his talents for war have never been successful'.[113] When Pitt was
reinstated in May 1804, following Addington's resignation as Prime
Minister, Banks was predictably disenchanted with both the manner and
the result of this political change reserving his sympathy for the King
whom he considered ill-used. 'We are here at present in a Compleat state
of anarchy', he told Boulton, 'I have never before known the fact of the
king's cabinet having been actualy stormd'. Banks concluded with yet
another affirmation of his political neutrality, adding with Olympian
detachment:

> you know [I] have always avoided all interference with Political Parties I never have
> lookd for advantage from Government & have therefore never sufferd less. I value
> myself as being the only man in England who is Quite free from party connexions
> or indeed from Party Bias a situation I should not boast of if both Parties had not
> allowed it.[114]

But Banks's political objectivity did not extend to the point of welcoming Pitt's return, something which prompted him to remark to the
Earl of Liverpool, a fellow critic of Pitt and hence a sympathetic listener,
that 'I have always held Mr Pits judgment as far inferior to his
Eloquence'. Banks, moreover, regarded Pitt's political associates – and,
no doubt, particularly, George Rose, Banks's *bête noire* – with some
distaste. Thus he warned Liverpool to be careful about associating with
some of the political servants whom Pitt had chosen 'as he himself seems
to pay too little attention to the opinions the Public may entertain of the
persons he chuses to employ'.[115] Liverpool needed little such advice since
the more he faded from political view the more critical of Pitt he became
(despite the fact that his son was one of Pitt's ministers). Indeed, shortly
afterwards, Liverpool informed Banks of his decision to withdraw from
the Committee for Trade since George Rose had formally become a
member. He concluded bitterly with a reference to Pitt's lack of courtesy
for not having advised him of such changes: 'Such are the manners of
the Man'.[116] Banks echoed his views since his indignation at Pitt was
further heightened by what he felt was the unfair treatment meted out to
his old friend, Boulton, by Pitt's cronies on the Board of Trade. 'I wish I
could reserve my seat at the Board', he wrote to Boulton in April 1805,

> but the new associates Mr Pit has provided for me do not act on the Principles I am usd
> to, they are ignorant & of course obstinate[.T]heir management in your case alone
> decidedly proves that I am right in declining to trust my character among theirs.[117]

Banks's tenuous relations with Pitt and his increasing disenchantment
with his administration do, at first sight, serve to confirm Banks's own

assessment of himself as a man who served the public without being ensnared in party politics. The few occasions on which he did serve Pitt's directly political purposes in his capacity as a Lincolnshire power-broker were in relation to national emergencies such as the Regency crisis or the need to mobilise for war – occasions which largely, though not completely, transcended party divisions. But, though Banks generally distanced himself from both Pitt and his political opponents, Banks was quite capable of political engagement – provided it was not too public. This, as we shall see, is most evident in his defence of the landed interest in the controversy over the export of wool where Banks worked assiduously behind the scenes in mobilising political support for his cause. Again, Banks's political battles on the Committee for Trade were largely fought for him by Lord Hawkesbury (the future Earl of Liverpool). For both men shared a common commitment to the maintenance of a system of mercantilist protection for British trade and navigation and to the exploitation for the benefit of British commerce of new products made available by scientific exploration. Banks may, then, have kept himself aloof from public political involvement but he was able to afford this luxury since he could work through intermediaries who were more willing to expose themselves to the dust of political battle. With Liverpool's political eclipse, and in the absence of another political sponsor, Banks's involvement in government declined accordingly – a decline that also owed much to his increasing age and infirmities.

After Liverpool's death in 1808, two years after that of Pitt, Banks's contacts with political life largely dwindled. But, as he grew older and more removed from the centre of power, he also in some senses became more politically partisan. Thus he became ever more opposed to reforming politicians, an aversion which was, of course, strengthened by the mood of reaction which followed the French Revolution. Banks, for example, greeted the downfall of the strongly Whiggish Grenville administration of 'All the Talents' in March 1807 with relief, viewing it as 'a little Political Hurricane which has taken the king out of the hands of a Whig administration & Placd him among Servants who are too good Friends to the Constitution & too little wedded to their own interests to wish to Reign over him'. In the same letter Banks made plain his natural Toryism writing that 'England is never itself but when she has a virtuous King & a Tory ministry'. He did add, however, (perhaps with a view to the future George IV for whom Banks, like most of his contemporaries, had little regard) that a 'Whig ministry is the natural check provided by the admirable Constitution we live under to Restrain the Evil wishes of a wicked King'.[118]

Banks particularly welcomed the change in ministry since it would weaken the reforming cause, writing that 'The demagogues like the Master Bulls in a Pasture are always few in number [.I]f you Suddenly take the Leaders away the Remainder Quarrel & Fight for some time before they can agree upon Successors'.[119] Banks had a particular aversion to the arch-Whig, Charles James Fox, and made no attempt to disguise his relief at Fox's death in September 1806 even in so public a document as a letter to Governor King of New South Wales:

> I trust that the fluctuations of Administrations will not act against you, and I trust it will not just now. I confess I have my hopes that Mr. Fox's death will drive all the profligates who now hold the keys of the Treasury into the Red Sea, and that we shall have a succession of honest and quiet men placed in their room.[120]

Predictably, Banks responded with particular vigour when the prospect of reform in the person of the radical Sir Robert Heron appeared on the Lincolnshire political landscape. Heron's first attempt to enter the contest for a county seat resulted in Banks rebuking him for 'your view on the subject of Elective Franchise ... [which] savors also not a little of Political Licensiousness'. Moreover, continued Banks, 'the disclosure you have made of your principles ... must bar all possibility of your future success'.[121] Banks's aversion to political radicalism was strengthened still further by his own experience of popular agitation. His prominence in Lincolnshire affairs led to his receiving in 1811 a letter on 'extension of the operations of the organised miscreants of Nottingham' – the Luddites of neighbouring Nottinghamshire – to which he responded by offering to government his own services and those of his steward.[122]

Popular discontent impinged even more directly on Banks when, in March 1815, the Corn Law rioters attacked Banks's Soho Square house. It was an attack prompted by his association with leaders of the landed interest such as Sheffield who had been the chief instigators of the new Corn Law. Banks, as he told Sheffield, regarded those who attacked him as 'hav[ing] been drilled by some of King Lud's Nottingham Regiment for they are Quite aware of the nature of the Armies they command'.[123]

At the election of 1818, the first general election since the end of the war, Banks continued to watch for signs of political radicalism rearing its head in Lincolnshire. This the more so since Sir Robert Heron again had entered the fray for a county seat acting as a focus for what Banks called the forces of 'anarchy, democracy, and ultimate destruction'.[124] However, he could report with satisfaction in June 1818 that 'we men of Lincolnshire shewed very little democracy'[125] and rejoiced that 'the democrats appear to be on the decline in Westminster'.[126] Predictably, in the following year when Banks's old adversary, Sir Robert Heron, attempted to arrange a county meeting to press parliament for an investigation into the Peterloo Massacre, Banks joined with other Lincolnshire grandees to oppose the plan. The events of Peterloo and the growing polarisation of society in the tense and hungry years after the end of the Napoleonic Wars made the aging Banks increasingly fearful of civil strife and more draconian in his views about how such a danger should be averted. In December 1819 he commented to Blagden that

> our Parliament is active & diligent in opposing our disaffected Reformers ... I feel & hope that the business will be closd without a Battle, some blood must be shed on the Scaffold but that I do not Regret if those only will suffer who deserve to suffer.[127]

But Banks had no doubt that, regrettable as it might be, the forces of order could, if necessary, crush the unruly and particularly his old foes, the Luddites. As he wrote to Blagden in December 1819:

> I am not now afraid of the Physical Force of our mechanic Levellers unless for the Shock of hearing that many of their lives must be lost if they attempt their now aborrd Plan of Dividing among themselves the Property which the Rich they say withheld from them unjustly.[128]

Banks's determination to avoid too close an identification with any one political party did not, then, preclude his having strong political sympathies of his own. Nor were his political sympathies as shielded from the public gaze as much as he would have wished. When the radical Sir Francis Burdett stood for Middlesex in 1802 Banks 'being known to be a Tory was of course much hooted and abused by the Mob'.[129] Banks, as Brougham described him, was, at bottom, 'a tory, and very firm in his opinions, both in Church and State' – particularly when the traditional constitution appeared under threat in the tense and troubled years that followed the end of the French Wars. But, though Banks was far from being politically indifferent (at least in private), Brougham could still describe him as being 'anything rather than a party man'.

Whatever his personal views, Banks played out the role of a de facto civil servant by accommodating himself to different political regimes. Like many administrators the qualities he admired most – stability, efficiency and order – inclined him to maintain the status quo almost irrespective of its political hue. As he remarked in 1818, when supporting a candidate for a Welsh constituency, his 'Politics are similar to mine, who always feel an inclination to support the existing Government'.[130] Banks came closest to showing his true political colours when he stepped out of his role as an adviser to the central government and assumed the more traditional one of a Lincolnshire landowner. But, in this capacity, too, Banks above all favoured stability and 'the peace of the County' rather than exhibiting a strong inclination towards any particular party. To cite Brougham once more:

> He never interfered in politics beyond using his legitimate influence in Lincolnshire and Derbyshire, where his property lay, to aid those country gentlemen whom he believed fitted to be useful representatives of the landed interest.[131]

PUBLIC SERVICE AND THE FIRST AND SECOND EARLS OF LIVERPOOL

In viewing political life largely through the spectacles of an administrator whose concern was with efficient and orderly administration, rather than in the clash of parties or principles, Banks had much in common with his most important political ally, Lord Hawkesbury. Both Banks and Hawkesbury viewed themselves first and foremost as the King's servants whose task it was to implement his business. Consequently, both tended to regard political manoeuvring as at best a tiresome necessity in the furtherance of these goals.

This might seem a paradoxical position for Hawkesbury as a lifelong practising politician and, after 1791, as a Cabinet minister. But, in an age when there was no clear distinction between politicians and civil servants, politics – in the sense of service to the executive – was still the most expeditious route towards high administrative office. The basis of Hawkesbury's political position was not his membership of any particular political faction but rather his long and close association with the King – just as Banks's standing in government circles largely derived from his close association with George III. Thus Hawkesbury's declaration to Lord Auckland towards the end of his political life that 'I have never in my life engaged or meddled in political intrigues'[132] – for all its glossing over much of the inevitable reality of his practice of politics – conveyed his sense of having remained outside the mainstream of party politics. 'Politically timid', writes Brooke of him,

> Jenkinson [Hawkesbury's family name] attached himself to the Crown as the one stable element in the political scene; a born bureaucrat ... his passion was for the detail of office. He never felt the excitement of the parliamentary game.[133]

Charles Jenkinson, first Baron Hawkesbury and first Earl of Liverpool. Portrait by George Romney, c.1786.
(By courtesy of the National Portrait Gallery, London)

Hawkesbury, then, constitutes an outstanding example of the way in which, in the late eighteenth century, 'the king's friends' performed a role which a later age would regard as the province of professional administrators.[134] For, in this period, such individuals could not find a permanent resting place within a civil service which was, by later standards, neither properly developed nor distinct from parliament and the political arena.

Much of Brooke's description of Hawkesbury also readily applies to Banks. Even more than Hawkesbury he felt little attraction for the 'parliamentary game' and he, too, regarded himself first and foremost as the King's servant. Like Hawkesbury, too, Banks was 'a born bureaucrat' with a 'passion ... for the detail of office'. The activities of both Hawkesbury and Banks reflected the ever-mounting need for government involvement in an age when the bureaucratic machinery of the central State was still inadequate for the task. Thus the bureaucratic vacuum for dealing with commercial and imperial affairs was largely filled by a reluctant politician in the person of Hawkesbury and a public-minded landed gentleman in the person of Banks – both performing roles which in a later age would fall to high-ranking civil servants.

Hawkesbury's rise to office illustrates the changing tenor of the late eighteenth-century British State as the need for administrative efficiency and regularity was given greater recognition in the face of the widening scope of government responsibilities. Jenkinson (as he was before 1786) had to bear the political opprobrium of having been closely associated with George III's ill-fated first minister, Lord Bute, whom he served as private secretary. Bute's attempts to distance himself from the ruck of party politics led to unrelenting hostility from politicians of all hues as an attempt to subvert the constitution. However, this conception of politics as being the path to service to the King, above the din of political battle, continued to shape the thinking of Jenkinson (and, indeed, Banks). Such a conception of politics also helps to explain why, despite the considerable political cost involved, Jenkinson maintained his connection with Lord Bute, George III's early teacher and mentor, leading to the accusation that he was 'the favourite's confidant, and the chief agent of his invisible influence'.[135]

But, despite this lead in his political saddle, Jenkinson's abilities as an administrator eventually propelled him upwards. Early service as an Undersecretary of State (1761) and Secretary to the Treasury (1763–5) was followed by a long period in the political wilderness as atonement for his connections with Bute. But, with the elevation in 1779 of Lord North as Prime Minister, Jenkinson's political stocks began to rise again assisted by North's sympathies for 'the king's friends' and his cautious attempts to advance administrative reform. As Secretary at War from 1778 to 1782, Jenkinson confirmed his reputation as one of the most competent administrators in political life advancing his career, as he himself put it, 'by industry, by attention to duty'.[136] His handling of this position put him in the vanguard of the movement for administrative reform.

Appropriately, however, given his distaste for many aspects of the parliamentary process, he was to demonstrate that at least some elements of the executive could reform themselves before the prod of the legislative became more pressing from the mid-1780s. Under the shadow of impending national humiliation at the hands of the American colonists, Jenkinson declared in 1780 that 'though the present times disastrous as they are, will not admit of any great and hasty reforms, yet I shall always think it my duty to pay the utmost attention to Publick Oeconomy'.[137]

His labours at the War Office not only brought him growing recognition among the politicians of the day but also increasing contact with the King in his capacity as head of the Army.[138] The King not only came to rely more and more on his administrative abilities but also came to use Jenkinson as his eyes and ears in the political intrigues of the day – Jenkinson virtually assuming the role of a 'royal spy'.[139] The collapse of the North administration in March 1782 led to Jenkinson being again cast into the political wilderness but administrative competence and, no doubt, royal favour led to his being appointed to the Privy Council Committee for Trade and the Plantations when it was established in 1784. This he used as a platform for formulating British policy on trade with the infant United States – a key area in the reconstruction of British commerce after the debacle of the American War.

This reflected a long-standing interest in commercial and imperial affairs which was more and more to become Jenkinson's chief concern. In 1772–3 he had been one of the chief architects of an early version of the India Bill which, when finally passed in 1784, established a Board of Control as an instrument for better overseeing the actions of the East India Company in the interests of the British State. Such an increase in the scope and competence of government action was well suited to Jenkinson's conception of the proper role of the British State. As early as 1764 he had remarked on the political and administrative anomaly of allowing the affairs of a body as important as the East India Company to be controlled by a body independent of parliament – or, as he himself put it, 'The affairs of this Company seem to be become much too big for the management of a body of merchants'.[140]

From 1784, with his appointment to the Privy Council Committee for Trade, Jenkinson became more and more the leading authority in commercial and imperial matters and Pitt's chief lieutenant in the reconstruction of the British Empire after the American Revolution.[141] Recognition of Jenkinson's role as 'the *primum orbile* of the commercial interests of this great nation'[142] (as one of his correspondents put it) came with his appointment by Pitt as President of the Committee for Trade in 1786 and (with the King's hearty approbation) elevation to the peerage as Baron Hawkesbury. It was a post that Hawkesbury retained until 1804 when he finally retired from politics. At his death in 1808 George III acknowledged his long and loyal service as one of the foremost of 'the king's friends' by writing to his son (the future second Earl of Liverpool and Prime Minister) that he had 'known and experienced, during a period of 48 years, his integrity and fidelity in the able discharge of his duty'.[143]

Banks and Hawkesbury – both born administrators whose sympathies lay with the executive rather than the legislative organs of government – formed a long and productive partnership. It was a partnership which even survived Hawkesbury's policy of providing rather less political support for the landed interest than Banks and his allies such as Lord Sheffield or Arthur Young could have wished. In the midst of such debates Banks could still assure Hawkesbury that 'your Friendship as a man & as an able man I shall ever wish to retain'.[144]

Both Hawkesbury and Banks shared a common dedication to the aggrandisement of Britain's commercial standing and hence its strategic and military strength. Both also took the view that as far as possible the trade and shipping of Britain's expanding empire should be moulded to suit the needs of Britain itself. And both brought to government a determination to get things done – to cut through the inherited bureaucratic muddle and to impose order on government action. This applied particularly in the field of imperial affairs which, by default, largely fell to the Committee for Trade. This was Hawkesbury's chief political base and, as the friendship between Banks and Hawkesbury ripened, it also became more and more Banks's main path to the inner workings of government.

This long and fruitful association between the two men did not begin until the late 1780s, long after both of them had achieved considerable public stature. Their first correspondence on imperial or commercial matters came at the end of March 1787 when Banks recommended a botanist for a joint East India Company–Committee for Trade expedition to search for useful plants in India.[145] The tone of their partnership was further established when, at the same time, Banks advised Hawkesbury about the details of what eventually became the *Bounty* expedition to transfer breadfruit from Tahiti to the West Indies.[146] From such beginnings the mutual advantages of a partnership became increasingly evident – Banks supplying the scientific expertise and Hawkesbury access to the processes of government. For, as Banks himself put it in 1799, Hawkesbury 'has the confidence of the Minister [Pitt] on all matters in which the commercial interests of this Country combine themselves with the political ones'.[147]

Banks responded to requests for advice on a growing range of subjects as Hawkesbury used the Committee for Trade to respond to the increasing diversity of British commerce and industry in the age of the early Industrial Revolution. A brief list of some of the major subjects about which Banks and Hawkesbury corresponded conveys the range of the Committee for Trade's activities – reflecting the more general growth of the British State and its range of responsibilities in the late eighteenth century. Banks was requested to provide advice on species of cotton and of tea which might grow in lands under the British flag, on metallurgical problems at the Mint, on the threat of Hessian Fly infection in wheat, on methods of producing saltpetre, on the supply of wheat and of cinnamon, on proposals for producing alkalis, on extraction of gold from Africa, on the manufacture of beet sugar and the growing of hemp[148] – and so the list of products and processes which might be utilised for the promotion of British commerce continued.

The partnership between Banks and Hawkesbury rested on a shared ethic of public service – something which helped to bind together the landed oligarchy who controlled the political process giving the different organs of government, whether local or central, some unity of purpose. Hawkesbury's request to Banks in 1789 for information on a botanical expedition to India was accompanied by a tribute 'to the Zeal you always manifest when your Talents can be of any Use to the Publick'.[149] The object of Banks's and Hawkesbury's endeavours was, of course, first and foremost the advancement of Britain's commercial interests but this could, at least in Banks's view, also coincide with the benefit of humankind more generally. The botanical specimens brought back from India, wrote Banks to Hawkesbury in November 1789, provided the opportunity for providing new crops for the British colonies in the West Indies – something which benefited both the British and the West Indians. 'I hold firmly the opinion', wrote Banks, 'that furnishing a Countrey with Esculent Vegetables unknown to it but which will thrive there, is conferring an Obligation of the First importance on the inhabitants'. To translate these Baconian hopes of science acting for 'the relief of man's estate' required political patronage – hence Banks's request that Hawkesbury's 'influence in the West Indies may prove them a Fair trial'.[150]

So identified did Banks become with Hawkesbury at the Committee for Trade that, as the latter's political star faded, so, too, did Banks's involvement with the Committee for Trade and the processes of government more generally also waned. By 1800 what Banks considered the increasingly cavalier treatment of the Privy Council and, with it, Hawkesbury and the Committee for Trade, prompted him to express his outrage to Liverpool (as Hawkesbury became). Such indignation, he wrote, 'would surely have burst out, had not your Lordships example of Patience restraind me'.[151] When Liverpool was finally replaced at the Committee for Trade in 1804 so, too, did Banks's involvement with that body largely cease. In 1804 Pitt's political lieutenant, George Rose, was appointed as Vice-President of the Committee and hence as Liverpool's virtual successor (for the President, the Duke of Montrose, was merely a figure-head). This prompted Banks both to pay tribute to Liverpool's wide conception of the province of the Committee for Trade and to lament that this tradition would not be maintained. For, as he wrote to Hawkesbury, he feared the waning of

> those comprehensive views of your Lordships on which the office was originaly formd for the improvement of the Resources of the Countrey by encouraging new adventures of Commerce, assisting the Progress of manufacture & Releiving trade from difficulties which the Lapse of time may have brought upon it.[152]

Banks's determination largely to retire from the Committee for Trade was, of course, further strengthened by his indignation at the treatment accorded to his old ally. As he wrote to Liverpool, he was prompted to remove himself from the Committee by 'a sense of the double impropriety of your Lordship's being exiled from a board which you have for so long & so eminently conducted, & the appointment of Persons wholly incompetent to the business'.[153]

Though after 1804 the long and productive partnership between Banks and Hawkesbury largely ceased – in a political if not a personal sense – Banks's association with the Jenkinson family continued to bear some further fruit through Hawkesbury's son, the second Lord Liverpool and Prime Minister from 1812 to 1827. It was, for example, to him that Banks turned in May 1814 to secure the appointment of a new Astronomer Royal, complimenting him on his interest in matters scientific. 'On all subjects', wrote Banks, 'that relate to the advancement of Science I always address your Lordship with pleasure, well knowing that your Lordships inclinations on that head are at least as strong as my own'.[154]

In the Liverpools, both father and son, Banks found politicians who could share something of his enthusiasm for applying scientific knowledge to practical ends. Of all Banks's political patrons the first Earl of Liverpool was to be the one with whom he worked most closely in integrating his scientific and imperial expertise with the actual workings of government. This political partnership rested on a common commitment to the advancement of Britain's commercial and hence strategic standing and a determination to shape imperial policy to further such ends. Banks and Liverpool, then, shared to a large degree a similar conception of the role the British State should play in advancing trade and in controlling its imperial possessions. Both, in their different ways, could be described as neo-mercantilists. For both regarded the State as playing a critical role in the shaping of economic policy and both regarded economic considerations as subordinate to other national goals – whether strategic or for the maintenance of public order. It is the purpose of the next chapter to explore the ways in which such a mercantilist conception of the State was, for Banks and other members of his circle, closely allied to the defence of the landed interest in an age when the interests of the landed and commercial classes were beginning to diverge: a foreshadowing of the social divisions which were to re-shape Britain's ancient constitution in the following century.

CHAPTER FOUR

Neo-mercantilism and the Landed Interest

ARISTOCRATIC IMPROVEMENT AND NATIONAL ECONOMIC POLICY

Though the British State was growing in size and reach in the late eighteenth century it rested on deeply traditional social foundations. For it was very largely the artefact of a landed oligarchy, the remote origins of which lay in a feudal military class but which had, over the centuries, shown a remarkable capacity for adaptation and renewal. Since the Glorious Revolution of 1688, in particular, the upper echelons of this class had consolidated both their political and social power. The growing parliamentary restraints on the actions of monarchs and their ministers reflected the determination of an increasingly self-assured oligarchy, acting through both the House of Lords and the House of Commons, to prevent any renewed monarchical attempts to challenge their privileges or prerogatives.[1]

Such political power rested, in turn, on the growing economic power of at least the better endowed members of the landed classes. As Cain and Hopkins write: 'The period 1688–1850 owes its unity to the economic and political dominance of a reconstructed and commercially progressive aristocracy which derived its power from land'.[2] The agricultural developments of the eighteenth century favoured the large-scale landholder, for agricultural improvement required both considerable capital and economies of scale. Agricultural improvement, in turn, multiplied the number and the significance of tenant farmers for it rested on a partnership between landowner and tenant farmer: the one providing capital and incentives for innovation and improvement, the other the organisation and the labour to implement such change. And, as the network of tenants expanded, so, too, did the landowner's political reach and his significance in both local and national affairs.

Moreover, the experience of improvement became contagious as the success of agricultural innovation prompted improvement in other areas of the nation's economic and social life, whether in commerce, manufacture or social policy towards endemic problems such as the treatment of the poor.[3] The ancient and all too demonstrable view of this life as a vale of tears and the human condition, in the Hobbesian phrase, as being 'nasty, brutish and short' was weakened by the evident benefits that improvement brought in its wake. Improvement, in short, offered the possibility of progress – first and foremost in the most fundamental area of social and economic life, the production of food. From these beginnings the experience and benefits of improvement rippled out to other areas, further weakening the hold of tradition and the natural human aversion to change. Improvement, too, was closely linked with the Baconian goal of utilising science for 'the relief of man's estate'; for improvement both drew on, and confirmed, a faith in the importance of empirical methods.

Though traditional in their origins, in many of their attitudes and in their claims to ancient lineage, eighteenth-century Britain's landowners were, then, increasingly open to the possibility of change. This was true, at least, in the sphere of economic affairs and, by extension, in the realm of social policy. Predictably, such an openness to change was much less apparent in political affairs for to accede to change and reform was likely to weaken the power of the elite. But, though the landowning oligarchy may have resisted major concessions of political power to other social groups, such as the commercial and manufacturing classes, they were nonetheless sympathetic to their needs and sensitive to their significance.

The experience of successful agricultural improvement made such landowners willing to sacrifice tradition for economic benefit, a cameo example being the alacrity with which the Duke of Bridgewater tore up his ancestral park to install a coal mine and a canal linking the mine with eager customers in Manchester. Banks, too, extended the size and effectiveness of a mine on his Overton estate using the latest technology provided by Boulton and Watt. The benefits accrued through investment in the improvement of one's estate and, by extension, the improvement of the transport linking one's estate with markets, both national and international, naturally intensified the traditional landowning oligarchy's appetite for profit. And, as the eighteenth century wore on, such landowners became increasingly aware that profit could be derived from sources other than land. Investment in commerce, particularly through the monopoly trading companies such as the East India Company, offered one increasingly popular route to such profits. More spectacular, though more precarious, profits could be made from service to the State for, as the domain of the State's activity expanded, so, too, did the possibility of realising large sums by handling State finances or

The Duke of Bridgewater and his canal. A print of 1767.
(By courtesy of the British Museum)

contracts. The late eighteenth-century British State may have rested on a traditional base in the form of a landowning class but it was a class eager to promote commercial activity and the possibility of augmenting both individual and national wealth.

The desire for commercial gain, then, became a major consideration in the framing of national policy. For a class which, like the European aristocracy generally, was still permeated by its military origins the most obvious route for the expansion of trade was to employ military and naval strength to weaken one's opponents. The quest for commercial advantage, too, strengthened the natural tendency of States to vie with each other. 'Commerce', wrote the arch-mercantilist, Colbert, as a loyal minister of Louis XIV, 'is the means to augment the power and grandeur of his Majesty and to lower that of his enemies and rivals'.[4] But, as we have seen, the increasing scale and expense of war transformed the character of such States as traditional dynastic disputes gave way to tussles between nations with better developed governmental machinery and, *pari passu*, better developed methods of extracting taxes from their populations. War and commerce, then, were more and more linked in a reciprocal relationship: war helped in the capture of new markets and imperial possessions while such increased sources of wealth enabled states to fight bigger and better wars.

Such a view of commerce was, of course, predicated on the view that commerce existed to serve government and was largely amenable to government control. In other words, the link between commerce and warfare was closely allied to what Adam Smith derisively termed the mercantilist system in which commerce had largely to accommodate itself to the Procrustean bed arranged for it by the State. For Smith, mercantilism represented such a patent and menacing reality which was embodied in a whole framework of legislation that he devoted the largest section of the *Wealth of Nations* to a critique of its stultifying effects on the relations between nations.[5] But mercantilism was too deeply linked with the needs of a State seeking to establish authority both at home and abroad to be readily overthrown. As Heckscher wrote in his classic work on the subject 'the states stood at the centre of mercantilist endeavour as they developed historically: the state was both the subject and the object of mercantilist economic policy'.[6]

In the manner of a form of government and a governing class shaped by the needs of war, mercantilism reflected the belief that one nation's commercial advantage represented another's loss. The most tangible symbol of victory was the inflow of bullion to one's own kingdom while its outflow represented national loss and disgrace – hence bullionism became for Smith the ultimate expression of mercantilism.[7] In mercantilist thinking, then, international commerce was a cake of fixed size so that the bigger the slice taken by one's own State the smaller was that enjoyed by other States.[8]

In late eighteenth-century Britain such a dog-eat-dog view of international economic life had been weakened by the increasingly evident fact that international trade was not of finite size but rather could continue to grow to the benefit of all. Moreover, economic relations between nations, like those between individuals, could work to enrich all parties. Hence Smith's scathing attack on mercantilism which he saw as corroding the natural association between trade and domestic and international co-operation. 'By such maxims as these', he wrote of mercantilism, 'nations have been taught that their interest consisted in beggaring all their neighbours. Each nation has been made to look with an invidious eye upon the prosperity of all the nations with which it trades'. The consequence, then, was that 'commerce, which ought naturally to be, among nations, as among individuals, a bond of union and friendship, has become the most fertile source of discord and animosity'.[9]

But, though such Smithite views of international trade were beginning to influence the views of late eighteenth-century British statesmen,[10] more traditional conceptions of the links between commerce and the imperatives of government were too deeply engrained to be readily dismissed. For a landowning oligarchy, commerce was to be encouraged because it was a source of individual and national wealth but also for the strategic advantages it conferred in the most traditional occupation of any aristocracy: the waging of war.

The agrarian roots of this oligarchy's wealth and social and political significance also served to strengthen such attitudes. The view that agriculture was too vital to the nation's welfare and too closely tied to its traditional social fabric to be exposed to the vagaries of international trade was a deeply rooted one – so deeply rooted that it remains a major factor in international commerce to this day. Agrarian improvement may have greatly increased the productivity of eighteenth-century British agriculture but landowners continued to oppose the importing of food on the grounds that this would weaken local production – a view that became increasingly difficult to maintain in the face of a rapidly growing population which less and less could be fed solely by British agriculture. Landowners naturally, then, continued to favour governmental controls over trade in agricultural produce, an attitude of mind which strengthened long-standing beliefs in the importance of governmental regulation of commerce more generally.

Mercantilism and the defence of the landed interest were, then, closely aligned in a polity still largely controlled by a landowning oligarchy. And, in late eighteenth-century Britain, the landed interest was beginning to become more insistent in the defence of its position in the face of what it considered the growing governmental favour for the commercial and manufacturing classes. Though government might be the province of a landed oligarchy it was one ever mindful of the importance of commerce. Lord Shelburne went so far as to write around 1765 that 'It has ever been the Maxim of all polite Nations, to regulate their Government to the best advantage of their trading Interest'.[11] The late eighteenth century, then, sees the beginning of the conflicts over free trade in agricultural products which, in the nineteenth century, were to transform Britain's ancient constitution as the growing economic power of classes other than the landowning oligarchy began to achieve growing recognition in the realm of politics.

But in the late eighteenth century such transformations seemed remote, as the commercial and manufacturing classes were still largely prepared to leave the conduct of national and international affairs to the traditional landowning class. For, in general, the interests of merchant and landowner seemed to be largely congruent – both favoured policies which at the national and the international level would increase national wealth and significance. Indeed, it was the frequent complaint of such largely self-appointed leaders of the landed interest that even their fellow landowners were not sufficiently mindful of their own interests. For a class whose wealth derived from both landed and commercial activities there was a natural conflict within their own ranks in balancing the demands of the landed and commercial interests. Commercial interests were also frequently linked with strategic concerns which again had to be weighed against the agrarian interest which, *prima facie*, was the most natural concern of a landowning class.

Those men, such as Banks and his close collaborators Lord Sheffield and Arthur Young, who saw themselves as defending the landed interest came to form one among a number of competing lobby groups which shaped the conduct of the British State's economic policy. It was a lobby group, too, the activities of which had wider implications than simply policy towards agriculture. For, as we have seen, the defence of the landed interest naturally tended to strengthen the still deeply engrained mercantilist attitudes among those conducting the policy of the British State towards international commerce and imperial affairs. Since agriculturalists were wary of the effects of Smithian principles of free trade on their own interests they also tended to act as a brake on the dismantling of governmental controls over other areas of the British economy – particularly in the realm of international trade where free-trade principles might be in conflict with the strategic or military imperatives of government.

Banks was to play a significant role in forming the landed interest into an effective lobby group – a reminder that he was not as remote from the political arena as he often claimed. For the growing organisation and stridency of the landed interest in the late eighteenth century reflects a more general movement of the age: the increasing tendency to form associations for particular political ends, whether these be to achieve political reform, maintenance of penal laws against Roman Catholics or the advancement of the interests of the landed, manufacturing or commercial classes.[12] The growth of a landed interest as a political force reflects the fact that this class could no longer assume that parliament, despite its preponderance of landed gentlemen, would naturally act in its interest. For, by the late eighteenth century, government was having to acknowledge the economic and political significance of other interest groups, particularly those deriving from the increasingly important commercial and manufacturing sectors of the economy.

The concept of a landed interest – which was to loom so large in the politics of the nineteenth century – was a creation of the eighteenth. It surfaced during the wars against Louis XIV with their resultant burden on landowners in the form of the Land Tax, but faded as the Peace of Utrecht (1713) brought with it an abatement in taxation.[13] But the changing demands of government and the growing diversity of the economy in the late eighteenth century brought with them a renewed and much more long-lasting sense of the landed interest as something distinct and in need of vigilant defence.

THE RISE OF THE LANDED INTEREST: THE WOOL BILL CONTROVERSY

The first major illustration of the limitation of the political power of the landed classes came with the controversy over the export of unprocessed wool in the 1780s – an episode which did much to strengthen both the landed interest's sense of grievance and its *esprit de corps*. Ironically, it was an episode in which the landed interest appeared to be agitating for a dismantling of mercantilist controls – though, as we shall see, this was to be only a very partial and tactically-based move towards free trade as the ensuing agitation over the Corn Laws was to make abundantly clear. The fundamental distinction between the two episodes was that in the controversy over the export of wool the landed interest was advocating measures which could easily be accommodated within a mercantilist framework since they involved the sale of goods abroad and hence the augmenting of the wealth of the nation. By contrast, the importation of corn involved both an assault on the landowners' livelihood and a diminution of the nation's wealth in paying for exports.

The need to be vigilant in defence of national autonomy in the realm of agriculture, then, coloured the landed interest's cautious attitude towards free trade and helps to account for its reluctance to embark on any thorough-going dismantling of the State's traditional controls over the economy. It was an attitude of mind that was one among the range of influences that helped shape government policy abroad as well as at home. For the landed interest was among the most vocal groups urging the view that the economic life of the Empire should be arranged, where possible, to augment the wealth, autonomy and strategic strength of the mother-country. By doing so, the landed interest tempered the adoption of free-trade notions which it considered might weaken the utility of the colonies to Britain. In mobilising the landed interests at home and translating its concerns into the realm of imperial policy Banks – for all his claims to be above politics – was to play a critical role.

A study of the way in which the landed interest mobilised support in the two major episodes which brought it to birth as a political force in the late eighteenth century – the controversy over the controls on the export of raw wool and those over the Corn Laws – serves to point to a number of morals. First, and most obviously, it indicates the increasing assertiveness of the landed interest as government policy reflected the demands of a range of interest groups apart from the landowners. Secondly, it is a case-study of the formation of another lobby group, a notable feature of late eighteenth-century politics. Thirdly, and from the point of view of the theme of this chapter, most importantly, it illustrates the ambivalence towards free-trade economics which was to be a feature of the landed interest and its influence on government policy. Though laissez-faire ideas had become sufficiently accepted to be invoked where possible, the landed interest was too committed to the concept of national self-sufficiency ever to adopt them in any thorough-going manner. And when, as in the case of the Corn Laws, the landed interest's own needs clashed with free-trade principles its fundamental attachment to mercantilist conceptions of national economic life became manifest.

In the agitation surrounding the bill regarding the export of wool – controversy which did much to create a sense of common identity within the landed classes – agricultural improvers such as Banks, Lord Sheffield and Arthur Young took a prominent part. Agricultural improvement, then, did not always lead to a happy conjunction of interests between the landed and commercial classes. In the case of the Wool Bill the attempt by the manufacturers' lobby to restrict the export of wool was regarded as a brake on an area of agriculture which had played an important part in promoting productivity through the techniques of mixed farming with which sheep husbandry was associated. Less consistently, the long-running Corn Bill controversy led to the improving spokesmen of the landed interest portraying the threat of foreign imports as undermining national self-sufficiency in so vital an area as food – self-sufficiency which the endeavours of the agricultural improvers had done much to promote. Generally speaking, the ethic of improvement helped to bind together England's commercial and landed elites but as the century drew to an end both groups were becoming more aware of their separate identity and interest. As Banks's steward, Benjamin Stephenson, presciently remarked to his master in 1782: 'It has a long while been a political Maxim, that if Trade be encouraged & flourishes the Landed Interest will rise; but I am strongly of opinion their interests are not so compatible as that Maxim suggests'.[14]

Stephenson's remark was prompted by the early stages of the controversy – one which did much to imprint the truth of his view on the minds of many of the landowning classes. It was a controversy, then, which strengthened the self-consciousness of the landed interest as a distinct and somewhat embattled element within the body politic. Since the fifteenth century the English State had included in its mercantilist armoury a prohibition on the export of raw wool in order to stimulate the domestic cloth industry.[15] Such restrictions had become increasingly irksome to producers over the course of the eighteenth century, the

'Ram letting from Robert Bakewell's breed at Dishley, near Loughborough,
Leicestershire', 1810, by Tomas Weaver (figure fourth from door frame is
Sir Joseph Banks).
(By courtesy of the Tate Gallery)

result being a series of inconclusive measures intended to loosen the
traditional mercantilist strait-jacket.[16] But, with the depression in the
wool industry brought about by the collapse of exports during the war
with America, agitation for some relief from the restriction on the export
of raw wool reached a new intensity as growers attempted to bolster their
declining income by selling to foreign manufacturers.

Banks's county of Lincolnshire was at the forefront of such demands
since it was particularly dependent on the trade in heavy wools of the sort
traditionally used by worsted manufacturers.[17] Banks's response to this
economic crisis took a number of forms. In the long term he hoped to
introduce into England (and, in particular, into Lincolnshire) sheep
derived from Spanish merino strains which would provide the fine, light
wools which were increasingly in demand as the wool industry had to
compete ever more strenuously with the rapidly burgeoning cotton
industry. Fundamentally, then, Banks's goal in this area as in most fields
was to work towards national self-sufficiency: to ensure, in mercantilist
fashion, that British wealth and autonomy would not be weakened by

reliance on foreign imports. But such a transformation of centuries-old practices could not solve Lincolnshire's more immediate problems. Consequently, Banks, for all his much-vaunted political independence, became more and more the moving spirit behind a major lobby group based in Lincolnshire but with allies in other counties – its aim being to loosen the legislative control of the manufacturers over the export of wool. For the export of products – something which would bring wealth into the kingdom – was in accord with Banks's fundamental preoccupation with increasing Britain's self-sufficiency and standing. In the course of the campaign Banks enlisted the vigorous support of Lord Sheffield and Arthur Young and this triumvirate was to do much to create the rhetoric and sense of identity of an imperilled landed interest.

The campaign began with a county meeting at Lincoln in October 1781 which resolved to attempt to persuade parliament to allow some temporary and 'limited exportation' as 'the only measure w[hi]ch can give relief adequate to the present distress'. In support of this they argued that 'the old laws prohibiting the exportation of wool were made upon the principle of a scarcity of that commodity for the use of the manufacture at home'[18] – by contrast, there was now a glut. Thus they accepted the mercantilist premise that the State should intervene to ensure national economic self-sufficiency but argued that it no longer applied in this instance. The fact that the landed interest's arguments did not involve any fundamental break with mercantilist thinking is underlined by their attempt to couple the weakening of State controls over the export of wool with the prohibition on yarn imports.

The Lincolnshire committee also published an invitation to other graziers to join their cause – thus helping to create the sense of a common identity and shared grievances within the landed interest: 'Whereas the County of Lincoln has hitherto stood forth as the first power in this business, & we are willing to concur and co-operate with such other counties or persons as think themselves aggrieved in a similar manner'.[19] The landed interest, then, was adopting similar tactics to the contemporaneous movement for political reform, which also was heavily reliant on county petitions – an instance of the way in which the formation of the landed interest as a lobby group reflects the increasingly assertive political culture of the age. The sense of the landed interest as a constituency in need of defence and political mobilisation had been highlighted by Banks's correspondent, the Lincolnshire landowner, Henry Pacey, in a pamphlet of the same year. In it he had decried the fact that 'The policy of this nation should seem to have taken a bias, for some time past, in favour of trade, to the depression of the landed interest'. Pacey also made high claims for the landed interest since land was 'the resource from whence the wealth of the nation springs'.[20]

The manufacturing interest responded promptly and vigorously to this attempt to weaken such advantageous regulations with a meeting in Leeds in December.[21] The resolutions passed included a tactically astute attempt to split the wool producers by arguing that such mercantilist defences worked to the benefit of both the landed and commercial interests. After moving that 'the Landed Interest be applied to for their Assurances and Support', the manufacturers attempted to persuade some of the wool producers that they, too, would be weakened if exports were permitted. Such effective counter-measures from the manufacturers led the Lincolnshire squire, Charles Chaplin, to bemoan to Banks the political feebleness of the landowners in the face of such 'an infamous combination & Monopoly'. That 'people of property', he wrote, '[are] so idle & dissipated that they will not think of, or attend to any business, is an intolerable grievance'. This, together with the fact that 'We are certainly in an awkward situation for a Leader in the House', made him all the more grateful for Banks's role as leader – hence his comment that 'Your Country will be greatly indebted to you for your exertions'.[22]

The disparity between the political skills of the two sides was evident again in meetings held in London in early 1782. These meetings also made it apparent how little success the Lincolnshire wool-growers had had in rallying support from landowners throughout the country for their cause. Predictably, the graziers' proposed bill collapsed, its demise quickened by the formation of the Rockingham ministry in March 1782 which, as Charles Chaplin complained to Banks, had 'long since declared against our Wool Bill'. But, as Chaplin acknowledged, the more fundamental reason for defeat was 'the irresolute, pitiful and weak conduct of many of our Countreymen'[23] – the landed interest's disunity[24] and initial lack of ability to master the tactics of association and lobbying which the political crises were to do much to shape and develop.[25] Earlier, however, Chaplin had acknowledged that the failure of the landed interest was no fault of Banks: 'We are all sensible that if any thing should be done for us it will be entirely owing to your able & animated exertions in our favour'.[26]

It was Banks, too, who did much to rally the cause of the landed interest – both within Lincolnshire and throughout the country as a whole – when the issue of the export of wool again surfaced as a political issue in 1786. This time it was as a result of an initiative of the manufacturers who, perhaps emboldened by their earlier success, attempted to ensure that the traditional controls on the export of wool were enforced even more rigorously.

By 1786 the wool industry had recovered from its war-induced doldrums, though the Lincolnshire wool-growers still faced the long-term problem of a decline in popularity of their heavy wools. What prompted the woollen manufacturers appears to have been largely the fear that the commercial treaty between Britain and France would open the gate to an export of raw wool to France.[27] The experience of the wool controversy of 1781–2, together with the formation of the Chamber of Manufacturers as a result of the lobbying that surrounded the Irish trade proposals of 1785, had rendered the manufacturers an even more

formidable force. However, the draconian nature of the proposed
bill (with such proposals as a register of wool producers within fifteen
miles of the sea and penalties, including imprisonment, of offenders)
prompted the landed interest to act more vigorously than in 1781–2.
Once again the result was to be a defeat for the landed interest – albeit of
a qualified kind; but it emerged out of the controversy with a stronger
sense of purpose and common identity.

Along with Banks, the leaders of the landed opposition to the bill were
Lord Sheffield and Arthur Young, who complemented Banks's behind-
the-scenes lobbying with forthright public statements of the landed
interest's grievances. In particular, Young's outpourings did much to
increase the self-consciousness and sense of grievance of the landed
estate. As the title of his article, 'On the Necessity of County Associations
of the Landed Interest', suggests, Young saw the Wool Bill controversy as
highlighting the need for the landed interest to organise itself more
effectively. To prompt such action he enlarged on its grievances: 'The
history of the internal policy of this kingdom, in relation to trade and
manufacture', he wrote, 'would be a recital of the injustice and op-
pressions which have, uniformly, been heaped on those classes in the
community, commonly called the landed interest' – the needs of which
he saw as being 'sacrificed in favour of the manufacturing interest'.
Young emphasised that the success of the manufacturers in having a

John Holroyd, first Earl of Sheffield. Pencil and wash
drawing by Henry Edridge, 1798.
(By courtesy of the National Portrait Gallery, London)

revised version of the bill passed by parliament made the need for the
landed classes to organise even more urgent for it showed that
'Manufacturers are *combined*, and therefore respectable – the landed
interest discredited, and therefore contemptible'.[28] So combative had
Young been in his depiction of the oppression of the landed interest by
the manufacturers that he had earlier been burnt in effigy, prompting
Banks to send a congratulatory letter: 'I give you joy sincerely at having
arrived at the glory of being burned in effigy; nothing is so conclusive a
proof of your possessing the best of the argument'.[29]

Young combined such manifestos on behalf of the landed interest with
direct personal canvassing, both at the county and the national level, to
defeat the Wool Bill. Reflecting the move towards county associations for
specific political purposes, which had been stimulated by the opposition
to the American War, Young assumed the leadership of the Suffolk
movement. As he wrote in his autobiography this 'united [him] with Sir
Joseph Banks, who was deputed by the county of Lincoln for the same
purpose'.[30] But, to Young's dismay, few other counties followed suit, as he
wrote to Banks at the end of 1786:

> Lincolnshire in particular & the publick at large are highly obliged to you for the
> noble & active part you have taken on this occasion. Lord Sheffield has been very
> spirited in Sussex but what are the rest of the Kingdom about? Surely asleep.[31]

Though Banks was more sparing in his public pronouncements than
Sheffield and Young it is apparent that his two fellow champions of the
landed interest looked to him for guidance. Sheffield, for example,
deferred to Banks's opinion on whether he ought to call a meeting in his
home county of Sussex, writing that 'If you recommend it & I find I can
obtain a respectable Meeting in this County, I shall propagate & promote
it . . . Instruct me & I shall obey'.[32] After the county meeting was held – at
which characteristically Sheffield 'thought it best to move vigorous
Resolutions'[33] – he again deferred to Banks, writing that 'I am very glad
you approve the Proceedings at our Meeting'.[34] It was a political partnership cemented by the two men's common enthusiasm for agricultural
improvement, especially in regard to sheep – hence Sheffield's comment
to Arthur Young in October 1787 that 'No experiment has pleased me
better than Sir Joseph Banks relative to wool. I am now perfectly satisfied
we may improve the quality greatly'.[35]

Young's deference to Banks's leadership in the Wool Bill controversy
was less apparent (or less documented) but he, too, plainly depended on
Banks's behind-the-scene activities and well developed system of intelligence. Thus in February 1788 he sent Banks 'A thousand thanks for
your information: I must continue to depend on you for intelligence of
ye motions of the monopolists [the manufacturers]'.[36] Within Lincolnshire, Banks's role as the county's major advocate and organiser was
unchallenged. One Lincolnshire squire accompanied his request for
a subscription 'when the business comes before Parliament' with an

Arthur Young. Pencil drawing by George Dance, 1794.
(By courtesy of the National Portrait Gallery, London)

acknowledgment that 'it cannot be in better Hands than Sir Joseph Banks's, who is perfectly Master of the Matter & is indefatigable in rendering this County every Service in his Power'.[37]

Though Banks took a leading role in the campaign he nonetheless showed some reluctance to be too publicly – or, at least, too con-spicuously – identified with the brawl with the manufacturers. No doubt this reflected his view that the President of the Royal Society should be seen to be above the political fray. Thus he was reluctant to publish under his own name a pamphlet on the subject, despite the urgings of Sheffield that it was 'extremely essential that your name should be put to it' since the work would 'teach the torpid landed interest to think & reason'.[38] The pamphlet was never published though much of its substance appeared in Young's *Annals of Agriculture* under Banks's initials.[39]

Banks's role in the campaign was more that of a lobbyist than a publicist, one of his chief political assets being his recent association with

Lord Hawkesbury, President of the Committee for Trade, whom he attempted to persuade to modify the bill when it came before the House of Lords in June 1788.[40] Hawkesbury co-operated to some extent but not enough to assuage the landed interest. For although the bill, as eventually passed, amounted to little more than a consolidation of previous legislation, its passage in any form was regarded by the landed interest as evidence of parliament's subservience to the manufacturers. Thus one of Banks's correspondents wrote that he 'was sorry to find Ld Hawkesbury so decided an Advocate for the Manufacturers in the House of Lords'; he did, however, compliment Banks on the fact that the wool-growers 'certainly owe much to your exertions and vigilance that it [the act] was not infinitely more oppressive'.[41]

But a number of Banks's associates expressed the hope that out of the ashes of defeat would rise a more vigorous landed interest strengthened and sustained by the efforts that Banks, Sheffield and Young had devoted to the campaign. Young optimistically affirmed that 'The manufacturers experienced so determined and vigorous an opposition that they would hardly engage again in any similar attack upon the landed interest'.[42] Banks's fellow Lincolnshire grazier, Henry Shepherd, looked forward to 'some future Crisis [which] may favour a more direct attack on the monopolising spirit of the Manufacturers'.[43] With unwarranted optimism Banks's steward, Benjamin Stephenson, had hoped for a victory but linked such hopes with a tribute to the way in which Banks's 'unwearied diligence & perseverance' had 'rouse[d] up the Landed Interest'.[44]

In the course of the campaign the landed interest had learned to deploy a number of ideological weapons. Firstly, it appealed to the rhetoric of improvement. In his draft pamphlet on the Wool Bill, for example, Banks likened the wool manufacturers to an unimproving farmer who

> holding his Land at too low a rent to have livd idly on the profit which accrued without much industry & neglected to make those improvements in his Farm which his Landlord from the example of the rest of the Countrey had a right to expect of him.

Banks continued on to contrast the energetic improving spirit of the rapidly burgeoning cotton industry with what he regarded as the sluggish ways of the wool monopolists – an example that the woollen manufacturers should have emulated since 'every mechanical invention which has been adopted to the improvement of the Cotton [manufacture] is equaly applicable to the Woolen manufactory'.

Predictably, Banks regarded the slowness of the wool-growers to adapt and change with a more indulgent eye since 'the stagnation of price for so long a series of years as has now been the case has precluded all encouragement to improvement'. Like Young and Sheffield he bemoaned the supine character of 'the Landlord interest' which 'have for so long a time born this burden oppressive to themselves & impolitic to the nation at large'.

A second ideological weapon the landed interest had learned to employ was that of laissez-faire economics. As Carter points out, the campaign had shown the way in which the defenders of the landed interest could, when it suited their interests, speak 'clearly, as reforming agriculturists, in the authentic language of "the new Science of Political Economy"'.[45] Thus a pamphlet of 1782 attributed to Banks with the title, *The Propriety of Allowing a Qualified Exportation of Wool Discussed Historically*,[46] took as its motto a ringing declaration of belief in free trade from the writings of Lord Coke: 'Freedom of Trade is the Life of Trade and all Monopolies and Restrictions of Trade do Overthrow Trade'. Henry Pacey, the Lincolnshire landowner and pamphleteer in the cause of the wool-growers, also invoked the support of the clerical economist, Josiah Tucker, who anticipated some of Adam Smith's arguments against monopolies. Pacey informed Banks that 'his [Tucker's] sentim[en]ts were yt an exportation of wool under due regulations & restrictions w[oul]d be beneficial to ye state'[47] – a statement which, with its insistence on the continued need for government restrictions on trade, underlines how partial was the move towards a belief in free trade among the landowners.

The great Adam Smith himself had, in a section of *Wealth of Nations* on the theme of the 'Mercantile System', attacked the way in which the woollen manufacturers had

> not only obtained a monopoly against the commoners by an absolute prohibition of importing woollen clothes from any foreign country, but they have likewise obtained another monopoly against the sheep farmers and growers of wool by a similar prohibition of the exportation of live sheep and wool.[48]

Arthur Young invoked such passages in Smith in arguing that the Scot had shown how 'The country gentlemen ... have always been duped by a set of men much more active, connected and sagacious, than themselves'.

But, continued Young, the tide was now beginning to turn, largely as the result of the enlightened writings of political economists such as Adam Smith who had stripped away the rationalisations which allowed monopolist manufacturers to use parliament for their own ends:

> But the present age is too much enlightened for this commercial mummery of smoak-ball phrases to pass any longer, without opposition and detection. The ablest political writers, at present in Europe, have with one voice, condemned the commercial monopolies, which take place no where to such a degree as in England'.[49]

Elsewhere Young even more firmly linked the cause of the wool-growers to that of free trade, writing that 'Regulation may destroy, but it can never make commerce; and this kingdom has grown great, not by her numerous restrictions, but *in spite* of them'.[50]

Needless to say, such resort to the language of political economy in defence of the wool-growers was largely tactical, for the landed interest showed no compunction about abandoning free-trade principles when it suited their ends. The demand by the Lincolnshire wool-growers in late 1781 for a relaxation of the laws forbidding the export of wool was combined with an attempt at reinforcing a form of mercantilism: a prohibition of Irish yarn imports.[51] Lord Sheffield's vigilant defence of the landed interest later led him in 1811 to attack as a 'sacrifice of the landed to the manufacturing interest' not only the ban on the export of raw wool (which was not to be abolished until 1824), but also 'the free admission', without tariff, of foreign wool. Such imports he described, with a characteristic appeal to mercantilist principles, as 'a sacrifice of essential interests in favour of foreigners, which can not be supported by any principles of justice or sound policy'.[52] Sheffield, then, was in favour of free trade for some exports but wanted to retain controls on imports which might affect the landed interest – a position in accord with traditional mercantilist theory about husbanding the wealth of the kingdom.

THE BEGINNINGS OF THE CORN LAW DEBATE

The landed interest's fundamental suspicion of free trade – at least in agriculture – was to be transparently evident in the controversy over the Corn Laws, an issue which was, of course, more and more to dominate political life until their eventual and highly divisive repeal in 1846. For the Corn Laws commanded a degree of political, and even symbolic, significance which transcended their immediate economic importance. Since no commodity was more vital than food the controls on the import and export of grain embodied in the Corn Laws were at the heart of the mercantilist system. Thus the Corn Laws were to act as the hardiest and most strongly defended outpost of that system with its assumption that the economy ought ultimately be controlled by the State. Moreover, the Corn Laws also reflected the power of the landed interest acting through parliament and so the laws' vicissitudes were regarded both by their advocates and their detractors as an index of the waxing or waning power of the landowners.

The plentiful harvests of the first half of the eighteenth century defused the issue of the control of the import or export of grain but, as population grew in the second half of the century, so, too, did the pressure on the available supply of domestically-produced grain. As a consequence, in 1773 the traditional armoury of legislative controls (which dated back to 1360) was strengthened by the addition of Thomas Pownall's Corn Law which had the effect of preventing exports when the domestic supply was low.[53] The issue of the control of the movement of grain was again catapulted into political prominence by the poor harvests of 1789–1790 which resulted in pressure for a new bill after parliament both forbade the export of grain and permitted its controlled importation. Such legislative interference in the workings of the market in grain helped to inflame the increasingly militant landed interest, fresh from its bruising encounter with both the merchants and parliament over the export of wool. In any case, corn-growers were increasingly resentful that the 1773 act did not permit them to benefit as much as they might from the increasing prices that grain was commanding. Where the landed interest had accepted the compromises involved in the 1773 act with a degree of grace, by 1790 its chief representatives were demanding greater legislative protection for their interests.[54]

The political figure at the eye of the storm was Lord Hawkesbury, President of the Privy Council Committee on Trade, who had already alienated landed opinion by supporting the Wool Bill of 1788. As the tribunes of the improving landowners began to close with Hawkesbury so, too, their suspicions increased. Arthur Young, for example, reported to Lord Sheffield in 1790 that 'I had a conf[erence] with Lord Hawkesbury on ye new corn bill ... wch. appar[antl]y [will] not [be] too good for ye L[anded] Int[erest]'.[55] Hawkesbury's draft proposals were printed in Young's *Annals* together with a generally critical commentary reflecting the increasing militancy and bitterness of the landed interest. 'God send the time may not soon arrive', wrote Young, 'when the nation shall feel the mischiefs of our shallow policy, of sacrificing the landed interest on every occasion, to favour the trading and manufacturing ones'.[56] Predictably, Banks also shared Young's sense of outrage on behalf of the landed interest. As early as 1787 he had drafted some comments on the 'structure of the present Corn Laws' bemoaning the fact that since the burden of taxes fell chiefly on the farmers who 'are the Principal source of our Prosperity' landowners therefore found it difficult to compete against imported grain. Banks could foresee, too, that the problem of the supply of grain was likely to become more acute for 'There is not more Corn now then there was (I think there is Less) yet from increasd Population & enlargd opulence there is a greater demand for it'.[57]

By late 1789 Banks was involved in some of the preliminary discussions about a new bill, though, characteristically, he operated as far as possible out of public view. When his Lincolnshire neighbour, John Linton, wrote to him in November 1789 about reports that he had 'had a Conference with one of the Secretaries of State, on the subject of the new Act relating to Corn' Banks replied that

> I trust my Conversation with Mr. Grenville is not publickly talked of ... as I am anxious at all times when I do business which ought more regularly to be done by the County members to keep myself as much as possible in the back ground to avoid jealousy.[58]

Naturally, Banks was also closely in touch with Lord Sheffield who, like Young, was critical of Hawkesbury's proposals and particularly those concerned with controlling the export of grain which, as he told Banks, he regarded as 'the most compleat system that can be imagined for utterly preventing a Trade in Corn.[59]

Sheffield's solution to the shortage of grain was that of Banks and other representatives of the landed interest: to increase domestic supply of grain (or, if necessary, other foodstuffs) in order to ensure self-sufficiency. Hence his reply to Banks that

> I do not subscribe to the Doctrine that we cannot raise Corn enough for our use – if it is true, we shou'd be highly alarmed, & ins[tead] of checking Agriculture by low[er]ing the exporting or importing price we sho'd raise both & encourage the growth of Corn by every means possible.[60]

It was a position that Sheffield spelt out at greater length in the following year (1791) in a pamphlet entitled *Observations on the Corn Bill*, in which he argued that the effect of the proposed bill was to make England 'in great measure dependant on foreign countries for subsistence'. The pamphlet also included the sort of invective that was increasingly to characterise the relations between the landed and manufacturing interests. Thus Sheffield envisaged a situation where a harvest failure in Europe would reduce 'the manufacturing interest who calculate nothing beyond a temporary cheapness' to 'look[ing] up to the landed interest for their daily bread'.[61] Banks may also have had a hand in producing this pamphlet while adopting his familiar reluctance to appear in too public a guise on issues linked to party politics. When Banks's neighbour, John Linton, thanked him for sending on a copy of the work, Linton added that he was even more grateful 'for the Share I am convinced you have had in contributing Materials for many Parts of his Essay'.[62]

For Banks, too, shared the view that government policy was encouraging imports at the expense of stimulating home production, as his pointed rejoinder to Hawkesbury about the proposed Corn Law a month later indicates:

> The Policy of the present bill is evidently to feed the inhabitants of this great Agricultural Country upon Foreign Corn ... [which] arises from an opinion that the manufacturers in it either cannot or will not without commotion pay the price that the native Farmer is obliged to demand.[63]

Banks even felt the need to drive home this message to Arthur Young whom he regarded as having become too inclined to view Hawkesbury's proposals favourably. Thus in a letter to Young he envisaged the possibility of 'a general famine in Europe' which would 'teach ... us by direct & absolute starvation that we are dependent on other nations for that which at a fair Price we should have grown for ourselves'.[64] Sinclair, the arch-agricultural improver and moving spirit in the creation of the Board of Agriculture in 1793, was of the same mind as Banks and Sheffield on this point. Thus he wrote in his *Address to the Landed Interest, on the Corn Bill* that 'if we cannot supply ourselves with bread we are not an independent nation'.[65]

In the event, the landowners displayed their increasing political muscle by extracting an important concession: the lifting of the maximum price level before exports were permitted – something that was embodied in the act that was eventually passed in May 1791, much to the outrage of the manufacturing interest.[66] But, though Sinclair could write to Banks in May 1791, congratulating him 'on the progress we have made in the Corn Bill though it is still far from being perfect',[67] the leaders of the landed interest remained fearful of government intentions. Thus, two days after Sinclair's letter, Banks could attribute the landed interest's compromise on the bill as being better 'than [to] experience any more of the unfair opposition of Mr. Jenkinson [Hawkesbury]'.[68]

The greater the possibility of competition from imported grain, the more the leaders of the landed interest redoubled their efforts to promote agricultural improvement at home as an alternative to relying on foreign supplies. Banks and other leaders of the landed interest continued to advance the increasingly unrealistic argument that domestic agriculture could supply the entire population if improvement were allowed to proceed under the umbrella of government protection. As he wrote to Hawkesbury, his old sparring partner on issues affecting the landed interest,

> if the Just price whatever it may be is allowed, I have no doubt that the Farmers of this Island are able to Preclude Famine & even high Price, for greatly as the Population of this Countrey has of Late increasd, I think it Certain that the improvements of agriculture have kept Pace with it, & are likely to Continue still to keep pace with its future increase.[69]

But Hawkesbury remained sceptical of the claims of Banks and also those of other improvers like Sheffield who argued that England's food difficulties could be solved by measures such as the cultivation of waste lands (one of Sheffield's pet projects[70]). 'I am convinced', he wrote to Banks in September 1800, 'that the Population of this Country increases much faster than the Cultivation of it, though more than Ninety Inclosure Bills were passed in the Course of the last session of Parliament'.[71] Banks, however, was not to be discouraged and his efforts to ensure domestic self-sufficiency continued: in 1801 the shortage of grain prompted him to suggest to Lord Carrington that the spread of potatoes might 'remedy the temporary deficiency we at present experience'.[72] Another solution which he energetically advanced was the spread of spring wheat which would alleviate the problem of periods of dearth 'which will occasionally happen as long as the manufacturing interest insists on keeping the price of corn, in a plentiful harvest, below the actual cost of growing it'.[73]

The approach of the end of the French Wars brought the issue of the Corn Laws to renewed political prominence. Because the wars had disrupted the export of wheat from Europe the price of domestically produced wheat had soared, a situation which the landowners sought to perpetuate by ensuring that parliament continued to discourage imports. In the agitation for such a change Lord Sheffield was a loud and insistent voice. As early as December 1813 he was urging his fellow agricultural improver, Lord Egremont, to join him in such a crusade to curtail the importation of corn since 'There never was a period so favourable to this essential improvement in our Corn Laws'.[74] As always, however, Sheffield found his fellow landowners too quiescent – in familiar terms he complained to Young the following year that 'the landed interest is a torpid race ... I am shaking off all such business as much as I can'.[75] Despite such protestations, Sheffield continued his campaign and his pamphlet of 1815 on the Corn Laws did much to promote the passage in that same year of a new Corn Law which was to dominate political life for some three decades thereafter.

His pamphlet was a clear statement of the mercantilist faith on which his efforts as both an agricultural improver and a major voice in the formulation of imperial trade policy had been based. He protested that he had been 'early and always ... the zealous friend of the commercial and manufacturing interests of the United Kingdom' for he had attempted to ensure 'their right to the monopoly of the home and colonial markets, and to protection against the admission of foreign manufactures, in competition with our own'. With both his impartiality and mercantilist principles thus established, Sheffield continued on to argue that landowners were entitled to no less protection than that which he had endeavoured to obtain for the manufacturers: that what he was endeavouring to do was 'to secure the home market to the home grower, as all other manufactures are secured'.

He also reiterated the fundamental arguments on which the landed interest had so long based their case for a protection of agriculture from foreign imports: 'that the greatest mischief that could happen to the United Kingdom, would be a dependence on foreign countries for our subsistence; and that the United Kingdom is capable of growing more than sufficient for our consumption'.[76]

Sir John Sinclair, the founder of the Board of Agriculture, also contributed a pamphlet to the campaign, taking as its motto a quotation from Dr Johnson: 'Agriculture is the great art, which every government ought to protect, every proprietor of land to practise, and every inquirer into nature to improve'. Writing as 'one who has anxiously endeavoured, for so many years past, to promote the improvement of the country', Sinclair portrayed the effects of the recent peace as having had a disastrous effect on the income of farmers – so much so that 'It now rests with government, to prevent the probable destruction of the landed and farming interests'.[77]

Banks's contribution to the debate took a characteristically private form: a long letter to the Prime Minister, Lord Liverpool, dated 10 February 1815. In it he argued that Napoleon's Continental system had, paradoxically, 'increased its [the nation's] strength & extended its resources to a height they had never before attaind' – this being particularly true in relation to 'all Articles of Agricultural Produce'. By contrast, the return of peace had brought with it the situation where 'Corn [has] fallen below the Cost incurrd in raising it'. In Banks's analysis, then, government action to secure the income of the farming interest was an urgent necessity. Such a move would, he argued, ultimately be of benefit to society as a whole for it was the land that was the basis of the nation's economic well-being – or, as Banks himself put it in an extended organic metaphor calculated to impress on the Prime Minister the primacy of the landed interest:

> The Political State of a Nation may be compard to a Tree, the Roots of which are the Farmers, the lower Branches the Retale Traders, the upper ones the Manufacturers, the Flowers & Fruit to the Gentry & Nobility; if we cease to supply the Roots with Manure, the Branches Leaves Flowers & fruit must fade & wither, but in fact the more effectually the Root is nourishd the more vigorously the whole that is above it, will thrive & prosper.

Banks drove home the importance of the landed interest by some aspersions on the manufacturing interest. This had 'formerly [been] dependant for success upon cheap Food' but this was no longer true since more and more unskilled labour was being 'performd by Fire [steam] Engines whose Food is Coaks & not Corn'. Indeed, if the manufacturers but recognised it, it was in their interests, too, to maintain a healthy agricultural sector for, as Banks put it with another stock organic metaphor, 'to sap the foundations of the home market by reducing the incomes of the purchasers must produce the same consequences as to reduce the strength of the Limbs by denying food to the Stomach'. Moreover, continued Banks, with an appeal to mercantilist principle, if England became more dependent on imported grain 'the whole of the Sums we pay for Food will not only be withdrawn from the support of our Manufactures, but will become aliment [food] to the Manufacturers of the Rival Nations who feed us'.[78]

The increased unity and political power of the landed interest is brought out by the fact that such representations by its leaders did result in the new Corn Law of 1815 which, by banning the import of foreign wheat until the home price reached eighty shillings a quarter, went a long way towards meeting their demands. The act also had the effect of heightening the divisions between the landed and the manufacturing interests and of fomenting social division generally, one minor consequence of which was an attack by rioters on Banks's house since it belonged to someone identified with the new Corn Law.[79] But, needless to say, the landed interest's sense of grievance was not fully allayed: in 1818 Banks complained that he felt 'Rather severely the diminution which the Price of all the Produce of the Land' had undergone 'on the Return of Peace'.[80] True to form, Sheffield regarded the new Corn Law as inadequate and pressed for a revised bill which would even more securely safeguard the landed interest – though he thought it prudent to defer such a campaign in the immediate aftermath of Peterloo.[81] Behind Sheffield's demands and those of the agricultural interest generally lay the same assumptions that Banks had developed in his letter to Lord Liverpool: that the land and those who tended it were the chief source of wealth for society as a whole. Hence Sheffield's remark to the Earl of Egremont in 1820 that the distress of the 'Agriculturists' had resulted in 'that of all other Classes of Society'. Predictably, Sheffield's panacea was a revised Corn Law to discourage further imports from countries not subject to the same taxes 'as the British Farmers are'.[82]

ADAM SMITH AND THE LANDED INTEREST

In all these debates about the Corn Laws the name of Adam Smith figured prominently as a synonym for those free-trading principles which the leaders of the landed interest opposed in relation to the sale of grain – even though they might rather tentatively and partially embrace them as a tactical weapon when fighting other battles, such as the promotion of the export of wool. The *Wealth of Nations* contained a critique of the arguments that had been mounted in defence of the Corn Laws. It had described 'The high duties upon the importation of corn, which in times of moderate plenty amount to a prohibition' as giving a near monopoly to the home producers. Smith acknowledged this could produce some domestic benefits, but overall he argued that this simply amounted to a re-direction of capital to one particular sector rather than an addition to the sum total of society's wealth 'and it is by no means certain that this artificial direction is likely to be more advantageous to the society than that into which it would have gone of its own accord'. He argued, too, that 'the free importation of foreign corn could very little affect the interest of the farmers of Great Britain' since corn was such a 'bulky commodity'. Furthermore, contended Smith, 'To prohibit by a perpetual law the importation of foreign corn and cattle is in reality to enact that the population and industry of the country shall at no time exceed what the rude produce of its own soil can maintain'.[83]

Not that Smith was unsympathetic to the landed interest which he saw as less of a brake on society's economic development than the manufacturers. 'Country gentlemen and farmers', he wrote, 'are, to their great honour, of all people, the least subject to the wretched spirit of monopoly'. Where manufacturers sought to impede their rivals 'Farmers and country gentlemen, on the contrary, are generally disposed rather to promote than to abstract the cultivation and improvement of their neighbours' farms and estates'. With the sociological insight characteristic of the Scottish Enlightenment, Smith pointed out one of the basic reasons for the relative political weakness of the landed interest as it stood in 1776 before the controversies over the trade in wool and corn made it a more potent force:

> Country gentlemen and farmers, dispersed in different parts of the country, cannot so easily combine as merchants and manufacturers, who, being collected into towns, and

accustomed to that exclusive corporation spirit which prevails in them, naturally endeavour to obtain against all their countrymen the same exclusive privilege which they generally possess against the inhabitants of their respective towns.[84]

Such favourable sentiments towards the landed interest may help to explain why Banks and Smith evidently regarded each other with respect for, in a letter of 1789, Smith thanked Banks for 'The very great politeness and attention with which you was so good as to honour me with when I was last in London'.[85]

Though the landed interest adopted Smithian-style principles when it suited them in the 1780s in support of the relaxation of legislative restraints on the export of wool, they became more and more qualified in their attitude to Smith as the Corn Law issue assumed ever greater importance. Arthur Young regarded Smith's work as a useful weapon against the entrenched interests of the merchants but argued that, though free trade was the ideal system, it was impossible to implement it properly in relation to agriculture. Hence his equivocal description of the *Wealth of Nations*:

> I hardly know an abler work than Dr.Smith's, or one (it is no contradiction) that is fuller of more pernicious errors: he never touches on any branch of rural oeconomy, but to start positions that arise from mis-stated facts, or that lead to false conclusions.[86]

As the Corn Law issue became more and more pervasive so, too, did the leaders of landed opinion become more inclined to take Smith to task, a transformation reflected in Banks's increasingly critical comments on Smith. In a memorandum on the state of the economy in 1799 Banks attributed the high cost of provisions to the fact that the application by government of free-trade principles had resulted in the lifting of traditional controls on the sale of grain with the result that the grain merchants had engaged in profiteering. This prompted a bitter tirade by Banks against the Scottish political economist (even though Smith himself had included some caustic remarks on the machinations of grain merchants in his work[87]):

> Thus much for the Principle of a Free Competition in Trade which that profound Theorist Smith[,] where every page proves him to be absolutely unpractical in the ways of men a very monk in a Scottish university[,] asserts to be a safe remedy against all Exhorbitance of Price. Well would it have been for us had his book been long ago stigmatized with the disgrace which daily attaches itself to his numerous Errors but for a reliance placed by those who govern us in the infallibility of his maxims Corn might now have been bought at a Reasonable rate and abundant Errors of different kinds remedied which are still corroding our System & must by degrees be curd if we expect to continue as we are an opulent & a respectable nation'.[88]

As these inflammatory remarks suggest, Banks's indignation against Smith arose out of the way in which his work had influenced governmental policy. In particular, Banks regarded Smith as having had a pernicious effect on the thinking of Hawkesbury who, as President of the

Privy Council Committee for Trade, had been largely responsible for formulating a response to the problem of dearth. Hawkesbury had been chiefly responsible for the Corn Law of 1791 which had attempted to promote as far as possible a free trade in grain – at least within England – to facilitate the movement of grain from areas of plenty to those threatened by famine.[89] Hawkesbury was, however, much less doctrinaire than Banks's comments might suggest. As the spectre of widespread famine became more of a possibility he became increasingly inclined to balance the ideal of free trade against the need to ensure that the population was properly fed. As he wrote to Banks in September 1800: 'I am also convinced that the commerce of the Necessaries of Life cannot be conducted on the same free Principles, as the Commerce in Luxuries, Conveniences, and all indifferent Articles'. This despite the fact that 'Dr.A.Smith, in his Book on the Wealth of Nations, has so possessed the World with an Idea of the Freedom of Commerce, that no one wil allow of any Exception or Restraint'.[90] Banks, of course, enthusiastically endorsed the waning enthusiasm of Liverpool (as Hawkesbury had become) for Smith, though the two men continued to disagree over the extent to which Britain should import grain to ward off possible famine – a move which Banks regarded as likely to depress prices and thus to discourage domestic production and self-sufficiency.

In the counter-revolutionary atmosphere of 1800 Smith's work could be regarded as being akin to the products of the French Enlightenment with their love of the speculative and contempt for tradition. 'Smith's Principles', wrote Banks to Liverpool, 'like those of the French Revolution breath nothing but unqualified Liberty and are as little Founded in Reason & Experience as the French are'.[91] Others damned Smith in a similar manner – an 1800 pamphlet by Alexander Dalrymple on the subject of 'the present high price of corn' spoke of Smith as one who was an infidel in religious matters and who 'was strongly tinctured with *French Philosophy* and systime'.[92] Even the whiggish Robert Heron – whom Banks strongly and successfully opposed when he later stood as an MP for Lincoln in 1812 – described Smith's work as being the product of French 'grand theory' and as providing some of the inspiration for Paine's subversive *Rights of Man* – a 'book [which] only repeats, and applies to all parts of the controul of our Government, the commercial principles of Smith'.[93]

But, for all this denigration of Smith, the rhetoric of free trade had been too firmly established as a mark of an enlightened and properly limited form of government to be lightly cast aside. In this, as in other respects, while the reaction to the French Revolution might have qualified the attitude of England's elite to its Enlightenment heritage, it did not altogether undermine it. Free trade remained a creed to be generally embraced in principle – though its application to specific areas, notably agriculture, might be called into question. Sir William Young, a loyal supporter of Banks's African Association, was candid enough to write of Smith in his pamphlet of 1800 on the Corn Laws: 'He is tenacious of his principle of *free trade*, to the very extreme. I admit and approve his principle, but in its operation I contend, for exceptions in respect to the corn trade'.[94]

Though Liverpool might argue for some modification of the full rigour of Smithian principles he, too, where possible, attempted to justify his policy in relation to the corn trade within the context of free-trade principle. As he wrote to Banks in October 1800 when defending his proposal to import corn:

> Though I am for a free Trade in Corn, I wish to resist Combinations, for these Combinations are in my Judgement destructive of a free Trade ... I know of no proper Method of resisting these Combinations but by introducing Competitors, who shall assume a share in the Trade & thereby defeat these Combinations.[95]

When asked to comment on matters outside the sensitive area of agriculture even Banks would adopt much of the language of free trade. In 1810 he responded to a proposal for government intervention in the iron industry with the comment that he doubted 'the policy of the interference of Government in any Shape with the natural Course of Trade'.[96]

The natural flow of the current of opinion, then, was increasingly towards free trade – to dam or modify such a current took more and more of the energies of an increasingly organised and strident landed interest. And, in the nature of politics, militancy begot militancy as the manufacturing interests began to organise and to generate the rhetoric of distinctively middle-class interests – something which had been largely absent in the eighteenth century. Thus the simmering conflict between the landed and manufacturing interest was transformed into the nineteenth-century battle between a traditional landed class and an increasingly self-confident middle class who characterised as 'Old Corruption' the networks of patronage and political influence by which the landed class maintained its position.

But, for all the tensions between the landed and manufacturing interests in the late eighteenth century, such disputes seemed only a small wrinkle on a political landscape which was still very largely the province of a landed class. It was a landed class ever mindful of the benefits that would accrue to themselves as individuals and to the nation as a whole from the cultivation of commerce and manufacture. Hence the irony that self-appointed leaders of the landed interest such as Banks, Sheffield and Young, saw themselves as battling to be heard by a political establishment composed very largely of fellow landowners. The message to which such tribunes of the landed interest returned again and again was the need for national self-sufficiency, whether in corn or in other areas of agriculture. It was a message that combined only partially and inadequately with the increasingly prevalent emphasis on free trade.

It was, too, a message that had wider implications than the conduct of domestic agriculture. For it was also to colour British imperial policy by emphasising the need to use imperial possessions to strengthen national economic and strategic self-sufficiency. Agricultural protection at home and mercantilist policies within the Empire were naturally complementary in the minds of landed gentlemen who regarded the Empire as an extension of the agricultural and commercial wealth of Britain. After all, had not the elder Pitt considered 'the sugar islands as the landed interest of this kingdom'?[97] The increasing emphasis on the need to regulate the economies of Britain's imperial possessions to suit the needs of Britain itself both reflected and strengthened the authoritarian character of the British Empire after the revolt of the American colonists had illustrated the dangers of granting too great a measure of colonial self-rule.[98] Moreover, with the loss of the American colonies the British Empire became less a partnership between white English-speaking subjects at home and abroad as the peoples under the British imperial flag became more diverse in race and language.[99] Thus the traditional pattern of establishing colonial replicas of Westminster rule was weakened and more direct and even authoritarian forms of government became more prevalent.

IMPERIAL POLICY AND THE NAVIGATION ACTS

For Banks and his contemporaries the all-pervading question in late eighteenth-century imperial affairs was how best to reconstruct British power abroad in the wake of the American debacle. The morals to be drawn from the loss of the American colonies were various and inconsistent. In the long term, the fact that trade between Britain and the newly-independent United States actually increased became a formidable argument for the virtues of free trade. The United States purchased twice as much from Britain in the early 1790s as it had thirty years before[100] while yoked to the British economy by a series of restrictive Navigation Acts. But, in the short term, a contrary moral could be drawn: that the American revolt was the result of allowing colonies too much freedom, whether political or economic. Moreover, the fact that the feats of the British Navy during the War of American Independence had spared the nation even greater humiliation strengthened another traditional justification for that system of economic control over the colonies, the Navigation Acts: the insistence that British colonial trade should be carried in British ships or 'bottoms' was a way of ensuring a pool of trained seamen on which the Navy could draw in times of national emergency.

In putting the view that the American revolt strengthened rather than weakened the need for such traditional economic controls the most insistent voice was that of Lord Sheffield, Banks's close comrade-in-arms in the defence of the landed interest. To Sheffield, the maintenance of economic controls over Britain's remaining colonies was of a piece with the protection of the landed interest. In both cases the interest of Britain and its economic and strategic self-sufficiency were being protected against a dangerous dependence on foreign interests. Such a position was, as we shall see, consistent with some bowing to the increasingly fashionable winds of free trade, especially when dealing with trade outside the British Empire. However, for Sheffield, as for his fellow defenders of a revised and revitalised version of the traditional commercial system held together by the controls embodied in the Navigation Acts, free trade was not an absolute good. It was but one among a number of *desiderata* which had to be balanced against the more pressing priorities of economic and strategic self-reliance.[101]

In voicing such views Sheffield was to be the most vigorous and outspoken representative of a group of largely like-minded individuals with whom Banks, as one of the major advocates of agricultural improvement, was to be closely associated. As public propagandist for the cause of imperial self-sufficiency Sheffield was frequently assisted by Banks's old schoolboy friend, William Eden (after 1789, Lord Auckland), who shared with Banks the ambition of restoring Britain's autonomy as a wool-producer by introducing new breeds of sheep. Though less prominent in public debate on imperial policy Arthur Young, the best-known apostle of agricultural improvement, was to be another voice in urging policies to achieve agricultural self-sufficiency at an imperial as well as at a domestic level.

Most significant of all in the actual implementation of such policies was to be Banks's chief political ally, Lord Hawkesbury. This despite the fact that, as we have seen, Hawkesbury was not always as doughty in defence of the landed interest as Banks or Sheffield could have wished. Nonetheless, he shared with them a belief in the need to subordinate colonial trade – and, indeed, trade in general – to the strategic needs of Britain. As he wrote in 1797, 'the extent of our navigation is to be preferred in general, to the Extent of our commerce, for on the first depends the security of everything'.[102] His conception of imperial policy was largely shared by Henry Dundas who, as President of the Board of Control from 1793 to 1801, was, along with Hawkesbury, one of the major architects of the second British Empire. Though Banks's association with Dundas was more tenuous than that with Hawkesbury, a shared enthusiasm for agricultural improvement at home and within the Empire at large drew the two men together.

The issue of the future direction of British imperial policy in relation to colonial trade was largely prompted by the needs of the West Indian colonists in the wake of American independence. Should such colonies, on which so much British commerce depended, continue to draw their supplies from the Thirteen Colonies, now the independent United States outside the pale of the British Empire? Lord Shelburne, who was largely responsible for the terms of the American peace, had foreshadowed a commercial treaty between Britain and the infant United States largely based on free-trade principles or, as he put it, founded 'upon grounds of mutual advantage and convenience'.[103] Such a position was consistent with his more general imperial policy which was encapsulated in the remark that 'We prefer trade to dominion'.[104] However, Pitt's attempt to follow in the footsteps of Shelburne by enacting the proposed American Intercourse Bill of 1783 which would have permitted trade between the United States and the British colonies in the West Indies was largely to be defeated by a spirited campaign led by Lord Sheffield and William Eden.

In his pamphlet, *Observations on the Commerce of the American States* (1783), Sheffield laid down some of the basic planks of the neo-mercantilist platform. Hence the praise of his close friend, Edmund Gibbon: 'The Navigation Act, the palladium of Britain, was defended and perhaps saved by his pen'.[105] For Sheffield argued that the bitter experience of defeat had addled his compatriots' brains, prompting them to adopt wholly new policies in the place of the traditional commercial system and its foundation stone, the Navigation Acts, which had been proved by time and experience:

> the independence of America, has encouraged the wildest sallies of imagination; Systems have been preferred to experience, Rash theory to successful practice, and the Navigation Act itself, the guardian of the prosperity of Britain, has been almost abandoned by the levity or ignorance of those, who have never seriously examined the spirit or the happy consequence of it.[106]

Two years later Sheffield also played a major part in defeating another of the early initiatives in Pitt's prime ministership: the attempt to dismantle some of the controls on the trade between Ireland and Britain. Such moves again stung Sheffield into print in defence of the Navigation Acts. 'The colonial system of navigation laws', he declared in his *Observations on the manufactures, trade & present state of Ireland* (1785), 'very properly gives the supply of the plantations and colonies to the British dominions alone'.[107] As so often for Sheffield the cause of Empire and that of the landed interest were closely intertwined. The possibility of cheap Irish agricultural imports, he told Banks, represented 'the sacrifice of the landed interest of England'.[108]

For Sheffield – as for other neo-mercantilists such as Hawkesbury – the significance of the Navigation Acts lay in the fact that they subordinated commercial concerns to other more primary national goals, such as defence. Hence Sheffield's description of these laws as 'the support and stay of the naval strength of this nation and as essentially interwoven with its commercial superiority'.[109] It was, moreover, an issue on which he could quote Adam Smith, the scourge of mercantilism, to his own ends. Hence Sheffield's citation in his pamphlet on the American trade of Adam Smith's remark that: 'As defence, however, is of much more importance than opulence the act of navigation is, perhaps the wisest of all the commercial regulations of England'.[110] He was, however, critical of the fact that Adam Smith did not pursue the full logic of this position by acknowledging that such naval advantages had to be purchased by the commercial restrictions of the mercantilist system which Smith had so vehemently criticised. Against 'this generally excellent writer [Smith]', Sheffield objected that 'we know not how to condemn the trade as commercially injurious, which produces such important and profitable effects'.[111]

Sheffield's attitude of mind reflected the traditional self-confidence of a landed class that it was for them, rather than the trading classes, to shape national policy. True, the interests of trade should be a compelling voice in the formulation of policy, but such concerns had to be balanced against other national priorities, especially that which was uppermost in the minds of an aristocracy: the demands of war and national prestige. As Sheffield boldly stated, 'Defence and independence are more important than wealth'.[112] Hence his rather reproving tone about the demands of merchants with the strong implication that they should know their place when it came to matters of government, the natural prerogative of the landowning classes: '*freedom of commerce* is not a power granted to merchants *to do what they please*'.[113]

Consequently, for Sheffield and his neo-mercantilist allies, the trade of the West Indies and, indeed, of British colonies generally needed to be controlled by the system of Navigation Acts because of what Sheffield called their 'essential importance' as 'to the commerce and independence of the nation'.[114] In an age when naval power depended very largely on the number of trained seamen, any measure which a State could command which maintained or increased the number of British vessels and their crews was a significant advance for British naval power. As Sheffield put it with characteristic directness: 'The great object of the Navigation Laws of this country is maritime strength'.[115]

It was Sheffield's hope that an insistence that the West Indian colonists should be supplied by 'British bottoms' would work not only to the advantage of Britain but also to the advantage of the remaining British colonies in North America (the future Canada). Trade between these colonies, it was hoped, would stimulate the growth of new forms of commerce to replace those previously supplied by the Thirteen Colonies. Sheffield, then, envisaged some amendment to the traditional colonial system but the ultimate goals remained the same as those that had always shaped the Navigation Acts: the achievement of British economic self-sufficiency through its Empire and the promotion of its naval and strategic strength.

In such a scheme of things colonies existed as a means of promoting trade and, with it, maritime strength. It followed, then, that colonies of settlement were to be discouraged, particularly in view of the lamentable example of what had happened to the Thirteen Colonies. As Sheffield later acidly remarked, 'From the day we plant a colony we may date its progress towards independence, whenever it may suit the interests or passions of the colonists'.[116] For a nation such as Britain, with a much smaller population than its traditional rival, France, emigration represented a loss of strategic and, in Sheffield's view, commercial power. Hence he urged in 1819 that the best customers of our manufacturers are the people of the United Kingdom. Every emigrant, consequently from being the best customer, becomes infinitely less so ... and from being a soldier or a sailor, who may be brought forward on the day of danger, ceases to be of service to the State in any shape.

Such considerations led him to insist that 'It is full time we should have learned the impolicy of founding colonies, and of extending ourselves in foreign settlements and dependencies'.[117]

In Sheffield's neo-mercantilist conception of empire, then, colonies could be justified by the extent to which they stimulated trade and naval power or if they promoted national economic self-sufficiency. By both criteria, the West Indian colonies remained of particular significance. 'The system of colonizing', he wrote,

except West Indies Islands, always appeared to me to be highly impolitic: West India colonies may be protected and maintained by our fleet; they furnish what we cannot produce in this island; they never can produce nor manufacture the same articles as we do.[118]

Whether in domestic policy in his defence of the landed interest or in imperial policy in his defence of the Navigation Act Sheffield's goals remained the same: national self-sufficiency and the avoidance, both for economic and strategic reasons, of reliance on foreign suppliers, particularly in such basic areas as the supply of foodstuffs or naval supplies. To a remarkable extent the goal of national self-reliance in food had been achieved at home by the practices of agricultural improvement. (Though rapid population growth put the ideal of complete self-sufficiency out of reach – something Sheffield and his allies were loath to admit.) Sheffield hoped, too, that within the Empire agricultural improvement could work to the same ends.

Hence his hope that Britain would be discriminating in utilising the colonial gains made in the Napoleonic Wars, retaining those colonies which would produce products not available to Britain elsewhere. He therefore welcomed the British capture from the Dutch in 1796 of the South American colonies of Surinam and Demerara and their 'rapid improvement', since they could supply products such as cotton and coffee. They were also capable of 'producing any quantity of Sugar', a crop Britain already obtained from the West Indies. But, since they thereby had the potential to undermine the prosperity not only of the British but also the Dutch and French colonies in the West Indies, 'It is highly essential that England should retain them if possible'.[119]

The plantation system on which these crops were dependent rested on 'the importation of Negroes'. This serves as a reminder that Sheffield's defence of the British plantation-owners – the landed interest abroad – extended to a defence of the slave-trade, a form of moral callousness he shared with other architects of neo-mercantilism such as Hawkesbury and, to a degree, Banks.[120] In the minds of those who shared Sheffield's conception of Empire the link between the slave-trade, maritime strength and the prosperity of the colonies was an indissoluble one. Hence we find one of Sheffield's admirers linking his praise for Sheffield's efforts to defend the slave-trade with the exhortation that he continue to be heard 'in support of the Commerce and Navigation Laws of the United Kingdom'.[121] Hawkesbury was of like mind writing of the slave-trade in 1788 that he wished 'to preserve as great a Share of it as possible to this Country' subjecting it only to such 'proper Regulations as shall manifest a due attention to motives of Humanity & Justice'. In the same year Liverpool, the chief slave-trading port, awarded the future first Earl of Liverpool with the freedom of the borough in gratitude 'for the essential Services rendered to the Town of Liverpool by his Lordship's late Exertion in Parliament in Support of the African Slave Trade'.[122]

Like that of Hawkesbury, Sheffield's defence of slavery formed part of his overall conception of the way in which the Empire ought to operate. Anything which promoted the maritime, and therefore the naval strength, of Britain was to be supported and defended. Colonial activities which promoted British economic self-sufficiency, such as plantation-based crops with which slavery was linked, were also to be promoted. Such a view of empire explains Sheffield's early stand on the West Indian trade in 1783, an issue which helped to strengthen the hold of neo-mercantilist policies. In arguing for the need to keep trade with the British West Indian colonies within the strait-jacket of the Navigation Acts Sheffield had the support of a number of allies who, like him, were suspicious of those who wished to divorce the movement of trade from the political controls embodied in these acts.

For William Knox, the former Under-secretary of State for America from 1770 to 1782, the need to maintain controls over West Indian trade was heightened by the experience of the revolt of the American colonists. On such a view the American Revolution showed the conse-quences of lax and fluctuating colonial controls. To prevent a repetition of such occurrences Britain must hereafter be more assertive in main-taining its just prerogatives within its colonies. In particular, the colonies should be required to play their part in bolstering British maritime strength on which the nation's commercial and strategic standing de-pended. As he had told Lord North, the basic principle on which imperial policy should rest was 'that it was better to have no colonies at all, than not to have them subservient to the maritime strength and commercial interest of Great Britain'.[123] Knox implemented this prin-ciple by drawing up in July 1783 an Order-in-Council which insisted that all trade to the West Indies should be carried in British ships and that American imports should be restricted as much as possible. By success-fully urging such a measure Knox hardened the divide between Britain and the infant United States and undermined Fox's attempts to frame a commercial treaty with the new republic.[124]

It was, of course, an order that received the enthusiastic blessing of Sheffield who looked on Knox as one of his staunchest allies. 'It gives me sincere pleasure', wrote Sheffield to Knox on 3 July 1783, to find the order of Council has passed exactly as you drew it ... I know no man who deserves better of the Republick than you do at this moment. The Country had very nearly suffered the greatest mischief, but our carrying Trade, consequently the foundation of our Navy is now safe.[125]

Knox shared the same rather apocalyptic view of the gravity of the issue writing that the order should be engraved on his tombstone 'as having saved the navigation of England'.[126]

From the perspective of the landed interest Sheffield also had the enthusiastic support of Arthur Young.[127] Previously, in 1772, Young had enunciated his views on the role of colonies in a manner that put him squarely in the mercantilist tradition of viewing colonies as weapons in the economic struggle between nations:

> The great benefit resulting from colonies is the cultivation of staple commodities different from those of the mother country; that, instead of being obliged to purchase them of foreigners at the expence possibly of treasure, they may be had from settlements in exchange for manufactures.[128]

Consistent with such a view of empire, Young, like Sheffield and Knox, was eager to defend what he called 'those sound principles of navigation, the great foundation of our naval power'.[129] Predictably, too, he saw the system of Navigation Acts as a way of ensuring that the West Indian colonists would be supplied with British produce to the benefit of the landed interest. Young was, however, to become more of a convert to laissez-faire principles, perhaps because he observed that the loss of the American colonies enhanced rather than detracted from British trade. As he wrote in his *Travels in France*, it was 'one of the most remarkable and singular experiments in the science of politics that the world has seen; for a people to lose an empire of thirteen provinces and to GAIN by that *loss* an increase of wealth, felicity and power'.[130] Needless to say, however, Young's enthusiasm for free-trade principles did not extend to allowing them to encroach on that great symbol of the power of the landed interest, the Corn Laws.

Along with Knox and Young, Sheffield's fulminations on the importance of maintaining the West Indian trade within the framework of the mercantilist system had the public support of William Eden, an active member of the Privy Council Committee for Trade who was closely associated with Knox.[131] The arguments that Eden employed in his parliamentary speech of 7 March 1783 attacking proposals for reciprocal trade between Britain and the United States largely rehearsed the familiar mercantilist nostrums about the dangers of conceding any trade advantages to rival states. 'This Bill', he declared, 'would introduce a total revolution in our commercial system, which he was afraid would shake it to its very basis'. But the issue on which he, like Sheffield, discoursed most passionately was the potential dangers to British naval power if the West Indian trade were allowed to pass into the hands of the Americans, something which would result 'not only to the great decrease of our revenue, but the absolute destruction of our navy, arising from the destruction of that great nursery for seamen'.[132] The Eden–Sheffield combination went into battle once again, shortly afterwards, in defence of similar mercantilist principles in relation to the proposed commercial treaty with Ireland in 1785.[133]

Yet, despite such views, Eden was to be best known for his success in bringing to fruition a commercial treaty with France in 1786 which was the most concrete tribute paid by the late eighteenth-century British State to the virtues of *freer* trade if not free trade *tout court.* The difference was, however, that France was not a part of the British Empire and that therefore arguments based on the need to maintain British naval power did not apply since there was no possibility of maintaining a British monopoly of the carrying trade. A year before the Anglo-French trade treaty was signed, Auckland amply demonstrated his continued allegiance to neo-mercantilist principle in the colonial sphere. For he vigorously opposed measures to permit the British-based Newfoundland fishermen from settling permanently in North America or, still worse, allowing them to import supplies from the United States. For, he insisted in parliament, he must oppose the introduction of 'systems, by act of parliament, contrary to that monopolising system, which, however described by theoretical writers, must be considered as the rock of salvation and strength of this country'. If Newfoundland were permitted to become a settled colony it might well follow the path of the American colonies appropriating 'every benefit to itself, without regarding the naval advantages of the Mother Country'.[134]

Moreover, though the Anglo-French Treaty may have appeared to be a significant concession to the cause of freer trade, it was framed to allow only freer movement of a restricted range of goods which each country considered would not weaken their home industries.[135] From the perspective of a neo-mercantilist like Sheffield the treaty was a notable victory since it offered an opportunity to increase greatly the wealth of the kingdom in return for relatively unimportant concessions. As he wrote to Eden in October 1786: 'I like the idea of supplying twenty-four millions of people and through them in a certain degree a greater part of the world'.[136] Sheffield looked on the treaty with particular relish since he thought Eden had managed to persuade the French to agree to a treaty that was largely weighted towards British interests. Nor did Sheffield fear that Eden's apparent concession to free-trade principles in relation to the French would make him less sound on colonial matters. We find him, for example, sharing with Auckland in August 1794 his indignation 'that the West Indians have had the impudence lately to present to the Secretary of State a similar Petition to that which was so effectually opposed in 1783 and 1784'.[137]

Sheffield's alliance with Auckland was a natural one both because they shared similar neo-mercantilist principles and because Auckland, as a well-placed political operator, was able to promote such principles within the inner recesses of government. It was, moreover, a government which was strongly inclined to listen to such arguments. For, though Pitt showed some signs of sympathy for Shelburne-style policies to promote freer trade, the fact that he largely entrusted commercial matters to Lord Hawkesbury indicated that Pitt did not wish to challenge neo-mercantilist principles in any fundamental manner. Though Pitt some-times intervened in European affairs, he largely left imperial matters to Hawkesbury and showed no major reservations about the goals he pursued.[138]

After all, such neo-mercantilist principles were in accord with the increasing importance of the State and its machinery which Pitt's re-forms were designed to promote. It was difficult to extinguish mer-cantilism, the view that the economy should be controlled by the State in order to promote its wealth, power and prestige, in an age when the British State was being re-shaped to make it a more successful competitor in the struggle with other States. Free trade fitted well with the en-lightened rhetoric of promoting greater domestic and international wealth and harmony. But, though politicians could afford to indulge themselves in such enlightened rhetoric when there was little at stake, when things came to the point the old mercantilist habits of weighing commercial advantages against strategic considerations died hard.

In appointing Hawkesbury to the Privy Council Committee for Trade in March 1784 and making him President in 1786, Pitt ensured that someone long known for his mercantilist sympathies would have a major platform for the construction of state policies. In doing so, too, Pitt further strengthened his image as a Prime Minister determined to ensure efficiency and probity in the conduct of government business – for Hawkesbury was an exemplar of both. At the Committee for Trade, as a contemporary remarked, 'his intimate knowledge of trade, matured by experience and by communication with every source of information, rendered him an invaluable support to Ministers'.[139]

This virtual re-founding of the Board of Trade with Hawkesbury as its guiding spirit was largely prompted by the issue of West Indian trade – a matter which, as we have seen, did so much to fashion the imperial policies of the British State in the wake of the American Revolution on the basis of mercantilist principles. The petition of the West Indian merchants prompted the formation of this Committee of the Privy Council with Jenkinson (as Hawkesbury then was) as its chairman.[140] The Committee was originally charged to undertake a three-month investi-gation into the economic capacities of the Canadian colonies to supply the West Indies, thus maintaining the West Indian trade within the British Empire.[141] In the event, Jenkinson oversaw a comprehensive examination of the economic life of the British American and Caribbean colonies which largely determined future British policy in that region for the next decade. Jenkinson also largely accepted the over-optimistic assessment of the Canadian colonists that they could fill the vacuum created by the exclusion of the Americans. This was consistent with his hope that some of the economic damage caused by the revolt of the

Thirteen Colonies could be reversed by using the loyal British colonies as a base for trade throughout the region. The Committee for Trade was also to be involved in implementing schemes to promote new avenues of trade into the Pacific incorporating the British North American colonies, schemes which owed much to the expert advice of Joseph Banks.[142]

Such wide-ranging plans flowed from Jenkinson's view of empire in which colonies existed to promote national self-sufficiency and strategic strength in the conflict between states. It followed, then, that colonies should be ruled with a firm hand to ensure that they complied with such a role and in order to ensure that they did not come under the sway of rival governments. 'By the general law of nations', he asserted when dealing with the issue of West Indian trade, 'acknowledged by every European state, no nation has a right to have any trade with the colonies of another'.[143]

The great centrepiece of Jenkinson's imperial system was the Navigation Act of 1786 which attempted to reassert, with some concession to changed circumstances, the mercantilist principles embodied in past Navigation Acts. For Jenkinson saw himself as consolidating and adapting a commercial system based on over a century of proven experience. His edition of treaties, for example, describes the period 1648 to 1783 'as containing the whole of our Trade System, and whatever Alterations may hereafter be made, One or more of these Treaties must form the Basis of it'.[144] Appropriately, the full title of the 1786 Act – a bill 'for the Increase and Encouragement of Shipping and Navigation' – pointed to the motives which for Jenkinson, as for Sheffield, Knox or Auckland, underlay their determination to sacrifice free-trade orthodoxy to the cause of strategic advantage. To underline the message Jenkinson himself said of it that 'It is a Bill for the increase of Naval Power'.[145] It was a particularly pressing and understandable goal for a nation which, as a result of the result of the American rebellion, had lost some one-third of its merchant fleet.[146] It was, then, Jenkinson's overriding ambition to use commerce to restore Britain's greatness which had been tarnished by the bitter American defeat. Hence his statement in the Commons in support of the bill, that 'if proper means could be devised to secure the navigation trade to Great Britain, though we had lost a dominion, we might almost be said to have gained an empire'.[147]

The same year saw the successful implementation of Jenkinson's Newfoundland policy, building on the treaty of 1783 which defined zones for French, English and New England migratory fishermen.[148] His policy towards these fisheries embodied his fundamental views about the importance of navigation and the need to subordinate the interests of individual colonies to the grand design of promoting British commercial and strategic strength. The aim of Jenkinson's policy, which reflected that same post-American War wariness toward colonies evident in Sheffield's writings, was to ensure that the Newfoundland waters would principally be fished by ships based in Britain rather than Newfoundland itself.[149] Only then would it be possible to ensure, as Jenkinson put it, that the fishery remained a 'nursery of seamen'.[150] Once such fishermen were allowed to settle in Newfoundland, Britain would lose much of the benefit of their maritime skills and in the future possibly risk another colonial secession. Hence Jenkinson's firm tone in defining government policy on this issue as being intended 'to preserve it entirely a British fishery; and this could only be done by confining it to British ships, navigated from Great Britain, and by no means permitting any stationery settlement to be made on the island of Newfoundland'.[151]

Such a firm subordination of the interests of the colonies to the well-being of Britain itself further strengthened the personal bond between Jenkinson and Sheffield which had begun with their joint service to Lord North. Sheffield looked to Jenkinson as a natural ally in the neo-mercantilist cause of using the instrumentalities of government to control trade in the national interest, whether for economic or strategic reasons. We find Sheffield, for example, congratulating Lord Hawkes-bury on his elevation to the House of Lords in 1786, while lamenting that 'I do not know how your place can be supplied in the Lower House'.[152] Hawkesbury's appointment as President of the Privy Council Committee for Trade he saw as a long overdue recognition of the need for closer government involvement in the conduct of commerce. 'It is peculiarly absurd', he wrote to Hawkesbury, 'for a country like this to be without some kind of Board for the Management of the affairs of the Plantations & of Trade'.[153]

From 1792, as pressure mounted from the West Indian colonists to loosen the straight-jacket of the Navigation Laws because of the exigencies of war, Sheffield and Hawkesbury served as comrades-in-arms in resisting the anti-mercantilist tide. Indeed, Hawkesbury called on Sheffield to play his traditional role as pamphleteer and publicist in maintaining support for the Navigation Acts.[154] And so, in his *Strictures on the Necessity of Maintaining the Navigation and Colonial System of Great Britain* (1804), Sheffield once again publicly intoned the chief articles of the neo-mercantilist creed. Predictably, he wrote of the Navigation Laws that 'experience has learned to regard [them] as the support and stay of the naval strength of this nation, and as essentially interwoven with its commercial superiority'. Sheffield also paid tribute to Lord Liverpool (as Hawkesbury had become) as someone to whom 'this country is much indebted ... for his intelligent and persevering support of the question relative to the intercourse of the Americans with our colonies'.[155]

By this time, however, the hold of Liverpool and of neo-mercantilist opinion on government policy was beginning to weaken. The old orthodoxy was being undermined by the practical needs of the West Indian colonists and the increasingly evident fact that trade with the United States worked to the commercial benefit of all – that, though Britain had lost political control over its former American colonies, it could still benefit economically from fostering relations with them. Thus Hawkesbury failed in his attempt to sabotage Jay's Treaty of 1794 which regularised a series of issues in contention between the United States and

Great Britain and permitted the former greater access to the West Indian trade.[156] The Jay Treaty was, however, by no means a full concession to free trade: the United States was, for example, permitted only to trade with the West Indies in vessels of seventy tons and under and was not to re-export West Indian produce. Such restrictions prompted many within the United States Congress to refuse to ratify the treaty – a move which, of course, Sheffield greeted with enthusiasm.[157]

In the event, the treaty was narrowly passed by Congress but this did nothing to change Hawkesbury's view that trade needed to be controlled by government. He took such a stand not only for commercial and strategic reasons, but also to quarantine the British Empire from the subversive principles which had prompted the American and, more recently and more dangerously, the French Revolution. As he wrote in 1796:

> Our West India Islands will never be safe if the subjects of the United States are allowed to have a free Intercourse with them, and to import, among other articles, their Democratic Principles, into the Parts of those Islands.[158]

Since late eighteenth-century Britain lacked a department of government dealing specifically with colonial matters, the increasing volume of imperial policy fell within the ambit of either Hawkesbury at the Committee for Trade or Dundas, the moving spirit in the creation of the Board of Control (which controlled the East India Company) – a body he served as President from 1793 to 1801. It is a measure of the continuing strength and pervasiveness of the traditional view that, where possible, the economic life of the colonies ought to be controlled by the imperial government that the broad tenor of Hawkesbury's neo-mercantilist policies was also supported by Dundas. Appropriately, like Hawkesbury, Dundas had been a firm opponent of concessions to the American colonists as moves which would weaken the control of the British State.

As a loyal lieutenant of Pitt, Dundas was appointed in 1784, along with Hawkesbury, as one of the commissioners of the re-constituted Privy Council Committee for Trade, thus further strengthening his association with Hawkesbury and his policies. Another common link between the Committee for Trade and the Board of Control was Banks's lifelong friend, Lord Mulgrave, a member of both bodies and a major architect, along with Dundas, of the Anglo-French commercial treaty over India in 1786. In accord with mercantilist principle it was a treaty which closely tied trading rights with control over territory.[159] An even more explicit declaration of Dundas's agreement with Hawkesbury's view that strategic concerns took priority over commercial affairs came in the following year in Dundas's *Considerations on the Subject of a Treaty between Great Britain and Holland relative to their Interest in India*. It should be the main aim of Great Britain, declared Dundas, 'to maintain and preserve the Empire which she has acquired in comparison of which, even Trade is a subordinate or collateral Consideration'.[160]

Like Hawkesbury (and Sheffield), too, Dundas drew the moral from the American Revolution that where possible colonies should be maintained as trading posts and permanent settlement of British colonists should be discouraged as likely to produce eventual demands for autonomy. His speech to the House of Commons in March 1801, which emphasised the links between strategic and commercial power and hence the need for state control over the conduct of commerce and of the colonial system, could well have been delivered by Hawkesbury. 'Navigation and commerce', proclaimed Dundas, 'are inseparably connected, and that nation must be the most powerful maritime state which possesses the most extensive commerce'. In accord with mercantilist thinking, Dundas emphasised the possibilities of commerce as a weapon against the enemies of the British State arguing that 'We ought, as early as we can at the commencement of a war, to cut off the commercial resources of our enemies, as by so doing we infallibly weaken or destroy their naval resources'.[161]

This same determination to subordinate commercial considerations to other national goals was also evident in Hawkesbury's conduct of domestic affairs – particularly in relation to the critical issue of the supply of food on which so much of the social stability of the nation rested. And, to judge by a long letter from Liverpool to Dundas in October 1800, these were principles with which Dundas also sympathised. Liverpool was particularly anxious to point out the inadequacies of the principles of Dundas's fellow Scot, Adam Smith, when it came to such fundamental issues of government policy. 'From long Experience', wrote Liverpool to Dundas,

> as well as from deep Reflection, I have convinced myself, that Dr Adam Smith has pushed his principles to an extravagant length ... These Principles are the Favourites of all speculative Men, who are averse to resort to the dull Detail of Facts.

If free-trade principles were uncritically applied to the corn trade, he continued, the result might well 'be Insurrection of a very serious nature'. Under the counter-revolutionary shadow of the French Revolution Liverpool even associated Smith's position with that of the French *philosophes* who 'by the wild Principles in favour of political Liberty ... have destroyed the Government of their own Country'. Similarly, he feared that

> the French Oeconomists (from whom Dr Adam Smith has borrowed all his Doctrines), should, by Principles in favour of the Liberty of Trade, carried to as great an Extravagance, shake the Foundations of the Government of Great Britain.[162]

BANKS AND THE PROMOTION OF NATIONAL SELF-SUFFICIENCY

Such reservations about applying the purity of free-trade principles to the politically and socially critical area of the corn trade meant that

Liverpool shared much common ground with such tribunes of the landed interest as Sheffield or Banks – just as they inhabited the same ideological pasture as Liverpool in arguing for the control of trade within the imperial sphere. Liverpool's sympathies with the neo-mercantilist view that the State should intervene when necessary in commercial affairs to safeguard other interests meant that he had a natural affinity with the arguments advanced by the landed interest in relation to the Corn Laws. On the other hand, as a government minister, he had the obligation to attempt to reconcile diverse interest groups which were even more vociferous in domestic than imperial affairs; as a consequence, he did not always promote policies which were altogether pleasing to such self-appointed spokesmen of the landed interest as Banks.

In the discussions which preceded the revised Corn Law Bill of 1791 – a bill which made considerable concessions to the landed interest by lifting the maximum price level before exports were permitted – Hawkesbury sympathised with Banks about the fate of 'the landed Interest [which] was depressed, more than it ought, or than was necessary, even for the interest of the Manufacturers'. Significantly, Hawkesbury linked such moves with his attempts to foster measures which, in mercantilist fashion, would have had the effect both of benefiting home production and of strengthening the naval might of the nation. For, as he told Banks when explaining why 'I cannot venture to go further' in relation to the Corn Laws and the defence of the landed interest:

> I endeavoured last Year to check the Importation of oats from Holland and East Friesland by making it necessary to import them in British Vessels only. This measure would have been a Benefit to the Agriculture of this country, and at the same Time increased its navigation.

But, he lamented, 'Mr Pitt, influenced by Political Motives, obliged me to relinquish this Design' – an indication of the political limits within which he had to work. It was also, as he told Banks, a reminder to the country gentlemen that they had to do more to help themselves.[163]

But, as a government minister, Hawkesbury had to put the interests of social stability before those of the landed interest, especially when the problems of dearth were exacerbated by the strains of war. When the food supply situation dramatically worsened in 1795 Hawkesbury had to envisage the possibility of considerably expanding the importation of foreign corn – a measure which, predictably, Banks regarded with dismay. It was a situation which prompted Banks to don the garb of free trade with the important reservation that, though government should not intervene in the domestic market, it should act to curtail an international trade in grain. While Hawkesbury was prepared to concede that he was aware 'how improper it is for Government to interfere in any Branch of Commerce, particularly in one in which the Subsistence of the People depends', he urged Banks to consider that more fundamental national needs could outweigh such economic purity. For, he urged, 'not only the Subsistence but perhaps the Tranquility of the most populous City in the World, depend on the Measures which Government may now take'.[164]

For all his determination to protect the landed interest and to prevent the importation of foreign corn, Banks was prepared to concede to Liverpool the basic principle that the advantages of free trade could be outweighed by other social or political imperatives – particularly when it came to the sale of such a basic commodity as food. 'The Commerce of the necessaries', he agreed with Liverpool, 'cannot be indulged with that degree of freedom which other branches have hitherto enjoyd without detriment to the nation. Commerce like fire is a good servant but a bad master.'[165] It was an interchange that underlined their basic agreement on the neo-mercantilist principle that free trade was but one of a range of political *desiderata* which had to be balanced against other national goals. Liverpool and Banks gave differing goals greater priority: for Banks the protection of the landed interest and, with it, the maintenance of national autonomy in the supply of food loomed larger than for Liverpool, who was primarily concerned with avoiding social and political disruption because of the spectre of famine. But, for both men, the principles of free trade – as epitomised in the work of Adam Smith – represented a danger to the body politic if applied in such an uncritical manner that they weakened the nation's self-sufficiency or social stability.

This same underlying mercantilist framework of society and economics – which owed much to Banks's spirited involvement in the defence of the landed interest – is evident in much of Banks's thinking. These two strands – defence of the landed interest and support for neo-mercantilist principles – were joined in happy accord in one of the chief missions of Banks's life: the promotion within Britain and its Empire of fine wool which could compete with the increasingly popular merino wool imported from Spain and elsewhere in Europe. In Banks's view such an endeavour was an exemplary act of public service since it helped to free Britain from a humiliating and potentially dangerous dependence on foreign rivals. As he wrote to Thomas March, a British merchant in Lisbon, in September 1788: 'To depend upon a Country naturally unkindly to you for the Raw material of the finest branch of your Principal manufacture & to be in hourly danger of the privilege of Obtaining it being resumd is a humiliating consideration to a great nation'. It followed, then, that it was the highest reach of patriotism to promote British self-sufficiency in wool, or, as Banks put it to March, 'to put her [Britain] in possession of that Raw material then is an act deserving the best kind of Gratitude'.[166]

In pursuing such a goal Banks had the support of his old schoolfriend, William Eden (after 1789 Lord Auckland). For Eden's presence in France to negotiate the Anglo-French commercial treaty of 1786 gave him access to French woollen manufacturers and sheep-breeders and he came to appreciate the merits of Spanish wool. We find Banks thanking Eden for his friendship and loyalty in pursuing such Banksian initiatives in the midst of the multitude of other political and commercial tasks which fell to Eden. 'I am Fully sensible', wrote Banks to Auckland in February 1787, 'of the obligation conferrd upon an old Schoolfellow by being remembered in the hurry of the complicated negotiation you are conducting'.[167] Eden's subsequent appointment as ambassador to the Spanish court in May 1789 enabled him to obtain samples of pure merino wool and even to begin to explore the possibility of obtaining some of the sheep themselves. These plans, thanks to Banks, received the royal approval in 1790, being thereafter known as 'Lord Auckland's undertaking'.[168] After numerous vicissitudes a flock of Spanish merinos finally arrived in England in October 1791 – a flock which acted as the nucleus of the royal breeding stud at Kew. From there, merino sheep were disseminated throughout England and, more momentously, to another of Banks's pet projects, the infant colony of New South Wales. Predictably, a third participant in the Banks–Eden endeavour to divert Spanish and French agricultural advantage to the benefit of Britain was that insistent advocate of both the landed interest and neo-mercantilist principles, Lord Sheffield. On 17 October, for example, in a letter to Banks, he acknowledged 'The receipt of some samples of Spanish Wool from the Lord Auckland' – specimens which Sheffield regarded as 'finer than any I have seen'.[169]

Both Eden and Banks shared the same object in this and many other of their endeavours: to promote national self-sufficiency and autonomy. As Banks told Auckland in January 1791, 'My Ambition however will be satisfied if I can make England independent of Spain in the article of Superfine cloth'.[170] Auckland therefore encouraged Banks's other ventures which were intended to use Britain's imperial possessions as a means of promoting national economic independence. Thus Auckland looked with approval on the wide range of Banksian projects intended to turn British success in Pacific exploration to imperial advantage. As he wrote to Banks in 1790 of his 'benevolent attempt to introduce the Bread fruit of the South Sea islands into the West Indies' and to examine 'the Soil, Production, & Manners of the Inhabitants of the Regions Yclipd Nootka Sound' in Northwest America: ' "These are imperial works & worthy of our Sovereign" I most sincerely wish success to them'.[171]

Consistent with such a view of the Empire as an emporium of raw materials for the benefit of the mother-country, Banks was determined to ensure that the economic life of the colonies should work to the benefit of Britain. His paternal pride in the growth of New South Wales – a colony which he had done so much to initiate and sustain – was mixed with an impatience to see it grow economically to the point where it could contribute to the wealth of Britain. Appropriately, New South Wales was to serve as the chief means of realising Banks's goal of ensuring that Britain and its Empire became self-sufficient in the pro-duction of fine wool.

However, Banks was not as doctrinaire in support of the Navigation Acts as his close ally, Lord Sheffield. He responded rather equivocally to Sheffield's impassioned pamphlet of 1804 in defence of the Navigation Acts.[172] For, wrote Banks, though, in general, he supported the principles on which the Navigation Acts were based, nonetheless 'like Rules they cannot be so ably continued as to be without exception'.[173] Banks's willingness to adjust his mercantilist views to suit changing circumstances is evident, too, in his policy towards Newfoundland, one of the traditional shibboleths of the neo-mercantilist cause because of its importance as 'a nursery of seamen'. When Banks came to write on the subject in 1807, he took the view that, though the traditional policy of 'Retard[ing] the Fishermen from Settling themselves on Shore & keep[ing] up their annual migration' had substance, it had become unworkable:

> the impossibility of compelling these settlers to leave the island & migrate annualy to Europe is therefore manifest & without further argument it must now be admitted that Newfoundland is no longer a Fishery, that it has by degrees established itself into a Colony.

Banks even went so far as to entertain the notion that the colony should be permitted freer trade with the United States thus 'relieving our Colonists from the heavy expence of depending on the mother country for Provisions, which she can ill spare & naval stores which she herself does not produce'. But, in a more characteristic vein, Banks devoted most of his energies in relation to Newfoundland towards the promotion of self-sufficiency. Thus he argued that 'The most advantageous of measures that can be suggested is clearly to induce the settlers to grow their own Provisions'. He therefore suggested a range of crops suitable for Newfoundland, urging particularly the utility of one of his abiding interests, the cultivation of spring corn.[174]

THE RISE AND FALL OF NEO-MERCANTILISM

Banks's concessions to mercantilist principle in the case of Newfoundland were an indication of the increasing difficulty of maintaining the traditional nexus between political and economic controls that was central to that loosely-defined but nonetheless indispensable concept of mercantilism.[175] Though Adam Smith had, for debating purposes, attempted to elevate mercantilism to the level of a coherent economic doctrine[176] it was more a set of practices than principles. As Ehrman writes of the late eighteenth century: 'Mercantilism has proved a dangerous term to define. But the theory need not be currently in favour for statesmen to be mercantile in practice'.[177] Mercantilism reflected the political power of a landed class which – given its remote military origins and its disdain for involving itself too directly in the practice, if not the profits, of commerce – was naturally inclined to subordinate commerce to other national goals such as defence or the pursuit of national prestige.

Though, by the standards of the European aristocracy, the English landed classes viewed commerce in a particularly sympathetic light they expected the trading classes to know their place and, when necessary, to defer to such national goals as the promotion of British navigation and, with it, naval power. Commerce, too, was expected to play its part in the ancient dynastic conflicts between rival princes – something which again entailed that political control over trade which was the essence of mercantilism. The first Earl of Liverpool continued to insist in 1802 that trade was inseparably linked with the conflict between states arguing in relation to British navigation that

> Whatever we give, in this respect to the Dutch, Danes and Americans, we in reality take from ourselves … that it has been the great policy of this country during the course of many centuries, to prefer the Interest of our Navigation even at the Expense of our Commerce.[178]

The policies of Liverpool – which he shared with Eden, Knox, Dundas and, in large measure, with Banks – required, then, a continuation of what Smith scathingly termed the 'mean and malignant expedients of the mercantile system'.[179] This determination to maintain some of the traditional fabric of state control over trade in order to ensure that commerce served goals other than its own was encouraged by the growth of an increasingly self-conscious and militant landed interest with which Sheffield, Young and Banks closely identified themselves. Such copious and often shrill publicists more and more came to regard themselves as embodying 'the landed interest', even though they were by no means fully representative of the wide spectrum of interests associated with those on the land. 'The landed interest' endeavoured to ensure government action in order to keep in check the deleterious effects of free trade on agriculture, especially in relation to the politically highly-charged corn trade. Hence the tribunes of the landed classes were, on the wider platform of British imperial policy, attracted to the doctrines of neo-mercantilism with its insistence that the course of commerce needed to be kept in check by the State.

Their use of the lobby-group tactics, which were becoming more prevalent for a multiplicity of causes anxious to sway government in their direction, was an indirect tribute to the increasing importance of the political processes of the State in determining major issues of policy. Neo-mercantilism was, too, a doctrine in some ways in keeping with the growth of the British State both at home and in its imperial dimension. The growth in power and influence of the Committee for Trade under Hawkesbury's stewardship was indeed an instance of the increasing involvement of government in the conduct of commerce and an example of the way in which the machinery of the State was expanding to meet the wider range of its responsibilities. The counter-revolutionary tide set in motion by the American and, *a fortiori*, the French Revolution further strengthened the neo-mercantilist current with its insistence on strong government and wariness of notions of liberty, including freedom of trade. Government control was, too, as always strengthened and justified by the needs of war, particularly a war such as Britain waged against France which called for an unparalleled mobilisation of national resources.

The late eighteenth century, then, saw a number of movements which favoured a neo-mercantilist climate. By the early nineteenth century, however, other developments were more and more undermining the imperial apparatus which had been built around the traditional assumption that political and economic control could not be separated. Above all, it was the ever more demonstrable fact that free trade could work to the benefit of all that called many of the neo-mercantilist assumptions into doubt.[180] As trade with the independent United States grew to ever greater and mutually beneficial heights it became more and more difficult to argue that political control conferred economic advantages. One pamphleteer pertinently responded to Sheffield's 1804 pamphlet in defence of the Navigation Acts by observing that:

> If, as Lord Sheffield professes to deem necessary to our salvation as a commercial and naval nation, Britain had rigidly adhered to the navigation system of the seventeenth century, the consequence would have been, that we should have had much less than half the commerce and revenue to meet the arduous contest in which we were engaged.[181]

Such arguments that freer trade would actually benefit Britain, as the world's greatest trading nation, in its titanic struggle with France came to seem more and more plausible as Napoleon's Continental blockade forced Britain to find new markets. The importance of economic considerations in the long struggle with France, as Cookson points out, weakened the traditional preoccupation with naval superiority[182] and, with it, the neo-mercantilist reliance on devices such as the Navigation Acts. Gradually, then, the form of Empire for which Sheffield and Eden had lobbied and which Hawkesbury had done much to implement began to be eroded as the cause of free trade gathered momentum in the nineteenth century. Less and less was trade linked to such national goals as the maintenance of naval power or strategic advantage. Moreover, as the colonies developed and the pressing necessities of war receded, such imperial dependencies – or at least those with large European populations – began to demand a greater say in the running of their own affairs, thus further weakening the machinery of mercantilism.

It was the natural hope of the advocates of free trade that their principles would bring with them some check on the growth of government. And, indeed, the waning of imperial policies based on neo-mercantilist principles meant less direct control over the colonies by Britain and, with it, greater delegation of authority from the centre to the periphery. But, though the growth of government may have been partly attenuated, the imperatives for the growth of the State remained strong. The ever more urgent needs of a traditional society being rapidly transformed by the Industrial Revolution and soaring population increase helped to undermine the old hostilities towards action on the part of central government.[183] Even in the imperial sphere public opinion demanded more of the British State in advancing such moral crusades as the elimination of slavery and the fostering of representative forms of government (at least in areas of European settlement) – causes that fostered the growth of a larger, more competent and therefore more expensive Colonial Office.

Not even in the sphere of commerce could government altogether abdicate its responsibilities to meet the needs of a nation demanding an ever wider range and volume of raw materials. The Committee for Trade which the first Earl of Liverpool had largely created was gradually to shed some of the mercantilist principles which he had stamped on it, but it continued his endeavours to ensure that British industry and commerce would not be hampered by a shortage of readily obtainable raw materials. Such activities necessitated the increasing use of scientific expertise as the need to put to practical use specialist knowledge of Nature – whether of the animal, vegetable or mineral kingdoms – became ever more evident. In implanting in the deliberations of the Committee on Trade and the wider bureaucratic apparatus of the British State the early seeds of such a fruitful partnership between science and government Banks was to play a critical role, as the next chapter will attempt to demonstrate.

CHAPTER FIVE

Science in the Service of the State

The late eighteenth century, then, saw a revival of neo-mercantilist conceptions of the State as the English governing classes grappled with the problems of re-establishing British power at home and abroad in the face of the assaults attendant on the American and French Revolutions. Bolstered by the success of agricultural improvement, neo-mercantilists such as Sheffield, Jenkinson, Eden and, of course, Banks turned to the task of improving the British Empire in a bid to further the sway of British power. The apparatus of the State thus became linked to the course of imperial expansion though the direction of policy was often determined by individuals (like Banks) with little in the way of formal State office but who, thanks to the networks created by a land-owning oligarchic elite, were closely associated with the conduct of government.

In a State where the mechanisms of power were as complex and as malleable as in late eighteenth-century Britain, the routes by which Banks and his fellow neo-mercantilists shaped policy to link science with the conduct of empire were often diverse. Directly connected with the formal apparatus of the State was the Privy Council Committee for Trade which, under Jenkinson's direction, offered a very potent instrument for applying to the Empire the strategies of improvement which had trans-formed the estates and the wealth of the landowning oligarchy. At the very epicentre of the State's power lay the Admiralty and, through it, the Royal Navy, a major weapon not only of war but commerce – the two being closely linked in mercantilist thinking. Despite the Admiralty's long traditions and often inhospitable attitudes to outside bodies, it was, albeit in a much more limited way than that provided by the Committee for Trade, to serve as another point of access by which Banks linked science with the concerns of government.

Straddling the divide between a formal department of government and a private corporation was the Board of Agriculture. At an even greater remove from the central focus of the State were institutions such as the Royal Society, the Royal Institution and the Society of Arts which, though voluntary organisations, nevertheless in an oligarchic society such as late eighteenth-century Britain, were inextricably linked with those who held power. Also at a remove from the central machinery of the State, in an age when the border between the King's household and the apparatus of government was an uncertain one, was the Royal Gardens at Kew which for Banks represented the virtual laboratory for his schemes for imperial improvement. And, though jealous of their independence, the great trading companies, such as the East India Company, were too important to the wealth, power and prestige of the nation to be altogether independent of the controlling hand of government. It is the purpose of this chapter, then, to trace the way in which Joseph Banks, assisted by his fellow neo-mercantilists, used this complex array of institutions to link science to the cause of Empire.

THE FORMAL APPARATUS OF GOVERNMENT

The Privy Council Committee for Trade and Plantations

The ineluctable growth in the size and importance of the central government was reflected in the changing pattern of the channels through which scientific advice was conveyed to the government. The more informal methods, such as consultation with the Royal Society, continued to exist (as illustrated in Chapter Two) but a growing number of governmental agencies found that scientific and technological problems were forming part of the routine tasks of governmental departments. This applied most particularly to the Privy Council Committee for Trade, the branch of government most directly concerned with increasing the wealth, self-sufficiency and, ultimately, imperial might of Britain. It was through this increasingly important agency of an increasingly complex State, then, that Banks could do most to marry together politics and science. In doing so contemporaries recognised that he was obtaining for science an unprecedented degree of public recognition. Banks's elevation to the formal dignity of a Privy Councillor in 1797 (chiefly on account of his work on the Committee for Trade) prompted the congratulations of his Royal Society colleague, Richard Kirwan, not so much for himself 'for you are already more distinguish'd & Honour'd in every civilized part of the world than any of that body', but rather for its benefit to science.[1] In short, Banks had helped to make science part of the domain of government and, consequently, a path to public recognition.

Banks's path to these inner circles of government largely originated from his work as President of the Royal Society. This led to his becoming better known within the political establishment and, in particular, involved him with the concerns of the Committee for Trade. The re-establishment of this body in 1784 under the chairmanship of Banks's close ally, Jenkinson, was an indication of the ever-growing size of the central government since it came into being a mere two years after the abolition of the Board of Trade and Plantations in a vain attempt to stem the growth of the size of the executive. Jenkinson's appointment as President in 1786 marked his elevation to the position as Pitt's lieutenant in the task of restoring Britain's national pre-eminence on a sure economic footing. As Banks wrote in 1800, he 'has the confidence of the Minister [Pitt] on all matters in which the Commercial interests of this Country combine themselves with the political ones'.[2] Within a year of the Board's re-constitution, Banks and Jenkinson were co-operating on a plan to cultivate breadfruit in the West Indies as a cheap food for the slaves.[3] It was a plan that called for the co-operation not only of the Committee for Trade but also the Admiralty and the Home Office. In co-ordinating these diverse bureaucratic activities Banks's unofficial status on the Committee for Trade may well have been an advantage since his intervention was less likely to spark off the inter-departmental rivalries that are endemic to any large-scale bureaucracy.

In 1787, too, Banks was asked by the Committee for Trade to comment on specimens of Persian cotton which the Manchester manufacturers had suggested could be grown in the British colonies in the West Indies.[4] In thanking Banks for his active involvement, these manufacturers looked to him to promote the scheme both as President of the Royal Society and as someone with the ear of the political establishment, an indication of Banks's wide-ranging sphere of influence. For, as the manufacturers' spokesman wrote, it was a project 'which is certainly not only an object worthy of your attention but of the Learned Body over which you have the honor to preside, as well as every encouragement from the state'.[5]

In the same year the search for cotton plants which might flourish under British rule prompted the dispatch of Banks's Polish botanical client, Anton Hove, to the Gujarat territory, one of India's major cotton-growing regions. Hove was instructed by the Committee for Trade to 'conform yourself in all Respects to the Instructions you shall receive from Sir Jos. Banks'. It was hoped, too, that the 'weight of Sr Joseph Banks's authority' would persuade British planters to adopt the new plants which Hove might bring back.[6] Though Hove's mission had only limited success it further cemented the bond between Banks and Lord Hawkesbury (as Jenkinson became after 1786) in their common endeavour to strengthen British commercial self-sufficiency. When asking Banks for his opinion on Hove's specimens, Hawkesbury wrote that it was to Banks alone that he could turn 'To relieve me from this Difficulty' while 'I must trust to the Zeal you always manifest when Your Talents can be of any Use to the Publick'.[7]

Despite some disappointments, the Committee for Trade's efforts did help to contribute to a considerable increase in the output of West

Indian cotton – exports of which rose by almost fifty percent from 1786 to 1790.[8] As Mackay points out, such fruitful governmental intervention was a concrete instance of the link that could exist between science – in the form of imperial botany – and that most central aspect of the Industrial Revolution, the cotton trade.[9]

Along with the need to import cotton from areas outside British control another great drain on British resources was the evergrowing demand for Chinese teas. Though in one sense a luxury, the habit of tea-drinking was fast becoming entrenched in English homes and represented, from a mercantilist perspective, a vast drain on the national wealth. Hence the long memorandum which Hawkesbury addressed to Banks in 1788 bemoaning the loss of between £600,000 and £700,000 annually in silver bullion to China to pay for this indulgence. He reluctantly acknowledged, however, that 'There is no Possibility of preventing the Consumption of Tea, even to it's present Amount' and therefore 'As we cannot prevent the Consumption the only Object We can aim at is, to produce the Article ourselves' in territories under British control. With mercantilist pride Hawkesbury pointed to earlier successes in transplanting sugar and coffee, crops 'which We now produce in such Abundance in our Colonies'.[10]

Thus prompted, Banks conducted lengthy investigations (in the course of which he called on the expertise of Lord Sheffield[11]); the resultant plan urged the East India Company to undertake experimental planting with an ultimate view to large-scale cultivation in Assam[12] – an area which eventually, after Banks's death, became one of the great centres of tea-growing and hence of British imperial self-sufficiency. In developing his strategy to lessen Britain's dependence on the Chinese tea trade, Banks took into account the economic as well as the botanical and climatic considerations, arguing that India was appropriate since 'in the whole of India Labour appears to be as cheap as in China'.[13] In Banks's mind, then, the advancement of science and the advancement of British imperial interests formed a natural partnership.

Given that the Committee for Trade was concerned with the import of the most basic of all commodities, that of food, it was drawn into domestic as well as imperial politics. Predictably in this area Banks used his influence to advance the cause both of the landed interest and of the scientifically-based principles of agricultural improvement which had served it so well. As so often, Banks's links with one part of government led to involvement with other aspects of the apparatus of the British State. When the threat of a widespread wheat blight spreading from the United States to Britain threatened in 1788–9, the matter was of sufficient gravity to involve not only the Privy Council Committee for Trade but also the full Privy Council, who recognised the need for expert scientific advice and looked to Banks to provide it.

In 1788 Banks was called upon by the Privy Council to provide detailed advice on the origin of this so-called Hessian Fly blight and the best means of containing it. In responding to the emergency, Banks was able to use his position as President of the Royal Society to call on both British and French entomological expertise which he used to prepare a detailed report emphasising the gravity of the threat and suggesting methods for dealing with any wheat which might have slipped through the quarantine cordon.[14] Once the matter had been considered by the full Privy Council it thereafter largely reverted to the province of the Committee for Trade and its energetic President, Lord Hawkesbury, who naturally continued to seek Banks's expert advice. Thanks perhaps in part to the measures which Banks suggested, the threat passed and Britain was spared what Banks described to Lord Hawkesbury with some hyperbole as potentially 'the greatest scourge that Island [Britain] ever experienced'.[15]

When Britain faced an even greater agricultural crisis in 1795, when harvest failure was combined with the threat of foreign attack and domestic upheaval, members of the Privy Council were again 'desirous to avail themselves of your [Banks's] advice'.[16] Banks undertook lengthy researches on the matter concluding that the crisis could be avoided by using such expedients as more efficient milling with steam presses or by mixing the grain with Indian corn.[17] The issue continued to be closely monitored by the Committee for Trade, which devoted thirteen meetings from January to August 1795 to the shortage of wheat.[18] By August, however, the situation had greatly worsened and Hawkesbury asked Banks to prepare a submission for Pitt and the cabinet on the possibility of importing foreign grain. Hawkesbury, anticipating Banks's strong opposition to any measure likely to affect the interests of the country gentlemen, urged him to take into account 'the present Circumstances of this Country, and the very singular State of Europe'.[19] But, predictably, Banks, a strong supporter of the Corn Laws and agricultural tariffs, was opposed to imports until disaster stared the country in the face.

Though Banks was opposed to the free market operating at an international level in food stuffs and, as we have seen, vehemently condemned the application of Adam Smith's principles to agriculture, he used the language of political economy to argue against governmental intervention in the domestic market. Thus he argued that the crisis could possibly be avoided by stringent economies and by the use of substitute foodstuffs and that 'While there is any prospect of this being the case', he urged, 'it will surely be imprudent for Government to interfere in the market nothing but a well grounded apprehension of absolute want should ever induce them to be purchasers on their own account'.[20]

Banks's advice to government reflected, then, not only his importance as a scientific statesman but also his standing as one of the leading spokesmen of the landed interest, a position that had been confirmed by the active part he had played in vainly attempting to block the Wool Bill. In trying to persuade Banks of the necessity of imports Hawkesbury was also attempting to win over the political support of other landed gentlemen among whom Banks exerted considerable influence. Hence Hawkesbury's insistence in his reply to Banks's letter that the issue of imports raised basic questions of public order.[21] Banks's assessment passed to the highest levels of government. The Home Secretary sent Banks's 'very elaborate & satisfactory letter ... upon the state of the corn crops' to the King as a document produced by 'a person of such authority in matters of that sort'. George III replied by strongly endorsing Banks's views on the desirability of 'Avoiding at least till the season is farther advanced the buying corn by persons employed by Government'.[22] The royal response was an indication of the extent to which the King shared Banks's identification with the landed interest as well as his enthusiasm for agricultural improvement.

The experience of 1795 alerted Banks to the need to increase the supply of food for the rapidly increasing population of England. It also gave greater impetus to the arguments of the landed interest more generally that Britain should be self-sufficient in food.[23] Hawkesbury's view, as he told Banks in 1804, was that now that Britain had become a manufacturing country it had to accept that 'though our [Agri]Culture has of late Years greatly increased, our Population has increased in a much greater proportion'.[24] But Banks, ever resolute in the defence of the landed interest, took the view that the solution to such a difficulty was to work towards greater domestic self-sufficiency. But for such self-sufficiency to be achieved government had to allow domestic market forces to work, Banks having 'no doubt ... that this Island is amply capable of supplying its inhabitants with plenty of Corn, if its price is allowed ... to find its natural Level'.[25]

This striving for British independence from foreign suppliers was in the same mercantilist vein as Banks's response to the wool crisis that followed the American Revolution, when British wool was being outsold by fine Spanish merino wool – a situation which prompted Banks to attempt to breed varieties of merinos which could flourish in Britain or its Empire.

For Banks, then, the prevailing imperative was to promote national self-sufficiency – something which was of particular importance in the face of a crisis that threatened to make Britain dependent on a commodity as essential as food. Thus Banks sponsored a series of experiments through the Board of Agriculture and the Royal Institution designed to obtain better wheat yields and to foster alternative crops such as potatoes. But Banks was well aware that for farmers to plant such new or improved crops it must be economically advantageous for them to do so and this, he argued, would not be the case if cheap foreign corn was available. He took the view, therefore, that the political pressure of the manufacturers in opposing corn tariffs was impeding the introduction of the early sown and higher yielding spring wheat to which he attached such importance. Spring wheat, he thought, would not become properly established 'till a sowing in it becomes a matter of Political as well as of Economic importance'.[26] Thus Banks's scientific enquiries led him back once more to the political arena in which he had first become aware of the overriding importance of the need to increase England's supplies of food. Banks was therefore closely identified with the passage of the Corn Law of 1815 – so closely in fact that his house was attacked by an anti-Corn Law mob.[27]

Banks's involvement in the fundamental issue of supplying food to the nation illustrates a number of points about the nature of his political involvement. First and foremost it underlines the extent to which Banks, for all his interest in new technological processes and sources of supply for manufacture, was identified with the landed interest. Banks, like other members of the landed classes, was active in promoting England as a manufacturing nation and was on close and friendly terms with pioneering entrepreneurs like Boulton. However, he and others of his class expected such manufacturers to operate in a social and political order which gave ultimate political power to the landed interest which, when necessary, intervened on its own behalf. Thus Banks's scientific advice to government was not that of a disinterested technical expert – it reflected not only what he considered was possible in scientific terms but also what the politically pre-eminent landed classes were likely to regard as consistent with their interests.

Second, the number of institutions with which Banks dealt in relation to such issues – the Privy Council Committee for Trade, the Privy Council in general, the Board of Agriculture, the Royal Institution – illustrates the extent of his influence and the flexible manner in which he could operate to attempt to win over government to his way of thinking. Thus he employed both the formal mechanism of central government and institutions such as the Board of Agriculture and the Royal Institution which were more at the periphery of government but which nonetheless helped to shape the thinking of the government elite.

Last, the subject illustrates not only Banks's flexibility but also that of the British State more generally – though the central government may have lacked a formal organisation to examine issues such as the food supply, prominent establishment figures such as Banks helped to link the deliberations of voluntary scientific bodies (like the Royal Institution or the Royal Society) with the political process. In the absence of a central department for scientific and technological affairs, such personal networks also helped to give greater coherence and direction to this area of national policy than might have been expected to emerge from a seemingly random collection of independent institutions.

This same flexibility is evident in the way in which Banks helped to provide a bridge between the deliberations of the Committee for Trade – a body at the centre of the British State's decision-making processes – and other institutions and individuals when providing expert advice on matters that affected the conduct of war. For after the outbreak of war between Britain and France in 1793 the Committee for Trade invoked Banks's expertise on issues with a more direct impact on military concerns, such as the critical issue of the supply of saltpetre which was essential for the manufacture of gunpowder. Again Banks was able to use his influence at the Committee for Trade as a pivot around which he could draw in a number of institutions which collectively formed part of the domain of the British State. In 1794 Hawkesbury consulted Banks on the supply of potash to France which, Banks confirmed, enabled France to manufacture saltpetre by a new, albeit costly, chemical process. Consequently, he recommended that exports of potash to France should be stopped just as the East India Company had been required to cease exporting saltpetre.[28] In the following year Banks was also consulted on whether exports of nitric acid should also be stopped since it, too, could be used to manufacture saltpetre.[29] However, Banks recommended against this since he and his Royal Society colleagues – notably Blagden (who had become familiar with the French chemical industry during his time in France before the Revolution) – were doubtful that the French were manufacturing saltpetre in this manner.[30]

Though hemp was less obviously of military significance than gunpowder it was, for a maritime nation like Britain, of critical importance for maintaining naval power. Britain's dependence on the uncertain sympathies of Russia, traditionally its chief supplier, for such a vital commodity prompted the Committee for Trade to investigate possible sources of supply under British control. In doing so they naturally looked to Banks both to provide expert scientific advice and to facilitate the interconnections between the different arms of government necessary to promote such a project. Banks also had the advantage of being familiar with the production of hemp in his own county of Lincolnshire[31] – we find him, for example, in 1801 recommending to the Naval Commissioners the services of six Lincolnshire hemp dressers for service in India.[32] For, as with tea, British-controlled India was a natural location for attempting to produce a commodity so vital for national self-sufficiency. Banks with his characteristic ability to straddle the bureaucratic structures of the British State recommended such a project to the Committee for Trade in 1800 and then used his good offices with other bodies, such as the Navy and the East India Company, to bring it to fruition. However, the hemp trade, which, like the tea trade, became so vital to the Indian economy from the mid-nineteenth century[33] did not become a large-scale enterprise until after Banks's death.

The importance attached to promoting national self-sufficiency in hemp is reflected in the minutes of the Committee for Trade when, with Banks in attendance, the issue of hemp was again considered on 14 January 1801. For, it was urged, 'the Object we have at present in view is by no means merely commercial; it is for the purpose of relieving this Country from the entire Dependence on a Foreign power for an essential Article of Naval Equipment'. Along with the Indian venture, another possible source of hemp closer to home was in Ireland and, the Committee on Trade continued, 'the Navy Board should establish in Ireland a small hemp Farm' and 'this object could easily be effected by the able assistance of one of the Members of this Committee, Sir Joseph

Banks, who was ready to pay every attention to this subject'.[34] The importance of Banks as a bridge between the Committee for Trade and the Navy Board was underlined by another Committee for Trade resolution of a few months later recommending 'That the Navy Board be desired to consult with Sir Joseph Banks'.[35]

Along with the Navy Board, Banks continued to liase with the East India Company on the issue of hemp. In August of the same year he received a detailed report on the possibilities of hemp (both as a source of fibre and as a possible drug) and other useful commodities paying particular attention to 'getting substitutes in this Country for the materials which are brought from the northern nations for our navy'.[36] Two years later Banks was still pursuing the matter with the East India Company sending the Court of Directors a report compiled by the Committee for Trade regarding 'experiments made on the produce of the dependencies of the EI Company', paying particular attention to the successful outcome of investigations regarding Malabar hemp. On behalf of the Committee for Trade, then, Banks urged the East India Company both on grounds of patriotism and profit 'to encourage as much as possible the growth of strong Hemp'.[37] Reciprocally, Banks urged the Committee for Trade to make concessions to the East India Company by allowing them to import processed fibres duty free in return for which he thought the 'Court of Directors will agree to bring home a certain Quantity of the strongest Fibre undressed, and fit for the use of the Navy'.[38]

Ever anxious to enlist the new colony of New South Wales in the task of promoting British wealth and self-sufficiency, Banks used the Committee for Trade to promote the possibility of a hemp trade in that distant corner of the British Empire – the early fortunes of which were largely directed by Banks. The possibilities of New South Wales as a source of naval supplies had been canvassed even before British settlement in 1788. Two of the proposals for colonising the area – that of Matra in 1783 and Young in 1784–5 – spoke of the contribution that the proposed colony might make to British self-sufficiency through the cultivation of what Matra called 'the New Zeeland hemp or Flax Plant, an object equally of Curiosity & Utility' which, he contended, 'In Naval Equipments ... would be of the greatest importance',[39] while Sir George Young thought it 'may be obtained at a much cheaper route than those materials we at present get from Russia, who may perhaps at some future period think it Her interest to prohibit our Trade with Her for such Articles'.[40]

Though attempts to cultivate New Zealand flax proved disappointing, Banks continued to regard New South Wales as a possible source of naval supplies. Hence he used his position on the Committee for Trade to ensure that samples of hemp and flax sent from New South Wales were tested in government instrumentalities such as the Transport Board. However, though the initial experiments were encouraging enough for the Committee for Trade to declare in 1806 that they entertained hopes that 'a Trade in these Articles will be highly important to the Mother Country and extremely advantageous to the Colony',[41] New South Wales's future economic fortunes were to be tied to merino wool – another of Banks's enthusiasms – rather than hemp or flax.

Indeed, the promotion of New South Wales wool was an issue which the Committee for Trade had considered a few years before in 1803. Ironically, however, Banks, perhaps because of his dislike of John Macarthur, the main advocate of the industry, had been somewhat lukewarm in his support. He had taken the view that government should not become actively involved in the industry at this stage leaving it to private enterprise for the moment to demonstrate its profitability[42] – a stance that may also partly reflect his engrained suspicion of government intervention in the affairs of the landed interest. In the following year, however, Banks was involved in a resolution of the Committee for Trade to write to the Court of Directors to ensure that imports of wool and other commodities from New South Wales would not be adversely affected by the East India Company's traditional monopoly privileges.[43] In the conduct of colonial affairs, as of scientific, Banks was able to utilise his links with the Committee for Trade and other instrumentalities of the British State to advance his favoured projects.

Banks's influence on the Committee waned markedly after the departure of the first Earl of Liverpool (Charles Jenkinson) from active politics in 1804 (four years before his death). With the deaths of Pitt and Fox in 1806 and the collapse of the inaptly named 'Ministry of All the Talents' in March 1807, Banks's hopes for a politically more stable and more conservative administration – what he called an end of the 'profligates' and 'a succession of honest and quiet men'[44] – were realised. Consequently, he felt that he could once more act in the arena of government without being drawn into what he regarded as overtly party political activity – an indication of the extent to which Banks equated being apolitical with the maintenance of the status quo. Thus he greeted the formation of the Duke of Portland's administration in March 1807 with a sigh of relief as promising 'a Stable Administration'.[45]

Banks therefore began to be involved once more in the affairs of the Committee for Trade which from 1807 to 1812 was presided over by Earl Bathurst. The two men were linked by a common interest in agricultural improvement, for Bathurst's reputation as a sheep-breeder had earlier prompted Banks to send him a merino from his majesty's Spanish flock.[46] Predictably, their main area of mutual concern on the Committee for Trade was the import of merinos to Britain.[47] However, Banks *qua* Privy Councillor and Bathurst proved a much less fertile partnership at the Committee for Trade than had the longstanding working relationship between Banks and Jenkinson. Nevertheless, after Bathurst became Secretary of War and Colonies in 1812, Banks did look to that revitalised arm of government to achieve a number of his imperial and scientific projects[48] – a further indication of his estrangement from the Committee for Trade which had been for so long his chief link with the functioning of the British State. Banks last attended the Committee for Trade in November 1809[49] at about the time that the Portland administration was giving way to that of Perceval. Thus ended Banks's long involvement with the instrumentality of the British State which did most to realise his hopes that science might act as a loyal servant of empire.

The Privy Council Committee for Coinage and the Mint

Both Liverpool and Bathurst regarded it as part of their duties as Presidents of the Committee for Trade to regulate the nation's coinage and both relied heavily on Banks's advice on these matters – the association between science and the Mint having had the illustrious blessing of Banks's predecessor as President of the Royal Society, Isaac Newton. Liverpool, author of a work on coins,[50] took a particularly close interest in the nation's currency and, no doubt, it was at his instigation that a committee of the Privy Council was established in 1787 to deal with the issue of coinage. When Banks was formally made a Privy Councillor in 1797 he was appointed specifically to this committee as well as to the Committee for Trade and Plantations.[51] The establishment of the Privy Council Committee for Coinage reflected the inadequacies of the Mint which had become a breeding ground for sinecures, increasingly presided over by absentee Masters[52] – posts which were used to reward politicians for their activities elsewhere.

Liverpool and Banks both viewed the Mint's archaic practices with ill-disguised patience. They agreed in 1797, for example, that a recoinage of the silver coinage could not take place until the Mint was reformed which, Banks wearily commented, 'will be a difficult & Tedious Task'.[53] This drive for efficiency in the Mint was consistent with the two men's involvement in the reform and revitalisation of other areas of the creaky machinery of the British State. Nonetheless, one of the future sinecure Masters of the Mint was Liverpool's son, the future Prime Minister – an irony that serves as a reminder of the entrenched nature of 'Old Corruption'.

One of the major problems for trade within Britain in the late eighteenth century was the shortage of specie – a problem beyond the technical and administrative expertise of the enfeebled Mint. In order to overcome this Banks and Liverpool co-operated in organising a vast recoinage of copper money in 1797, with Banks acting as the intermediary between the Committee for Coinage and the industrialist, Matthew Boulton, at whose Soho works in Birmingham the recoinage took place.[54] Boulton, who had taken an active interest in coinage issues since 1773 when the need for recoining the nation's gold currency had become evident, had erected a private mint using steam power and had exported both coins and his mechanical expertise. Among his customers had been the East India Company an experience which, in 1789, prompted Boulton to suggest to the Committee for Coinage that his equipment might be used to deal with the ever increasing problem of the shortage of British copper coinage. His conduit to the Privy Council was Banks[55] – a cameo example of the way in which the technical abilities of the manufacturing classes and the political skills of the landed classes could complement each other. It also serves as another instance of Banks's ability to link the machinery of government with the emerging scientific and technological expertise of the period.

In the same vein, even before he had become a formal member of the Committee, Banks had provided scientific guidance on problems related to the wear of metals.[56] After his elevation as a Privy Councillor in 1797 this role as a scientific adviser became more pronounced and, in familiar fashion, he became the bridge between government and the Royal Society. In particular, Banks drew on the expertise of two of the Society's most eminent members, Henry Cavendish and Charles Hatchett; the latter conducted an important series of experiments on the wear of metal.[57] Once the study was complete, Hatchett was anxious to publish the results before the French, the traditional scientific rivals, anticipated his findings. This raised the issue of the extent to which experiments which impinged on confidential issues of State could be made available to the larger scientific world – a problem with a long future ahead of it. Lord Liverpool was, however, content to allow the needs of science to take precedence over political imperatives.[58] Such work was an indication of the British State's increasing need for scientific and technical expertise though, characteristically, the means of obtaining it remained informal and reliant on the personal networks characteristic of an oligarchy.

Like so many traditional governmental institutions, the Mint had its own traditions and fiercely guarded preserves of autonomy. The result was that the members of the Company of Moneyers at the Mint were not so much governmental employees as members of a virtually hereditary tightly-controlled guild which saw itself as possessing the exclusive right to produce coinage.[59] In 1789 the Company of Moneyers's traditional monopoly was breached when it vainly attempted to outbid Boulton for the contract to produce copper coinage[60] – an indication of government's greater willingness to break with tradition to achieve efficiency. The onset of competition did lead to the Moneyers showing some signs of bestirring themselves – as Boulton acidly remarked in 1798: 'There has not been a single Improvement made by the Moneyers in the Tower for this Century past; and whatever they may now make ought to be attributed to my having roused them from their Lethargy'.[61]

By this time Banks had adopted what Lord Bathurst called the role of 'Plenipo or rather Umpire and general pacificator between the contending interests'.[62] But, despite such improvements, the traditional status of the Moneyers as a virtually independent fiefdom reserving to itself the lucrative trade of coining was inconsistent with a government increasingly determined to have its servants more directly answerable to it. Their eventual abolition in 1850 was one indication of the drive by government to assert its direct authority over the running of the State.

One other result of the Privy Council Committee on Coinage's involvement with Boulton was a devastating report by John Rennie, FRS, one of Boulton and Watt's engineers, on the type of machinery used by the Mint. This eventually led to re-equipping the Mint with steam machinery of the sort pioneered by Boulton. This, in turn, meant that the Mint had to be re-housed and moved from its ancient home in the Tower – a move which helped to provide a suitable setting for a considerable administrative overhaul of its encrusted traditions under its first non-sinecurist Master for many decades, the dynamic William Wellesly Pole (brother of the Duke of Wellington), Master of the Mint from 1812 to 1823.[63] It was he who oversaw what Banks described, in Enlightenment fashion, as the transformation of 'an establishment [which] may have been [suitable] to the dark & half civilized times, when it was instituted' to one appropriate 'to the improved manners, the Public Credit, & the mutual Confidence of the age we live in'.[64] One indication of the extent of Pole's activities at the Mint was Banks's decision in August 1818 to donate to the Mint his substantial collection of books, coins and medals which 'I made when from the sinecurism of the Masters of the Mint I was one of the Committee of the Privy Council for Coins'. But now, he added, there was no such need for a Committee since Wellesly Pole was 'the most efficient Master I have ever heard or read of'.[65]

In its own small way, then, the Mint was undergoing something of the same experience as the East India Company – both were traditional monopolies which were coming under threat thanks to the growing size of the British economy. Both, too, were agencies which, though extremely important for the workings of the national economy, had traditionally maintained a substantial degree of autonomy. However, as Britain's government grew in size and governments became more assertive in the late eighteenth century, both institutions became subject to a greater degree of government direction. As the nineteenth century progressed, this was to lead eventually to their being subsumed within the formal apparatus of the central government. In the late eighteenth century, then, the traditional and often rather creaky bureaucratic machinery of old-regime England began to be overhauled and made more subject to the will of government – a process which can be seen both literally and metaphorically in the Mint's transition from horse power to steam power.

The Admiralty

Along with the Privy Council and its off-shoots, the Committee for Coinage and, most importantly, the Committee for Trade, the other most significant central agency of the British State through which Banks attempted to link science with the purposes of empire was the Admiralty.

In the period immediately after his election as President of the Royal
Society in 1788 it was a department of government where his stocks were
low, following his attempt to dictate to the Admiralty the terms of his
involvement in Cook's *Resolution* voyage of 1772 and the debacle of his
spectacular withdrawal when he was defeated in his attempts to bend the
Navy to his will.

But, by the time of the proposed breadfruit voyage in 1787, Banks had
mended his fences sufficiently to enlist the Admiralty's good offices in
linking the power of the British State with the practical benefits of
botany. As Sir Evan Nepean, Under-secretary of the Home Office,
remarked to Philip Stevens (Secretary of the Admiralty from 1763 to
1795), it was Banks 'who planned the Expedition undertaken by
Lieutenant Bligh in the Bounty Store Ship'.[66] Banks owed much to those
industrious civil servants Nepean and Stevens[67] – the latter of whom had
helped to secure Banks's place on the *Endeavour*[68]. Both were very much
in sympathy with Banks's plans for utilising scientific knowledge for the
benefit of the British Empire. Stevens was an FRS and Nepean took an
interest in economic botany for, while Governor of Bombay from 1812
to 1819, he sent Banks numerous examples of commercially valuable
fruits and spices.[69]

The organisation of the breadfruit expedition required the assistance
not only of the Admiralty but also the Home Office[70] which was largely
responsible for colonial affairs until the Colonial Office was properly
established in 1801. Thus Nepean at the Home Office and Stevens at the
Admiralty formed a partnership which enabled Banks to build up a
tradition of involving the British State in scientific exploration. Not only
did they facilitate Banks's sponsorship of the first breadfruit expedition,
but also the second, successful *Providence* expedition of 1791–3, the
organisation of which also largely derived from Banks. Hence Banks's
thanks to Lord Chatham (First Lord of the Admiralty, 1788–94) in 1793
for 'the honor of being intrusted ... with some portion of the Direction
of the Expedition commanded by Captain Bligh'.[71]

Before the *Bounty* expedition, Nepean had worked closely with Banks
in planning the epic voyage of the First Fleet to Botany Bay under
Captain Arthur Phillip in 1787–8[72]. Nepean's primary responsibility was
then to the Home Office, which often acted as a co-ordinating body
for major ventures which straddled a number of different government
departments.[73] There is little documentary record of such consultation since most of it was conducted by word of mouth, but there are
occasional hints as to the extent of Banks's involvement in the planning
for the First Fleet, particularly in any aspect that impinged on science.
Thus on 22 November 1786, Sir Harry Parker, the Under-secretary of the
Admiralty and Secretary to the Board of Longitude, sent Banks, at his
request, a list of the instruments to be sent to Botany Bay.[74] Banks also
advised Phillip about which plants to bring to the new colony.[75] While at
the Home Office Nepean, as his active involvement in the convict First
Fleet and the breadfruit expedition suggest, also exercised considerable

influence within the Admiralty and it was a natural progression for him to succeed Stevens as First Secretary of the Admiralty in 1795, a post he held until 1804.

During this time another of Banks's major scientific-cum-naval initiatives, the *Investigator*'s circumnavigation of Australia under Flinders's command, was planned and executed and, again, Banks and Nepean formed a close partnership. The extent of Nepean's confidence in Banks is manifest in his note to Banks of 28 April 1801, when he remarks about the *Investigator* expedition 'Any proposal you make will be approved. The whole is left entirely to your decision'.[76] The close relationship between these two industrious servants of empire is also evident in Flinders's decision to write to Nepean while Banks was ill, addressing him as Banks's 'friend' and as someone who was 'most capable of putting everything into a state of forwardness'.[77] Banks was, of course, actively involved in drawing up the instructions for Flinders emphasising both the scientific and potential commercial benefits to be obtained from the expedition. Banks's desire to strengthen his ties both with the Admiralty and the East India Company is probably reflected in the instruction to Flinders to be watchful for 'those Parts of the Coast most likely to be fallen in with by East India Ship on their outward bound Passages'[78]. It was a comment that underlined the close marriage between scientific and imperial-cum-commercial goals.

In this period not only did Banks have the aid of Nepean at the Admiralty but also that of William Marsden (second Secretary of the Admiralty, 1795–1804, first Secretary, 1804–7), who had been an enthusiastic participant at Banks's conversation parties in the 1780s and had published (with Banks's encouragement) a number of pioneering works in comparative linguistics; he also later deputised for Banks on the Council of the Royal Society when the latter was immobilised by gout. It was to Marsden that Banks turned when he wanted to ensure that the Admiralty treated both the men of the *Investigator* expedition and the collections that they had amassed with due respect.[79]

Quite apart from their personal interests in science and exploration, the chief officials of the Admiralty had good reason to take Banks seriously since he was well connected with their superiors, particularly a number of First Lords of the Admiralty. Banks's neighbour, close friend and early patron, John Montagu, fourth Earl of Sandwich, was first Lord of the Admiralty (1748–51 and 1771–82) and, although Banks's relations with the Admiralty were still then under a cloud following the debacle over the *Resolution*, he was active, as we have seen, in helping to make Banks part of the political establishment. He also assisted him in minor ways at the Admiralty, such as facilitating Banks's role in the publication of the journal of Cook's third voyage.[80] Among Sandwich's successors, Banks's ties were closest with Earl Spencer (first Lord, 1794–1801) who did much to reform and revitalise the Admiralty when the Navy faced its critical test during the French Wars.[81] Banks and Spencer shared many common interests – both were keen agricultural improvers and sheep-breeders[82] and Spencer served along with Banks on the boards of the Royal Institution and the British Museum. Appropriately, for a President of the Royal Institution, a Trustee of the British Museum and, subsequently, one of the founders and first president of the Roxburghe Club (a gathering of bibliophiles), Spencer also shared Banks's interest in scientific exploration. It was thanks to Spencer that the Admiralty agreed to Banks's proposal for the *Investigator* expedition – a subject on which he addressed a long memorandum to Spencer stressing the need for Britain to respond to the French expedition under Baudin in order to maintain its claim to the Australian continent.[83]

Under Spencer's sway such exploration became a path to naval advancement, something which had not always been the case under his predecessors. As Banks wrote to Lord Glenbervie (then the prospective Governor of the Cape Colony) when proposing a survey of the African coast, it was now no longer difficult to find naval captains willing to command voyages of exploration, something for which 'we may be thankful to the Liberal spirit of the First Lord of the Admiralty who by admitting that those persons who distinguish themselves in maritime surveys have a claim upon him for preferment'. Banks contrasted this with the situation that prevailed under Earl Howe (first Lord of the Admiralty, 1783-8) who, 'as brave a man as ever sat at that board, was certainly little addicted to the encouragement of science'.[84] One example of Spencer's sympathy for naval captains who assisted the cause of exploration was his willingness at Banks's request to assist in 1795 in Bligh's promotion.[85]

After Spencer's departure from the Admiralty in 1801 and from the cabinet in 1807, Banks's influence at the Admiralty waned for a time – something that also probably owed much to Marsden's resignation as Secretary of the Admiralty in 1807. In 1808, for example, he remarked to the Navy Board that 'I find it so impossible to obtein that access to the Commissioners at present that I was formerly usd to have'.[86] However, as his friendship with John Barrow (second secretary to the Admiralty, 1804–6 and 1807–1845) developed so, too, were his links with the Admiralty once again strengthened. The two men were, in many ways, kindred spirits: both shared an interest in natural history and in the promotion of empire through scientifically-informed exploration. This was a cause that Barrow continued to advance after Banks's death, thus helping to perpetuate the British tradition of naval-cum-scientific exploration. Barrow became a regular visitor at Banks's receptions at Soho Square and, by 1811, the two men had established a close working relationship. In that year Barrow helped to ensure that the Admiralty accepted Banks's offer to prepare Flinders's journal for publication – a task, as Banks noted, 'I had the honor to execute under the direction of the then Board of Admiralty, in the Publication of the third Voyage of Captain Cook'.[87] It was a comment that underlined both Banks's continuing role in the promotion of Pacific exploration and his long-standing position as an unofficial adviser to the Admiralty.

In 1815 Barrow was made a member of the Council of the Royal Society. Banks, reported Barrow, was of the view that 'one of the Secretaries of the Admiralty should always be in the Council of the Royal Society'[88] – a remark that reflects Banks's customary acuteness in linking science and politics. With Barrow's support at the Admiralty, Banks was able once again to persuade that department to undertake a major scientific expedition – the Buchan-Franklin Arctic expedition of 1818.[89] For both Banks, who was much influenced by William Scoresby, FRS, clergyman and former Greenland fisherman, and Barrow, the author of *A Chronological History of Arctic Regions* (1818), had a longstanding close interest in Arctic exploration.

Banks's influence at the Admiralty, then, helped to strengthen that association between naval exploration and scientific discovery which Banks's own highly publicised voyage on the *Endeavour* had done much to cultivate. For, though Banks was not the first English scientific explorer, and still less the first European, his famous expedition on the *Endeavour* also pointed the way to another means by which government could support scientific enquiry at little cost – namely by taking along a naturalist on a voyage which was generally prompted by concerns which the British State tended to think of as more peculiarly their own: such as exploration for strategic or imperial advantage. As Banks wrote, with pardonable pride:

> I may flatter myself, that being the first man of Scientific education who undertook a voyage of discovery and that voyage of discovery ... being the first which turned out satisfactorily to his enlightened age, I was in some measure the first who gave that turn to such voyages.[90]

Thus in 1780, Captain James King, a fellow of the Royal Society, wrote to him that 'it is with real pleasure and satisfaction that I look up to you as the common centre of we discoverers'.[91] And, of course, as Darwin's voyage on the *Beagle* and Thomas Huxley's on the *Rattlesnake* suggest it was a tradition that, thanks to Banks's efforts, became well entrenched in naval practice into the nineteenth century.

THE INFORMAL APPARATUS OF GOVERNMENT

The Institutions of Agricultural Improvement

While the Privy Council and its committees and the Admiralty formed part of the central core of the State there was a range of other institutions more removed from the epicentre of government which also formed part of the network through which Banks attempted to link the concerns of empire with those of science. For, just as the Royal Society could be said to be a part of the larger fabric of English government, so, too, a number of newer and smaller institutions with which Banks was associated also helped to shape governmental policy towards the increasingly important issues associated with the application of science, even though such institutions were not a formal part of the machinery of government.

The most important of these were the Board of Agriculture, the Royal Institution and the Royal Botanic Gardens at Kew – all of which shared a preoccupation with agricultural improvement. This was a central concern in a society dominated by a landowning class and presided over by a King who delighted in the sobriquet 'Farmer George' and who contributed articles (under a pseudonym) to Arthur Young's *Annals of Agriculture.* Though the Society of Arts was fundamentally intended to foster improvements in the trades it, too, played a role in promoting agricultural improvement and, in doing so, it also cultivated those informal links with the machinery of government which expanded the effective domain of the State. Hawkesbury, the President of the Committee for Trade, for example, was a member from 1789 and was elected a Vice-president in 1791 – links which facilitated the successful realisation of the Society's proposals for the removal of tariffs on products useful for domestic manufacture.[92]

The anomalous status of the Board of Agriculture, which was founded in 1793, is another indication of the transitional nature of the governmental apparatus in the age of Banks.[93] Pitt's government recognised the political importance of agriculture and the need for some state-sponsored patronage of plans for agricultural improvement, but at the same time limited the State's direct involvement to an annual grant of three thousand pounds per annum. But this ill-defined status also helped to bring about the Board's eventual demise. It was not sufficiently integrated with the inner workings of government to be taken seriously by Pitt and other practising politicians but it was sufficiently identified with government to limit support for it as a voluntary body and for its political freedom of movement to be circumscribed: thus its support for the political policies favoured by the landed interest led to the cutting off of government funds in 1821.[94]

Despite Banks's reservations about the possible competition that the Board of Agriculture might pose to the Royal Society he was eventually persuaded to take an active part in the Board's affairs. Moreover, his links with the inner core of government helped to some extent to offset the political ineptitude of Sir John Sinclair, the Board's founding president. In August 1800, for example, Banks was asked by his longstanding ally, Lord Liverpool, at a time when the government was concerned about possible food shortages, to undertake a survey of the quantity of land sown with wheat. In such an undertaking, Jenkinson saw the Board of Agriculture's anomalous political position as a positive advantage, for since 'the Board is less connected with Government than the Committee of Trade, the Measure when executed by them will create less Jealousy & Suspicion, and will be more readily complied with'.[95] Jenkinson's comment again underlines the fluid boundaries of the British State in this period – the Board of Agriculture, a partially private body, was, in effect, undertaking governmental business, not as the result of a formal governmental decree but rather through the personal associations developed between Banks and Jenkinson. Reciprocally, the Board of Agriculture also employed such informal connections with Banks acting as a convenient conduit back to the Committee for Trade and thence to the parliament. Thus Banks was requested by its president and members to request the Committee for Trade to arrange legislation to allow seed cake into the country duty-free as an aid to agriculture.[96]

The Royal Institution, founded in 1799, shared with the Board of Agriculture a strong interest in agricultural improvement, prompted particularly by the increasing levels of mass pauperisation. The two bodies had in common the active involvement of Sir Joseph Banks, who presided over the inaugural meetings of the Royal Institution, and it was under his chairmanship that the original proprietors in 1799 petitioned for a royal charter.[97] Banks also helped to persuade a number of prominent political figures – notably Earl Spencer[98] – to serve as proprietors. The Royal Institution was linked with the British State both by personal ties through individuals, such as Earl Spencer, and through the kind of projects it favoured. In particular its active involvement in agricultural improvement gave it public standing in a society dominated by a landowning class.[99] At Banks's initiative the Royal Institution helped to support and publicise Humphrey Davy's pioneering work in agricultural chemistry, an area where the Royal Institution came closer to the formal apparatus of the State through its association with the Board of Agriculture. When the Board of Agriculture lost its state funding in 1821 it was offered a home by the Royal Institution.[100] Though the Board declined the offer it nonetheless indicates the extent to which the Royal Institution was seen as pursuing similar goals to the Board of Agriculture.

Such close associations between the two institutions are an indication of the way in which the dominance of the landed class and their scientific interests helped to give some degree of cohesion to the seemingly diverse range of British institutions which impinged on science. The influence of prominent individuals such as Banks helped to ensure, too, that such institutions were not only linked to each other but were in contact with the central government. Banks, for example, used his influence with the Royal Institution to encourage Humphrey Davy to undertake experiments to show that *terra japonica* could be used as a substitute for oak bark in the troubled tanning trade.[101] The sample of *terra japonica* which Banks supplied to Davy in 1801 had been sent from India through the East India Company and obtained by Banks because of his work on the Committee on Trade on the state of the tanning industry. Thus England's colonial interests in India, together with its domestic interests in promoting a trade as dependent on agriculture as tanning, were promoted, thanks to Banks's agency, through the nominally independent Royal Institution – another instance of the loosely-defined nature of Britain's governmental apparatus in the age of revolution.

Kew Green with the road leading to the Palace in the mid-1760s. Drawing by
George Bickham.
(By courtesy of the Royal Botanical Gardens, Kew)

More obviously linked to government was the Royal Botanic Gardens
at Kew, though it was formally a personal possession of the King and did
not become subject to direct state control until 1841.[102] Under Banks's
de facto directorship (which dated from 1773 after the King inherited
the Gardens from the Princess Dowager in 1772[103]), Kew Gardens became virtually an institute for economic botany and it was there that
plants that were considered to be potential sources of additional income
for the British Empire could be cultivated and re-distributed. The
example of Kew Gardens, in turn, helped to stimulate the creation of a
network of colonial replicas with which Kew could exchange specimens
and it was generally left to Banks to help in the organisation and staffing
of such institutions.

Such gardens often had to negotiate a delicate passage between the
Scylla of the demands of the metropolitan scientific establishment at Kew
and the Charybdis of local political pressures. Banks represented the
demands of Kew and the metropolis but his room for manoeuvre in
shaping such colonial gardens to his own ends was often limited by local
interests. When Thomas Dancer, the Superintendent of the Botanical
Gardens at Jamaica, was in dispute with the Jamaican House of Assembly
in 1794 Banks declined to become involved[104] probably because he was
aware of how jealously the island maintained its tradition of local
autonomy. But where colonial possessions were more directly subject to
metropolitan authority Banks was able to use the machinery of the
British State to advance his scientific interests.

In contrast to Jamaica with its longer tradition of British settlement and local representation, the island of St Vincent was under the control of the War Office since it was virtually a garrison, having been captured by the French in 1762 and 1779 (though ultimately returned). As a consequence, Banks could use his standing at court and in the political establishment both to ensure its re-establishment in 1785 and to play a major role in choosing its superintendents. With Banks's encouragement, 'Farmer George' took a close interest in this institution for agricultural improvement – as the orientalist, William Jones, remarked in 1787:

> The King has much at heart his new botanical garden at St Vincent's; his object is two-fold, to improve the commerce of the West-India islands, and to provide the British troops on service there with medicinal plants.[105]

When the first superintendent was appointed he acknowledged to Sir George Young, the Secretary at War, the need to consult closely with Banks when planning the gardens[106] and this tradition of deferring to his judgement continued. In 1812, when the new superintendent, William Lockhead, was appointed, he acknowledged to Banks that his appointment owed much to his influence and that he had been ordered by the War Office 'to correspond with you as President of the Royal Society and with regard to exchange of plants, seeds & c with H.M. Head Gardener at Kew in the first place'.[107] Subsequently, the Secretary at War enquired of Banks if he had 'any additional Instructions ... by which the appointment in question can be rendered more advantageous to the Interests of Science'.[108] But, like so many superintendents of botanical gardens constrained by the parsimonious and unsympathetic local government, Lockhead favoured more direct control by the metropolitan government, particularly since this would increase the sway of the British State's de facto scientific adviser, Sir Joseph Banks. Hence he expressed the hope to Banks that the Secretary at War would 'see the necessity of rescuing the Botanic Garden altogether from the power of the Govt. and Council of St Vincent and attaching it entirely to the Army'.[109]

With Lockhead's death in 1815 Banks was invited to nominate a successor.[110] He choose that stormy petrel of botany, George Caley, whom Banks had sent as a collector to New South Wales where he had rapidly alienated all and sundry, from the Governor down. But once Banks had adopted a client he was reluctant to abandon him and Caley, like Bligh, continued to be given Banks's support despite his troubled record. Predictably, Caley was soon causing problems at St Vincent – within a year of his appointment he was complaining to Banks that 'if ever a man was in a hornet's nest, I am'.[111] Faced with such local opposition Banks was invoked in the attempt to protect the interests of the gardens against local incursions.

Banks duly used his influence in the corridors of power to defend the gardens persuading the Secretary at War to request the Colonial

View of the Botanic Garden at St Vincent from the superintendent's house.
Lithograph of a drawing by Revd Lansdown Guilding.
(From Lansdown Guilding, *Account of Botanic Garden in Island of St Vincent*, 1825)

Secretary 'to give strict injunctions to the Governor of St Vincents to exert his utmost authority in supporting Mr. Caley in protecting this part of the property of the Crown entrusted to his care'.[112] For, as Banks saw it, Caley was being vigilant in support of the gardens, whereas the previous superintendents had been 'much more inclind to seek for Favor from their neighbors by Granting to them indulgences at the Expense of the Establishment'.[113] Perhaps it was no accident that it was in 1821 – the year after Banks's death – that the government, weary of Caley's querulous ways, closed the gardens down.[114] On St Vincent at least, then, it was possible for Banks to bring to bear his links with government to serve the interests of science in the form of a colonial botanical garden though, as the counter-example of Jamaica suggests, local interests were not always so easily brought to heel by metropolitan political and, still less, scientific authority.

Perhaps Banks's experiences of the internecine conflict between the superintendents of botanical gardens and local authority in the West Indies accounts for his caution about choosing a suitably submissive superintendent when establishing the new botanical gardens in Ceylon in 1811. Banks's standing with government is evident in the way in which the second Earl of Liverpool (then Secretary for War and the Colonies) readily agreed to his proposal for such a garden and largely left its planning and the appointment of a superintendent to him.[115] Banks's plan envisaged the gardens fulfilling the customary functions of serving both science and commerce but it also made explicit its imperial dimension as a means of reinforcing European prestige for, he wrote:

> The institution of a Botanic Garden at Ceylon is much wishd for by the Governments there, who consider such an Establishment as a means of Raising the Character of the British nation in the estimate of the natives.[116]

As superintendent Banks nominated a former Kew gardener collector, William Kerr, whose humble origins and submissive character would ensure that he 'will have no extraordinary Pretences, [and] he will therefore be Easily controlled by the Governor in all cases of difference of opinion between them'.[117] High on the list of instructions to Kerr was the injunction that he must 'pay a Prompt & unconditional Obedience to the orders of the Governor'. Banks's own awareness of the tensions involved in balancing the local, largely commercial, purposes of a colonial garden against the scientific ends he was promoting from the metropolitan centre is apparent in his instruction to Kerr to make 'the interests of its inhabitants ... your first & cheifest duty' since the colony was paying for the garden. But, he hastily added, while this might be Kerr's first priority, 'the science of botany must not however be neglected'.[118] The establishment of the Ceylon Botanic Garden was, then, an instance of Banks's ability to influence the central government to adopt policies sympathetic to science, but the way in which it was run also points to the limitations of metropolitan authority – including that of science – at the colonial level. Banks was well aware that the conduct of science, like that of politics, was the art of the possible and that cultivation of science in the colonies involved a large measure of compromise with local interests.

The worldwide network of botanical gardens, ranging from the West Indies and St Helena to India, the Cape and New South Wales, gave Kew a great advantage in the Lilliputian version of scientific great power politics which Banks fostered in his determination to bolster British prestige by ensuring that the Royal Gardens were without rival in Europe. His main rival was the imperial gardens at Vienna[119] – hence his determination in 1792 to ensure that Bligh's second breadfruit voyage should be used to 'give His Majesty's Gardens at Kew the superiority in West India plants to the Gardens at Vienna'.[120] It was, then, Banks's proud boast that Kew has acquired a superiority over all Similar Establishments, which not one of its Rivals dares to deny; in fact it is the nursing mother of all the rest, who draw from England the greater part of the exotics they cultivate in their Botanic Gardens.[121]

Kew's relations with the central government again illustrate the elastic nature of the British governmental apparatus in this period – the ordinary running expenses of the gardens were met from the royal purse, but the Treasury was asked to meet the costs of some of the botanical collectors who were sent from Kew. This anomaly led to complaints of Banks's unwelcoming stance towards the general public at Kew. For, it was urged, 'the public have derived no benefit from this expensive Botanical Establishment' even though many of the plants were 'collected at the expense of Government on the scientific expeditions'.[122] In 1814, for example, Banks, through the agency of Liverpool, persuaded the Treasury to meet the expenses of the Kew gardeners, James Bowie and Allan Cunningham, the former of whom was sent to the Cape and the latter to New South Wales.[123] Colonial governors were also expected to meet some of the living expenses of the Kew collectors. Thus the Treasury asked Lord Bathurst, Secretary of State for War and Colonies, to instruct the Governor of the Cape to provide Bowie with a wagon and oxen.[124]

By and large such arrangements worked though, given their often ad hoc nature, there was naturally some friction. Banks had to be careful not to allow his collectors to undertake projects on such a scale that they would try the patience of the Treasury. Bowie, for example, was reminded that 'The Treasury are not Anxious for the promotion of Science'.[125] Colonial governors varied in their interpretation of what was an appropriate standard of living for collectors, who did not fit into the established hierarchies of colonial life. This was an issue which caused considerable tension between Allan Cunningham (the botanist) and Governor Macquarie of New South Wales and led to Banks invoking the authority of Lord Bathurst, Colonial Secretary, to pull the reluctant Macquarie into line. He also hinted that Macquarie could earn favour by being more accommodating to collectors by mentioning that, at the Cape, Kew's representatives had been provided with transport at the expense of the colony.[126] There was room, of course, for debate about what expenses belonged naturally to the Crown and what belonged to other governmental agencies though Banks could invoke the royal name to settle such potential disputes. The *mana* of royalty was also used to persuade the semi-independent East India Company to co-operate in advancing the interests of Kew. Thus in 1798 Banks commended the Company for their 'great inclination to promote the King's views in his Botanic Establishment at Kew'. He also assured it – with a subtle reminder of his own high standing with the monarch – that it was a 'mark of attention [of which] his majesty is very sensible'.[127]

Overall, then, Kew Gardens under Banks's directorship was a successful example of how an institution which was not part of the formal structure of centralised government nonetheless met many of the needs of imperial rule, thanks to the informal ties which Banks built up between it and other elements of the state machinery. For Banks, the Royal Gardens at Kew, with relatively generous funding and large degree of freedom from the complexities of parliamentary control, provided one of his favourite institutions for linking science with the cause of empire. Hence his encomium on the institution in 1814:

> the connection I have been permitted to form with the Royal Gardens at Kew is among those most grateful to my feelings, and I beg you to be assured that so long as I shall be permitted to continue it I shall cherish and improve it to the best of my power.[128]

The East India Company

At Kew Banks could benefit from the fact that the Gardens had largely grown up under his control and were a relatively small operation which affected few vested interests. Not surprisingly, he had much greater difficulty in bending the long-established East India Company to his purpose, both because it was much larger and because it had a long tradition of jealously guarding its privileges. The history of the East India Company in the eighteenth century is an indication of the pressures which were building up for an expansion in the size and range of responsibilities of the British State. Traditionally, foreign trade had been left in the hands of trading corporations from which the government extracted regular payments in return for the exercise of their monopolies but which otherwise largely ran their own affairs.

As the extent of British trade and colonial influence grew and as the challenge from foreign and, in particular, French rivals became more pressing so, too, did the need for direct governmental supervision of colonial affairs increase. For all the aversion to an expansion in the size and influence of central government, from 1730 the British government had had to subsidise the financially troubled Royal Africa Company to help maintain its forts against possible French attack and, by 1750, it had virtually dissolved it.[129] The vast East India Company presented far more formidable problems, though as early as 1764 Charles Jenkinson made the prophetic remark that 'The affairs of this [East India] Company seem to be become much too big for the management of a body of merchants'.[130] In 1772 it had to be propped up by what amounted to a loan from the State and its increasing financial problems and allegations of corruption led eventually to a partial governmental takeover in 1784 under the terms of the East India Act. Overall direction, particularly in matters relating to defence and foreign policy, was placed under a Board of Control consisting of six members of the Privy Council while the day-to-day administration of commercial affairs was left in the hands of the Company.[131] Liaison between the Board of Control and the Company became the responsibility of the Secret Committee made up of the Company's directors[132]. Thus, under the terms of this compromise, the East India Company maintained a nominal autonomy but even more clearly than in the past it was drawn into the orbit of governmental influence and formed part of the loosely connected network of institutions and influence which made up the British State.

The East India Company's economic importance made it a natural target for Banks's many projects to expand Britain's income. Thanks to the re-organisation of the Company's affairs in 1784 he had two routes to influence the Company's deliberations. In the first place through the Board of Control, which increasingly was dominated by Banks's ally, Henry Dundas, whose appointment as President of the Board of Control in 1793 was a belated recognition of his de facto role as the Board's dominant figure. Second, through the East India Company itself either through the formal government body, the Court of Directors, or through the more powerful virtual inner cabinet, the Secret Committee.

East India House, home of the East India Company in Leadenhall Street, London.
Engraving, c.1800. P. 2188.
(By permission of the British Library)

Banks had rather more success in influencing the East India Company through the first avenue. The Board of Control formed part of the inner workings of government with which Banks had become increasingly familiar and Dundas himself was one of a group of conscientious administrators with whom Banks naturally felt at home. The two men were also drawn together by their common membership of the Privy Council Committee for Trade and because Dundas took an interest in Banks's favourite avocation, the breeding of sheep.[133] Dundas's dexterous use of ministerial patronage[134] helped to ensure the election of directors amenable to his policies.[135] Under Dundas's watchful scrutiny the machinery of the East India Company was brought more closely under the control of the central State until the Board of Control began to approximate a department of government.[136]

Banks also had the benefit of close personal ties with Constantine Phipps (after 1775 Lord Mulgrave), another of the members of the Board of Control. His friendship with Mulgrave probably helped greatly in first introducing Banks to the inner workings of government, not only at the Board of Control but also at the Committee for Trade (of which Mulgrave was also a member). Not only were Banks and Mulgrave intimate friends but they also shared a common commitment to mercantilist theories of the economy[137] which those agencies of the British State, the Board of Control and the Committee for Trade, did much to implement. For, in his involvement with the Board of Control, Banks's goal was the same as that which underlay his activities in other areas of government: an increase of British wealth and power particularly by helping to promote economic self-sufficiency in areas where Britain had been, or was likely to become, dependent on products under foreign control. In Banks's mind such national goals could be combined with a determination to use science for human betterment more generally since material progress was only likely to come about if science benefited from the patronage of government. Thus, in a long letter to Dundas of 1787, he responded enthusiastically to proposals for the introduction into Bengal of new crops, such as sago and date palms, which would obviate the danger of famine and, having consulted the available literature, gave it his scientific *imprimatur* as a 'plan so freindly to humanity'.

But, as Banks soon emphasised, when he turned in the same letter to a related proposal for the establishment of a Botanical Garden at Calcutta, scientific improvement could not only be justified on 'testimony drawn from the first principles of humanity' but also of 'sound policy' since the gardens could be used 'for the purpose of Cultivating Plants likely to become usefull to commerce'. In a mercantilist vein he argued that this would help remedy the current situation where 'the greatest part of the merchandise imported from India have hitherto been manufactured goods of a nature which interferes with our manufactures at home' where 'our cotton manufactures are increasing with a rapidity which renders it politic to give them effectual encouragement'.

In Banks's view, then, India, where 'Labour [is] incredibly cheap' could produce not only cotton plants but 'Raw materials of many sorts . . . sure of a ready market & of producing a most beneficial influence upon the Commerce of the mother countrey'. India could thus not only serve England by supplying raw materials but it could also help to supply goods for sale in China and 'thus diminish at least if not annihilate the immense debit of Silver which we are annuely obligd to Furnish from Europe' – such a drain in silver in return for Chinese trade was a particular concern to Banks and others like him who, in mercantilist fashion, saw the loss of bullion as leading to a loss of national wealth and power. This same mercantilist strain of thought can also be seen in Banks's emphasis on national commercial rivalry and, in particular, the potential threat from the French who, he argued, in the cultivation of spices 'have taken the lead of us'. Nonetheless, England could recover it by implementing some of his suggestions especially 'if by these means we get possession of the chinese market the advantage of so doing will be to us almost beyond appreciation'.

Perhaps in an attempt to stir Dundas and the Board into action, Banks emphasised that such goals 'want only the encouragement of government to enable them to carry themselves into effectual execution' and he was encouraged to see that not only did they have the support of the King but also that of the first Governor-General of Bengal, Lord Cornwallis.[138] Cornwallis, whose appointment in 1785 represented a further strengthening of governmental control over the East India Company, had energetically set about transforming the Company's servants into 'a disciplined & effective civil service'.[139] Among those who benefited from his rule was Colonel Robert Kyd who had first put forward the proposal for the Botanic Gardens[140] – a proposal which had prompted Banks's long letter to Dundas and other scientifically-inclined officials such as James Anderson and William Roxburgh with whom Banks corresponded in his attempt to promote the goals he had outlined to Dundas. For Kyd, as for Banks, such a garden was a natural outcome of the increasing consolidation of British power in India. Britain, he argued, was obliged to provide some return for 'the accumulated Riches which have accrued to Great Britain, consequent to the acquisition of our Territorial Possessions in India'. One of the benefits that Britain could confer 'on the natives of India' was the cultivation of plants for protection against famine – a goal which the garden might help to advance.[141]

Thanks to Dundas and the Board of Control some of the measures which Banks had advocated in this letter were implemented. The Calcutta Botanic Gardens were opened in 1787 with the support of the Board of Control as well as of the Company.[142] Predictably Banks endeavoured to foster links between this new garden and existing colonial gardens, thanking Sir George Young, the Secretary at War, for example, for his 'plan of general benevolence' in 'setting a correspondence between that [the Calcutta garden] & his Majestys Garden at

Robert Kyd, founder of the Botanic Garden, Calcutta.
(From G. King, *Annals of the Royal Botanic Garden, Calcutta*,
IV 1895, i)
(By courtesy of Cambridge University Library)

St Vincents'. Such an interchange would facilitate the 'exchange between the east & West Indies those productions of Nature useful for the
support of Mankind that are at present confined to one or the other of
them'.[143] Under Banks's client, Dr William Roxburgh, Superintendent
1793–1813, it became a major centre of botanical research and a model
for other smaller gardens which were later established under the
Company's auspices in Madras and Ceylon.[144]

Through Roxburgh Banks received regular correspondence about the
gardens and by this informal means continued to watch closely its work
on such critical problems as the development of tea plants. But, as so
often in his dealings with the East India Company, Banks found it
difficult to exercise at a more formal level the degree of control that he
would have wished. Evidently, he hoped that he might shape the
development of the Calcutta gardens in the way he had done at St
Vincent. Thus he proposed to the Court of Directors that he should
receive regular reports on the gardens in the same manner as he
received them from the War Office about the gardens at St Vincent.[145]
But, while the War Office was part of the formal mechanism of government, the East India Company was more impervious to Banks's

wide-ranging political connections. Hence the rather plaintive tone when, in 1806, at a time when Roxburgh's future tenure looked doubtful because of his poor health, Banks attempted to intervene in the gardens' affairs. It was his object, he wrote, 'to make Trial whether I have sufficient interest with the very respectable body [the East India Company] to lay the foundation of a proper succession in future to an establishment in the welfare of which I feel a deep interest'.[146]

Underlying Banks's passionate interest in the Calcutta Botanic Garden was his hope that it might provide the key to free Britain from the drain on bullion to China produced by the British addiction for tea – a development about which the East India Company, with its vested interest in the China tea trade, viewed with some ambivalence.[147] Another way of dealing with this problem which was more palatable to the Company was to persuade the Chinese imperial court to exchange their tea for some commodity other than silver – hence the determination of Dundas, who shared Banks's enthusiasm for the abundant possibilities that could be opened for British commerce by such a trade, to send a trade mission to China. Along with the economic motives went curiosity about China and a sense that it should be opened to the cosmopolitan civilisation of an increasingly European-dominated world. As the author of an account of the embassy put it, China was a nation which 'would irresistably attract the attention of our enlightened country, to the only civilised nation in the world, whose jealous laws forbid the intrusion of any other people'.[148] When Dundas's first attempt to mount an embassy to Peking collapsed in 1788 because of the death of the ambassador, Lord Cathcart, he set about organising another under Lord Macartney, a former Governor of Madras.[149] Banks was closely involved with this mission from its beginnings and hoped to use Macartney's entourage as a cover for skilled craftsmen who could study Chinese manufacturing methods – particularly those relating to tea and porcelain – and establish them in England. This was something that had the enthusiastic support of Macartney, who sent back specimens of porcelain 'to Sir Joseph Banks with the view of having them compared under the eyes of Chemists and skilful artists with the materials used in England'.[150]

Another embassy to China in 1816–7 under Lord Amherst again vainly attempted to enlarge the East India Company's sphere of activities. Again, too, there was the hope that the mission might enable Britain to obtain commercially valuable information from China. Thus Banks was consulted by an officer of the East India Company as to the best means of transporting cotton and tea plants from China to India;[151] Lord Amherst also asked him to appoint a gardener from Kew as a member of the embassy.[152] After consultation with Amherst, Banks rather pointedly reminded the Company that it was 'a Duty due from them to the Public to make Provision for the advancement of the Science of Natural history on so interesting an Expedition'.[153] As a consequence of Banks's intervention the mission's medical officer had his brief widened to take on 'the office of Naturalist' and was equipped with 'all the apparatus for scientific research'.[154] Such activities were an indication of the continuing efforts that were being applied to bring about the goal that Banks had advocated so enthusiastically of making British-controlled India a supplier of as many basic commodities as possible for the home market.

In dealing with the Company itself Banks had to contend with its long tradition of jealously guarding its privileges and as much of its autonomy as the central government permitted – sentiments which were strengthened rather than weakened by the re-arrangement of 1784.[155] What appears to have been the first scientific contact between Banks and the East India Company came within a year of the establishment of the Board of Control and, significantly, at the initiative of the Company itself, though one may suspect that the Board of Control (and, in all likelihood, Mulgrave) played a part in prompting the Company to approach Banks. In April 1785 Thomas Morton, the Secretary of the Company, sent Banks seeds of hemp and flax requesting him to distribute them among those best qualified to conduct experiments with them, the object being to promote the growth of Chinese hemp in England as 'an object of general utility'.[156] However, it became evident to those guiding the British State that the supply of hemp – a necessity for a naval and maritime power – was too important a matter to be left to the often rather lethargic entrepreneurship of the East India Company. Consequently, as we have seen, the Committee for Trade, with Banks's active involvement, began to promote experiments in hemp-growing, though Banks – true to his de facto role as HM 'Ministre des affaires philosophiques' – tried to provide some co-ordination between the activities of the two different institutions. Despite the discouraging reports of William Roxburgh in Calcutta in 1803 about the growing of hemp there,[157] Banks continued to be involved in attempts to cultivate hemp in India conducted under the auspices of the Company and the Committee for Trade. In 1810, for example, Banks acted as an intermediary in disputes between one of the hemp-growers and his paymasters from these two institutions.[158]

The case of hemp underlined the potential importance of the East India Company in the supply of strategic commodities and in the development of trade more generally. After this initial approach by the Company, Banks was keen to cultivate his links with that often prickly body in order to use its vast resources to develop those botanical and scientific initiatives which he saw as the path to a wealthier and more powerful Britain. In 1787, in reponse to a request to evaluate the work of the botanist, the late Dr Koenig, who had been employed by the Company, Banks expressed his willingness 'to obey the Commands of the Court of Directors on any subject on which they think I am capable of giving them information'. In the same letter, too, he attempted to impress upon the Company the economic advantages that botanical investigation of the sort undertaken by Koenig could open up. Thus Banks passed lightly over 'the mere unprofitable satisfaction only of having been useful in the promotion of Science' which an appointment of a successor to Koenig would allow and dwelt instead on 'the more solid & substantial benefit of a real increase of investment [since] new Dying Drugs would in all liklyhood be discovered as that Branch of Knowledge is so much in its infancy'.[159]

In December 1788 Banks also attempted to impress upon the Company the boundless possibilities that might be opened up by the cultivation of tea in India under British control rather than importing it from China. Here, again, Banks was acting as a co-ordinator between the different arms of the State since the idea had originated with Jenkinson and the Committee for Trade but depended for its execution on the good will of the Company. Thus Banks outlined to the Chairman of the Company some of the measures that it could take to achieve his goals, such as the allocation of twenty acres in the Calcutta Botanic Garden for experimental planting and the sponsored migration of Chinese tea-planters to Calcutta.[160]

And at least some members of the company responded with enthusiasm to Banks's vision. In April 1789 Nathaniel Smith, a Director of the Company, wrote to say that he supported Banks's project for the cultivation of useful products in India; he also accepted Banks's proposal for the appointment of a new botanist at the Company's factory in Canton.[161] But the Company as a whole proved to be rather lukewarm about some of Banks's pet projects. The plans of Banks and the Committee for Trade for India to become a major source of raw cotton did not altogether appeal to a company which for so long had relied on importing from India handwoven cotton goods.[162] As a long-established monopoly, the East India Company was slow to promote innovation and its complex and unwieldy administration was a further brake upon change. Appropriately, the Company's future was to lie with its role as an administrator rather than as a trader since its commercial activities were wound up in 1833.

A further difficulty that Banks faced was that the policies of the Court of Directors varied with the changing political composition of that body, so that Banks's carefully cultivated links with one group might count for naught when their position waned within the Company. As he remarked to William Roxburgh in 1798:

> I am tir'd of promoting projects with a fluctuating body who are sure to be chang'd by the time I have convinc'd the first set of the propriety of any measure recommended to them ... in that fluctuating body no one can ever tell what interest he realy has, to have deserved well of one set of Directors does not at all ensure the good will of the succeeding set.[163]

As early as 1791 Banks was showing some exasperation with the Company's Byzantine ways, since he waspishly replied to a request for comments on some tea plants that 'when the Court do me the honor of asking my opinion on any particular subject, the whole of the materials sent home to them on that subject should be put into my hands'.[164] Banks's disappointment with the Company's sluggishness in promoting new products would have been strengthened by a letter he received the following year from Kyd, the virtual founder of the Calcutta Botanic Garden, who accompanied a specimen of indigo dye with the comment that the Court of Directors appeared to be reluctant to promote its manufacture.[165]

Banks himself found the same ambivalence in the Company's attitude to new dye substances in his long and tangled involvement with the Company over the introduction of cochineal insects to India. It was a project that clearly displayed the extent to which aggressively mercantilist policies still prevailed in Europe. The Spanish government regarded the cultivation of cochineal as a monopoly to be restricted to its territories but Banks was lured by proposals 'to render it impracticable for the Spaniards to transport so much as a single pound of Cochineal from Mexico'.[166] The French, too, had been involved in the surreptitious transportation of the insects[167] – a move which, like the French attempt to forestall the British in importing breadfruit to the West Indies,[168] was an indication of the way in which great power politics could be played out in the realm of economic botany. To further such imperialist ends Banks recruited someone willing (for a handsome consideration) to abscond with the insects from Mexico and thus risk the wrath of the Spanish authorities. Banks first raised the matter with the Court of Directors in January 1788, describing it in glowing terms as an 'object of national importance deserving the attention of the Company'.[169] He also linked its cultivation with larger imperial purposes, arguing that 'the present moment seems to me Favorable for the introduction of a valuable branch of Produce into India' – presumably a reference to the increasing consolidation of British power in India thanks to reforms such as that of Lord Cornwallis (Governor-General of Bengal, 1786–93).

At first the Company responded gratefully, acknowledging that it had 'been materially aided by the public spirit and communications of Sir Joseph Banks',[170] but the Company was, as so often, slow to act when a change in trade policy was involved. Banks's growing exasperation shows through in a private memorandum, made in August 1792, in which he noted that due to 'so many checks and so much inattention of the Directors' he was no longer so willing to support plans for obtaining cochineal from Mexico.[171] The reluctant Banks was again persuaded to lend his support but the 'alternate encouragement & neglect I have experienced from successive chairmen' and an indiscreet publication which alerted the Spanish to the plan finally resulted in his abandoning the project in 1796.[172] Similarly, though in 1802–3 the East India Company showed interest for a time in Banks's promotion of the seemingly promising plans for the import of catechu or *terra japonica* as a substitute for oak in tanning, ultimately this came to nothing – perhaps, as Berman suggests, because it was too useful within Asia where, among other uses, the Company employed it to adulterate tea.[173] Overall, the Company was in no hurry to change its traditional role as an importer of handicrafts to that of a supplier of raw materials.

Such abortive projects were indications of Banks's waning influence in the Company around the end of the eighteenth century. In May 1796, for example, he described the Court of Directors in a letter to the Deputy-Governor of St Helena as 'a very fluctuating body' adding that 'at the present juncture I have very few friends among them. I have not venturd to ask a favor except such as immediately respect the Science of Botany & the bringing home plants to the King's Garden for some years past'.[174] Banks's declining sway within the Company was probably partly due to the fact that, after 1793, when the Company's charter was renewed, the energetic Dundas's involvement in the affairs of the Company through the Board of Control was reduced – particularly during the period 1794 to 1801 when he was Secretary of War. With the reins of the Board of Control slackened the Company could once again start to assert its independence and a clique within the Company most strongly identified with the defence of its monopolist privileges came to dominate the Company in the same period .[175] Such keen monopolists were, as Banks found, unlikely patrons of scientific entrepreneurship; they were also impatient of interference from the central government, either of the Board of Control or from that active promoter of commercial expansion, the Committee for Trade – Banks being closely identified with both these bodies. When, in 1798, Banks's ally, the first Earl of Liverpool, attempted to dissuade the Company from buying copper at artificially high prices at a time when a re-coinage of copper money was being planned he had to report to Banks that although 'I have used all my Influence with the East India Company' he assumed that they would not comply since they had not even deigned to reply.[176]

Overall, then, Banks had little success in winning the East India Company over to whole-hearted support for his grand design to make India a source of as many raw materials as possible for the English market. Nonetheless, some of his ideas (such as the growing of tea or hemp on a large scale in India) did subsequently bear fruit. Moreover, as Mackay points out, his overall strategy of transforming India from a supplier of handicrafts to the source of raw materials for British manufacturers did encourage the Company to act as a patron of botanical and, to a lesser extent, zoological research through its gardens, its museums and as an adjunct to its administrative surveys.[177]

Changeable though they might have been, Banks's relationships with the East India Company were sufficiently substantial for him to use his good offices to further a number of his projects. In 1800 Banks intervened upon behalf of a group of London Missionary Society missionaries to ensure their passage to Tahiti on an East India Company ship (something which had seemed in doubt while Banks was unwell).[178] In the following year the Company – no doubt at Banks's prompting – contributed £1,200 to Flinders' *Investigator* voyage in order, as Banks told Flinders, 'to Encourage the men of Science to discover such things as will be useful to the Commerce of India & you to find new passages'.[179] And, in April 1803, Banks thanked the Director of the Company for assisting in the transportation of useful plants from China to the West Indies. He also succeeded in persuading the Company to meet the expenses involved in sending William Kerr, a Kew gardener, to Canton, though on this matter Banks could invoke royal support, suggesting diplomatically to the Company that it pay for this project as a compliment to the King.[180] All of these are instances of the way in which the East India Company, for all its traditional independence, nonetheless acted as part of the machinery by means of which British influence and colonial power steadily expanded with the active support of Banks.

SCIENCE AND THE BRITISH STATE IN TRANSITION

Banks's relations with the East India Company illustrate a number of points which apply more generally to the major themes of this work: the growth of the British State and Banks's endeavours to use this governmental machinery to advance both the cause of science and British power and prestige. First, and most obviously, Banks's involvement with the East India Company indicates the growing extent to which British economic interests were becoming dependent on expert scientific advice – advice which could not be provided directly by the apparatus of central government but which the British State provided through the more informal channels which were the natural milieu of Sir Joseph Banks. Second, the growing extent to which the affairs of the East India Company were coming under the scrutiny of the Board of Control and hence of the central government underlines the expansion in the formal mechanisms of government. True, as the informal arrangements that existed between the central government and such bodies as the Royal Society, the Royal Institution and Kew Gardens indicate, the British State – in contrast to France and many of its Continental counterparts – was able to accommodate a relatively loose, less formal structure of government and administration, relying on the ties which held together its landed, governing class. But, as Britain had to contend with the forces unleashed by the Industrial and French Revolutions, such informal methods also came under strain and the more important the institution the more pressing the need for a greater measure of direct governmental control. The East India Company, which controlled such a large proportion of England's trading wealth, was naturally more likely to become subject to state direction than the relatively more minor institutions with which Banks was more immediately identified. It was a natural progression, then, that the British government should continue to circumscribe the activities of the East India Company so that in 1813 the Crown claimed full sovereignty over its possessions and in 1833 its trading activities were abolished altogether, leaving it to act in all but name as an organ of government.[181]

But, as Banks found, though the East India Company might ultimately have been going down the path of becoming a department of State it was a gradual process which the Company attempted to resist. Its rearguard action in maintaining its privileges and autonomy was one of the reasons why Banks's attempts to mobilise the East India Company to embrace scientifically-based new products and enterprises had only limited success. Such a state of transition from a largely independent chartered company to a branch of government points to the more general changes in the character of the late eighteenth- and early nineteenth-century State as its need for centralised control and greater administrative and financial efficiency was strengthened by the burdens of war and rapid economic growth.

The fact that the British State had to deal with changing circumstances with often antiquated bureaucratic machinery called for a creative response in re-fashioning the inherited forms of government to achieve new ends. One such new end was to link science with the purposes of empire and it was Banks who largely succeeded in imprinting this goal on the apparatus of the British State by his ability to work through a range of different agencies, including both those (like the Privy Council and the Admiralty) which were a formal part of government and those (like the Royal Botanical Gardens or the East India Company) which were less directly at the centre of government. Banks's efforts to link science with the British State called for a campaign on many fronts. Though Banks's primary intent in promoting science in this manner was to advance British interests, this was not altogether inconsistent with the Baconian vision of science acting as an agent of human betterment. True, when the national and the international character of science clashed, Banks generally gave priority to the former but, as the next chapter attempts to demonstrate, he never altogether lost the vision of science as a cosmopolitan enterprise, the benefits of which transcended national boundaries.

CHAPTER SIX

Science in the Service of the Republic of Letters

THE IDEAL OF THE REPUBLIC OF LETTERS

For Banks, science provided a means of creating greater wealth and therefore greater prestige and power for his country. But his concept of science as a servant of British national and imperial interests did not preclude the view that science could also advance the interests of humankind more generally. In short, Banks retained some conception of Bacon's great hope that science might act for 'the relief of man's estate'; as Lord Brougham put it in his life of Banks, he 'applied himself vigorously to improving the discoveries successively made to the real use of mankind'.[1]

Needless to say, for someone such as Banks, who was so closely linked with the structures of British power, national interests in science or, more importantly, its applications tended to take precedence over international obligations to a scientific Republic of Letters. Nonetheless, in the many cases where the two were not in conflict, Banks saw it as part of his role as President of the Royal Society to foster the Society's ties with other scientific academies and to assist in the diffusion of information to a scientific community which transcended national boundaries. It was also a natural part of his conception of science that it should belong in the public domain, whether this be national or international. Thus Wollaston's decision to keep secret his researches on palladium in order to achieve a commercial advantage prompted Banks to make the withering remark that 'The keeping of secrets among men of science is not the custom here; & those who enter into it cannot be considered as holding the same situation in the scientific world as those who are open & communicative'.[2]

Banks's commitment to the claims of the Republic of Letters depended to a large degree on which of his many roles he was playing. In his most fundamental role as a Lincolnshire squire and agricultural improver the French generally appeared simply as competitors and potential or actual enemies. Nonetheless, he did welcome the Eden trade treaty between France and Britain of 1787 and 'the blessings of a mutual commerce between the nations who have been enemies these thousand years'.[3] As a servant of the British State, whether in his capacity as virtual director of the Royal Gardens at Kew or a member of the Privy Council Committee on Trade fostering British commercial or industrial advantage, he again tended to view other nations simply as competitors or, at best, sources of calculated exchange of information.

It was as President of the Royal Society, a body which was part of a European-wide network of academies, that his allegiance to the Republic of Letters was most evident. Partly the role was thrust upon him, since it was assumed by his foreign correspondents that they had some claim to his good offices as the head of Britain's leading institution devoted to that cosmopolitan pursuit, the advancement of learning. A Dutch correspondent, for example, urged Banks to continue his contributions to 'le monde des Savants',[4] a virtual synonym for the Republic of Letters. But Banks was more than an ex officio citizen of the Republic of Letters, for it became part of his programme for the betterment of the Royal Society and of science more generally to establish an international network of correspondence and exchange. He did so on a scale which foreigners recognised as exceptional and as betokening a real commitment to European rather than simply British science. Another Dutch correspondent, a professor of natural philosophy at Leyden, addressed him in effusive tones as one 'devoted to the progress of arts & Sciences, of which all Europe admires you as the Protector, its greatest Maecenas'.[5] Having in the previous chapter looked at length at Banks *qua* servant of the British State, the object of this one is to examine how far Banks could combine this national role with service to a cosmopolitan scientific Republic of Letters. In doing so it indicates that the consolidation of the apparatus of the British State during the age of revolution did not preclude the persistence of some forms of cosmopolitanism – though these became increasingly limited by the need to advance national interests.

The notion of a Republic of Letters embodied in partially secularised form the older concept of a united Christendom which transcended national and regional boundaries by maintaining a common faith and civilisation in the face of dynastic conflict. Like the ideal of Christendom, too, it was strengthened by the ties of aristocratic kinship and common culture which linked together the different European States. After the devastation wrought by the wars of the seventeenth century, engendered by a powerful brew of dynastic, religious and civil conflict between centralising monarchs and aristocratic intrigue, the notion of a Republic of Letters offered some consolation to an intellectual elite weary of strife.

It provided some re-affirmation of a common civilisation which maintained some of the higher ideals which all Europeans could share irrespective of their political or religious affiliation.

As the common medium of Latin declined it also helped to create a sense that European intellectuals shared a common language of ideas – if not a literal language – and that the use of a widespread language, such as French, could transcend national purposes. Not that all citizens of the Republic of Letters were always in happy accord, for one of its roles came to be to provide common ground, in the form of journals or pamphlet literature, on which to conduct scholarly battles in which personal and intellectual grievances were inseparably intertangled.[6] Such rivalries continued unabated into the eighteenth century, when d'Alembert in his 'Reflections on the present state of the Republic of Letters' described the citizens of this putative republic 'fight[ing] over glory just as men without government or laws fight over acorns'.[7]

The late seventeenth-century Republic of Letters helped, in turn, to give rise to the Europe of the Enlightenment – a movement which again sought to emphasise the cosmopolitan elements of European civilisation[8] in the face of a growing trend towards the consolidation of state structures. One of the central endeavours of the Enlightenment was, where possible, to analyse the workings of society in the detached spirit of disinterested enquiry which had been so conspicuously successful in the natural sciences. In theory, then, the true Enlightenment thinker should be willing to stand back from his own society and national loyalties and to arrive at a better understanding of both its strengths and weaknesses through a sympathetic comparison with other societies and cultures. Hence the pioneering sociologist, Montesquieu, could claim that he was 'human of necessity' but 'French by accident'.[9] Ultimately, too, the Enlightenment's emphasis on universal laws of nature and a form of reason which transcended national and cultural divides tended to stress the points of similarity rather than the distinctiveness between different countries.

With the Enlightenment, however, came the important change of attitude that learning should be used to change society – hence the contempt of the *philosophes* for the *érudits* of the old Republic of Letters who maintained the belief that scholarship was an end in itself and its audience fellow scholars rather than the general educated public.[10] Thus the Enlightenment maintained the cosmopolitan character of the seventeenth-century Republic of Letters with the addition of a sense of social and political engagement. Inevitably, however, such a sense of engagement often involved compromising international ideals for national ends. Like Voltaire and Diderot, who had to balance their international sympathies with the need to win over individual would-be enlightened monarchs, so too Joseph Banks sought to combine his goal of contributing to a cosmopolitan world of science with his strong sense of British patriotism. As one obituarist remarked of him, though 'warm with national patriotism, Sir Joseph still considered himself a citizen of the world in the cause of science',[11] while another remarked that Banks was a figure of European as well as British significance for he became 'a nucleus round which the scattered science of all countries might be gathered'.[12]

Banks's willingness to acknowledge the claims of a Republic of Letters which transcended national boundaries and loyalties varied according to the different roles he played. It was strongest in his role as President of the Royal Society and, naturally, weakest when he was acting as a servant of the Crown, whether as a Privy Councillor or as the de facto director of the Royal Botanical Gardens at Kew. When Banks acted as President of the Royal Society he was, of course, anxious to do all that he could to put science at the service of the British State but he was also aware of the importance of fostering an international audience for the Royal Society's deliberations. It was a tension which typified the situation of the Republic of Letters as it became more and more integrated with the world of the academies over the course of the eighteenth century and, as a consequence, its international loyalties were overshadowed by national interests.[13] Scientific advance depended on the flow of information across national boundaries and so national interest and allegiance to a cosmopolitan Republic of Letters could coincide in linking British science with its larger European (and, in particular, French) community of fellow specialists. As Banks's friend and Royal Society colleague, Edward Gibbon, put it:

> It is the duty of the patriot to prefer and promote the exclusive interest and glory of his native country but a philosopher must be permitted to enlarge his views and to consider Europe as one great Republic whose various inhabitants have attained almost the same level of politeness and cultivation.[14]

The Royal Society, like other European scientific academies, from its beginnings consciously linked itself with a European-wide network of journals, corresponding fellows and international visitors which helped to make the academies natural custodians of the ideal of a cosmopolitan Republic of Letters. The citizens of the Republic of Letters looked for the rewards of prestige and fame:[15] as the editor of the *Histoire de la République des Lettres en France* wrote in 1780 of the Republic of Letters, 'It is the empire of talent and of thought. The academies are its tribunals; people distinguished by their talents are its dignitaries'.[16]

In this cosmopolitan world, which was largely held together by the academies, Banks, the longest-serving of all presidents of the Royal Society, naturally became a major figure. Existing academies recruited his good offices by making him an affiliate while new academies looked to him to help build up their legitimacy as fledgling members of the Republic of Letters. By his death in 1820 he was a member of some fifty foreign academies.[17] Even before he became President of the Royal Society in 1778 his rising fame as a naturalist led to his being courted by foreign academies: in 1772 he became a corresponding member of the

Académie Royale des Sciences, the beginning of a long association with French science and with the Royal Society's main rival for the accolade of Europe's leading scientific academy. This was followed by his election in 1773 to foreign membership of the Royal Academy of Science (Stockholm) and the Batavian Society of Experimental Philosophy (Rotterdam), while three years later he was elected to the Royal Academy of Madrid, the Gesellschaft der Freunde für Naturforschende (Berlin) and the Physiographic Society of Lund – these being a mere foretaste of the long roll of foreign memberships showered on him once he became President of the Royal Society.

THE REPUBLIC OF LETTERS AND THE AMERICAN AND FRENCH REVOLUTIONS

When Banks took up the presidency in 1778 such a cosmopolitan ideal was under challenge from the American Revolution – an event which posed an obstacle to the continuing scientific relations between members of the Royal Society and those in the New World who were exploring the vast scientific possibilities opened up by European dominance of this land mass. Banks, despite his own conservative political views, was adamant, however, that such national disputes should not overshadow trans-Atlantic scientific fellowship. When Arthur Lee resigned from the Royal Society on the grounds that membership was incompatible with his rejection of the British Crown, Banks chided him by arguing that science and politics should be kept distinct since the objects of the former were universal 'belonging to the republic of letters, and to the community of man and mind'.[18] Lee seems to have conceded the point since he continued to maintain contact with British men of science throughout the War of American Independence.

Though Benjamin Franklin was one of the revolutionary leaders Banks continued to value his friendship and scientific enthusiasm. The two men shared a common vision of the place of science in human society as a means of improvement and, ultimately, of Enlightenment. Franklin's Baconian remark, 'What signifies philosophy that doth not apply to some use?',[19] was one with which Banks could readily concur. With the end of the war near, Franklin could write to Banks in September 1782 looking forward to the renewal of their common membership of the Republic of Letters and their mutual co-operation in the task of putting science at the service of human betterment. Thanking Banks for his letter, Franklin assured him

> that I long earnestly for a Return of those peaceful Times, when I could sit down in sweet Society with my English philosophic Friends, communicating to each other new Discoveries, and proposing improvements of old ones, all tending to extend the Power of Man over Matter, and avert or diminish the Evils he is subject to, or augment the Number of his Enjoyments.[20]

Dr Benjamin Franklin, FRS. Painting after Joseph Duplessis, 1783.
(By courtesy of the National Portrait Gallery, London)

Once peace was finally achieved in the following year Franklin wrote rhapsodically of the benefits that international scientific co-operation based on interchange between academies could achieve:

> Furnish'd as all Europe now is with Academies of Science, with nice Instruments and the Spirit of Experiment, the Progress of human Knowledge will be rapid, and discoveries made of which we have at present no Conception.[21]

And, indeed, Banks played his part in linking the infant United States with the larger Republic of Letters and the world of academies, accepting membership of the American Philosophical Society of Philadelphia in 1787 and both the Massachusetts and New York American Academies of Arts and Sciences in 1788.

Since the United States was very much Britain's scientific inferior Banks could afford a certain amount of *noblesse oblige* in his dealings with his former transatlantic brethren. However, relations with France, Europe's premier scientific nation and Britain's ancient and persistent foe, called for much more complex scientific diplomacy. It was, throughout his lifetime, Banks's goal to keep open the channels of scientific communication between Britain and France both for the larger good of the Republic of Letters and for the benefit of Britain itself. As so often with Banks, patriotism and allegiance to the Republic of Letters were, as far as possible, yoked together – though when the two were in competition it was Banks *qua* British patriot who took precedence. However, in his capacity as President of the Royal Society, Banks generally saw little patriotic difficulty in fostering ties with the Académie des Sciences and French science more generally, even while the two nations were at war. Science had little military significance[22] and both nations could gain from the prestige that scientific discovery conferred – so long as the practical benefits that could be gained from such scientific advance were as far as possible secured for Britain.

For Banks, France had a particular fascination as a state where science and government were more closely linked than in Britain. Indeed, it was France that first developed something approaching a 'science policy' for, as Gillispie writes of French science and government at the end of the old regime, 'What was particular to France two centuries ago is that the interaction became regular and frequent enough to be called systematic rather than episodic'.[23] Though Banks himself never visited France, Blagden acted as his virtual lieutenant there both before and after the Revolution. Blagden made him well aware of the extent to which in France science was given more recognition than in Britain, telling him in 1783 'that the Sciences are pursued here with more ardour than with us; there are more characters here who devote themselves entirely to the branch of learning they cultivate'.[24]

The flourishing state of French science made Banks particularly determined to cultivate an association between the Royal Society and the Académie des Sciences. This applied particularly since 1783 marked the formal end of hostilities between Britain and France in the War of American Independence. Such a proposal was one to which, Blagden reported, the Académie responded well. 'The plan of correspondence between the Royal society & the French academy of Sciences', he wrote to Banks in the same month, 'was well received by the Gentlemen to whom it was mentioned' adding, in the language of the Republic of Letters, that 'their views were just as liberal as ours' and that the interchange between these two bodies would provide a 'very honorable' example to the other academies of Europe.[25] But, in scientific matters, Britain needed France more than vice versa, a point that was underlined by the fact that, despite Blagden's urgings in 1784,[26] the Académie waited until August 1787 before bestowing on Banks the status of foreign member.[27] Banks, in as dignified manner as he could muster, made known his displeasure at this slight while attempting to continue to develop better scientific links with France. Thus in March 1786 he welcomed a scientific correspondence with the Marquis de Condorcet, Secretary of the Académie des Sciences, while tartly remarking that 'the

President of the Royal Society does not feel himself under any obligations to the Royal Academy'.[28]

By the following year, however, the Royal Society and the Académie
des Sciences could join together in scientific goodwill on the triangulation project[29] which was designed to ascertain with a high degree of
accuracy the relative positions of the royal observatories at Paris and
Greenwich. Like the observations of the transit of Venus of 1761 and
1769 and other such international scientific projects of the eighteenth
century, it was an enterprise which demonstrated the extent to which
the notion of a Republic of Letters held common currency even in the
relations between nations. It was to such ideals, for example, that
Blagden appealed when urging Banks to throw his considerable weight
behind the project, writing that 'it is equally our duty to co-operate with
the views of the French Government & of the Academy, in a matter that
so much concerns the common cause of humanity'.[30]

British royal support for the project took the highly tangible form
of a grant of £3,000, while Banks, as President of the Royal Society,
drew together the different instrumentalities of the State necessary to
accomplish the project and, thereby, to promote both British national
honour and the ideal of international scientific fellowship. Even after the
gruelling encounters of the Napoleonic Wars enough of such ideals
survived for a similar project involving accurate measurements from
Dover to Calais to be approved by the Royal Society in 1821 (a year after
Banks's death), 'both on account of the advancement of science & as an
undertaking honourable to both countries as tending to promote that
harmony & liberal intercourse between them so important for their
great interest & those of the civilized world'.[31]

Despite minor contretemps, then, Banks from the time of the Peace
of Paris of 1783 had laid the foundations for scientific interchange
between the two nations. But it was, of course, the coming of the
Revolution and the long period of warfare between the two nations
which followed in its wake which was to test fully Banks's ability to
balance the claims of patriotism with those of the Republic of Letters. In
the early years of the Revolution Banks, like most of the British establishment (with the conspicuous exception of Burke), looked on the
Revolution as an opportunity for France to rejuvenate its constitution
along acceptably British lines with benefits to science as well as politics.
In 1790 he received a cordial letter from France's leading man of
science, Lavoisier (who had been elected an FRS two years previously), in
which he assured Banks of his desire for good relations 'between the
enlightened nations' which he hoped to see linked by 'liberty and
philosophy'.[32] An enquiry in 1791 from a French nursery gardener
anxious to promote his cure for garden pests prompted Banks to praise
the 'regeneration' of the French government and acknowledge its
scientific credentials since it has 'attended with great liberality to the
Claims of all who have improved cultivation'.[33]

But by 1793, with the execution of the King and the declaration of war on England, Banks began to discover that he was in a new age where conflict between nations could imperil the bonds of common citizenship of the Republic of Letters. Thus in March 1793 Banks expressed his astonishment at the fact that a Frenchman declined to visit him to discuss their common scientific interests because of the possible political trouble it might cause. 'I cannot conceive', wrote Banks, 'that any one would consider as a political necessity to debar me from the acquaintance of a Learned man because he is of a nation with which we are at war'.[34]

The fact that France had entered a new period of history when the claims of the State transcended all else was underlined by the abolition of the Académie in 1793 as an institution tainted by its royal connection and this, together with the Terror, meant that Banks's contacts with France dwindled away. The re-foundation of the Académie in 1795 as the Institut National by the conservative Directory (which replaced the government of the Terror) provided at least the opportunity for republican France to resume once more its place in the Republic of Letters. However, it was not until 1797 that Banks canvassed with Pitt the possibility of 'opening a Communication with Paris for the reception of the Literary Production of the members of the *Institut National* & other scientific persons some of which are highly interesting to the Royal Society'.[35]

The channel through which Banks sought thus to renew the scientific relations between the two nations was the London-based Commissary for the Exchange of Prisoners, one M. Charretié, to whom Banks successfully appealed using the rhetoric of international scientific fraternity. '[S]uch communications', wrote Banks, 'cannot be but of material use to the progress of Science, and may also lay the foundations of a better understanding between the two Countries in future'.[36] And, by the end of the year, good scientific relations had largely been re-established between the two nations with one English scientific visitor to the Continent reporting from Lausanne that 'The Directory have lately been very much pleased with the approbation of the Royal Society to their various literary establishments'.[37]

Such overtures culminated in 1801, the year of the Treaty of Amiens, with Banks's election to the Institut National – his effusive letter acknowledging this honour leading to widespread criticism at home of his lack of patriotic restraint.[38] Unchastened, Banks continued to express his admiration for the Institut, if not for the regime with which it was associated. When Edward Jenner was elected in 1811 he congratulated him on 'obtaining a place among a body of men who have so little humbled themselves before the arbitrary dispositions of their Sovereign as to have retained the title of National, when that of Imperial was offered to them'.[39]

Along with Banks's endeavours to keep open the lines of scientific communication between France and Britain, even while the two countries were at war, went his activity in attempting to secure the release of men of science caught up in the toils of war. His most celebrated achievement in this regard was his successful intervention on behalf of the eminent geologist, Déodat de Dolomieu, who, after accompanying Napoleon to Egypt, was captured and held prisoner by the court of Naples. His release in 1801 was largely due to the support of the British government urged on by members of the Royal Society led by its President. In his effusive letter of thanks Dolomieu linked Banks's actions with the 'enlightenment and philosophy disseminated by' the Royal Society. This fostered loyalties which transcended national differences by 'mak[ing] common to all nations that blessed brotherly love which softens all political convulsions'[40] – in short, that science and learning promoted fellow feeling within the Republic of Letters. But Banks had to balance such supranational loyalties with his need to defend the patriotic credentials of the Royal Society as he made plain in his reponse to Dolomieu's letter. Thus he was anxious to disassociate the Society from any sympathy with the French government and, still more, with republicanism. '[W]e in England', wrote Banks to Dolomieu, 'are as firmly attached to Royal Government as you can be to Republican', nor did the Royal Society 'as a public body, [seek] to take matters of a political nature in any shape under our consideration'.[41] For Banks, correspondence with Dolomieu offered an opportunity to distinguish sharply between the claims of patriotism and those of the Republic of Letters as well as keeping the Royal Society firmly apart from Banks's own activities in the sphere of scientific diplomacy.

Nonetheless, though anxious to keep the Royal Society uninvolved in such politically sensitive undertakings, Banks himself continued to advance the claim that the world of science and learning could be regarded as a realm apart from that inhabited by warring nations. Thus a letter to the French Commissioner in London the following year invoked the full rhetorical force of the language of the Republic of Letters:

> I agree with you Sir wholly, the cooperation of those employd in enlarging the Limits of human knowledge ought not to be interrupted by the enmity of their respective nations, the armistice of science should ... be perpetual[42]

– a reference to the Peace of Amiens. Such fine sentiments were reciprocated from the French side later that year when Banks was thanked for sending an Australian natural history specimen to the Muséum d'Histoire Naturelle of Le Havre with a tribute to the worth of the 'Republic of Letters and sciences' as 'the most perfect of republics'.[43]

The renewal of war in May 1803 prompted Banks to re-affirm his position that war between nations ought not 'to compromise the more enlightened individuals'.[44] But Banks was soon to find that the claims of the Republic of Letters were subordinate to those of the State, particularly in time of war. An attempt to intercede on behalf of the French naval captain, Pierre-Bernard Milius, a former South Sea explorer, led to tributes from him to Banks's 'talents and enlightenment' and service to humanity,[45] but hostility from the Admiralty which regarded the exchange of naval prisoners as being its province. Thus in 1806 Banks was forced to withdraw from such attempts to realise a common fraternity between naturalists and explorers which could withstand the pressures of war. On the French side, too, there was increasing suspicion that such scientific fraternisation across enemy lines might be used as a ruse for spying and by 1807 Napoleon's regulations largely prevented Banks's continuing correspondence with France on any regular basis.[46] Ultimately, then, the modern state proved more powerful than the Republic of Letters though Banks did not abandon his belief in a cosmopolitan world of science. After the end of war in 1815 Banks was once more involved in attempting to resuscitate scientific fraternity between France and Britain expressing the hope in 1818 that there should be 'a Perpetual Friendship & Reciprocal good offices between the Profession of Science here & at Paris' as manifested in the relations between their two academies.[47]

NATIONALISM, INTERNATIONALISM AND EXPLORATION

The academies with their cosmopolitan connections were, then, the major repository of the belief in the Republic of Letters. A related area where the international claims of science could be recognised without too much strain on national loyalties was in relation to exploration. This applied particularly to the exploration of the Pacific which gathered pace in the late eighteenth and early nineteenth centuries. Some measure of international co-operation in this area was encouraged by the fact that in the Pacific the prizes were not sufficiently glittering to tempt rival nations into war over new territory.[48]

Such exploration, with its acquisition of new knowledge about both nature and humanity, was seen as the embodiment of the Enlightenment particularly since the relatively pacific exploration of the Pacific was contrasted with the earlier, more manifestly brutal Spanish subjugation of the Americas. As Kippis wrote in his contemporary life of Cook:

> There is an essential difference between the voyages that have lately been undertaken, and many which have been carried on in former times. None of my readers can be ignorant of the horrid cruelties that were exercised by the conquerors of Mexico and Peru; cruelties which can never be remembered without blushing for religion and human nature. But to undertake expeditions with a design of civilizing the world, and meliorating its condition, is a noble object.[49]

Gibbon went even further claiming that 'The five great [Pacific] voyages successively undertaken by the command of his present majesty were inspired by the pure and generous love of science and mankind'.[50] Such voyages were, moreover, something which were thought to bind together the enlightened population of Europe more generally.

It was to such ideals that Banks could appeal when arguing that the political differences between nations should not stand in the way of exploration which would benefit the Republic of Letters and, ultimately, all humanity. In 1780 he could compliment his kindred spirit, Benjamin Franklin, on the way in which he attempted to ensure (unnecessarily, as it turned out) that United States warships did not interfere with Cook's third great Pacific voyage at a time when Britain and the infant United States were at war (an example also followed by the United States's chief ally, France). When issuing this order Franklin appealed to the benefits that such exploration would bring to humanity in general as

> an Undertaking truly laudable in itself, as the Increase of Geographical Knowledge facilitates the Communication between distant Nations ... whereby the common Enjoyments of human Life are multiplv'd and augmented, and Science of other kinds increased to the benefit of Mankind in general.[51]

It was an act, wrote Banks appealing to the same ideals as Franklin, which showed him to be 'the Friend of disinterested discovery'.[52] Subsequently, when the war between the United States and Britain had ended, Banks conferred on him a Royal Society gold medal in recognition of 'those sentiments of general philanthropy by which I have observed your conduct ever actuated since I have had the honour of your acquaintance'.[53] Appropriately, the ideal of an international brotherhood of scientific explorers was recognised by an award from one of the academies which held together the Republic of Letters.

Banks's status as an international patron of Pacific travel was underlined by the way in which the Italian Alessandro Malaspina sought his help in 1789 when planning his great Pacific voyage on behalf of the King of Spain. Appealing to a cosmopolitan ideal of learning, Malaspina made bold to write to Banks 'on an equal basis, and with a keen desire to co-operate towards the progress of science'.[54] In return for Banks's help Malaspina offered to send Banks 'everything which pertains to botany and natural history in general from this kind of voyage'.[55] But the correspondence between the two also pointed to the complexities of balancing such elevated claims to the advancement of the Republic of Letters with the interests of the individual State. For Malaspina was being less than candid in describing the voyage as being actuated solely by the Spanish monarch's desire to advance science when, in fact, he also looked to the voyage to shore up the faltering Spanish Pacific Empire.[56]

It was, however, the outbreak of war between France and Britain which posed for Banks the greatest problems in balancing the cosmopolitan claims of scientific discovery with national loyalties. In 1791 relations between France and Britain were still sufficiently amicable for Banks to assist the d'Entrecasteaux expedition which was sent to search for the earlier Pacific voyage of discovery led by the Comte de Lapérouse, who had not been heard from since January 1788 when he called in at the early settlement at Botany Bay. Banks felt no patriotic qualms about giving the d'Entrecasteaux expedition's chief botanist, Jacques Labillardière, the benefit of his own experience in collecting botanical specimens in the Pacific and asked him, in the spirit of international enquiry, to pay particular attention to the flora and fauna of New Caledonia, if he should visit those islands, since they had been relatively overlooked on Cook's second voyage.[57]

Inevitably, however, relations changed after France and Britain were at war from 1793 and the aftermath of the expedition was to involve Banks in delicate manoeuvres to reconcile the international aspirations of Pacific exploration with the *realpolitik* of the relations between warring nations. For the vast collections accumulated by the expedition were captured by the British and it was Banks who attempted to persuade the British government to accede to the request made by the Directory in 1796 to restore them. In writing to Labillardière to assure him of his good offices in the matter, Banks invoked the customary language of the Republic of Letters in which scientific exploration transcended national disputes. 'That the Science of two Nations may be at Peace while their Politics are at war', he wrote, 'is an Axiom we have learnd from your Protection to Capt. Cook'.[58] When successfully appealing to the British government on the matter Banks again pointed to the example of earlier French respect for the cosmopolitan character of scientific exploration by exempting Cook's voyage from its blockade. He also sought a further instance of Britain's respect for the Republic of Letters by asking for free passage of a French ship travelling to the West Indies to collect plants on the grounds that 'all good men respect the extensive benevolence of increasing the food of mankind, by removing useful plants to countries where nature has not provided them'.[59]

When, in 1800, Napoleon approved another major expedition to the Pacific led by Nicolas Baudin the Institut National appealed to Banks to use his influence with the British government to ensure that it was not caught up in the conflict between the two nations. It was especially in time of war, it urged Banks, that 'the friends of humanity' should work to advance 'the limits of science and of useful arts' and thus they addressed him as 'one of the most distinguished members of the republic of letters'.[60] And such an appeal to the cosmopolitan ideal of disinterested scientific exploration was successful. As Banks told the French Commissioner in London, when requested by 'my friends the Commissioners of the National Institute instructed by their Government with the charge of recommending voyages of discovery likely to promote the progress of useful sciences' he applied to 'the King's Ministers here'. These showed 'every proper disposition to promote as all men of education ought to do the increase and improvement of human knowledge by whatever nation it may be undertaken'.[61]

Banks's support for the Baudin expedition made it all the more galling when the French authorities were slow to aid his attempt to have Matthew Flinders freed from French captivity. After his great voyage of circumnavigation of Australia from 1801–3, Flinders, on his return to

The *Géographe* and the *Naturaliste* as depicted on the writing paper prepared for the expedition.
(By courtesy of the Muséum d'Histoire Naturelle of Le Havre, Collection Lesueur)

Britain, had called into the Ile de France (Mauritius) in 1804 and was there imprisoned. Flinders's voyage around Australia, which was largely sponsored by Banks, represented in many ways Britain's response to the Baudin expedition to Australia – an indication that the politics of great powers could rarely be altogether divorced from scientific exploration. But the fact that the Baudin and Flinders expeditions were seen by Banks as having similar scientific-cum-political goals made the French intransigence over Flinders's imprisonment all the more vexing (even though the Flinders case was made more complex by the fact that he was carrying secret documents sent back from New South Wales by Governor King).

In Banks's view it was incumbent on the French to reciprocate his efforts in support of their exploration by freeing Flinders as one devoted to the cause of science. Hence the outrage evident in the letters of both Flinders and Banks when General de Caen, the Governor of the Ile de France, steadfastly refused to comply. In vain did Flinders appeal to the ideals of the Republic of Letters when he wrote to the French naval minister in 1800 urging that 'I am a man of peace; my business is not to destroy, but to add to the knowledge of one part of mankind, and alleviate the miseries of another'.[62] In a similar spirit, four years later Flinders expressed his dismay that he should be kept a prisoner though 'a commander of a voyage on discovery, whose labour is calculated for the good of all nations'.[63]

A few months later, Banks urged such considerations when attempting to seek 'the powerful interference of the Institut National'. He praised their nation for its past support 'to all Persons employed in usefull discovery' and reminded them of the help the British had provided for the Baudin expedition.[64] These were powerful arguments to an institution still imbued with the language of the Republic of Letters despite Napoleon's attempts to supplant it with an ethos based on national and individual fame.[65] Mindful of the moral claims of Banks on its goodwill, the Institut did attempt to intervene with the naval minister on Flinders's behalf as well as assuring Banks of its desire to do all in its power to remove those obstacles to science caused by the conflict between their two nations.[66]

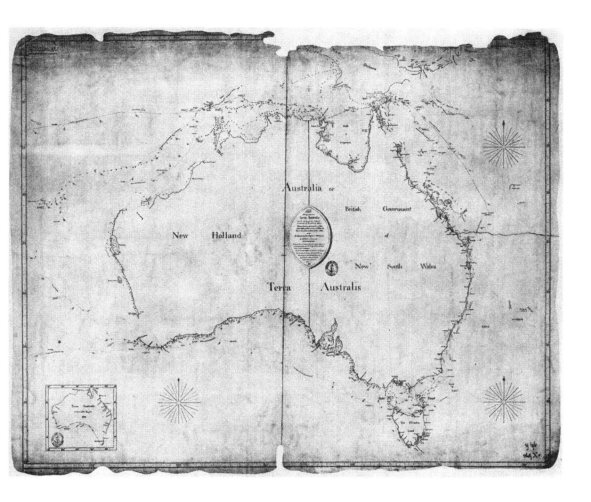

Matthew Flinders's *Chart of Terra Australis* . . . 1804.
(By courtesy of the Hydrographic Dept., Ministry of Defence, Taunton, England)

Though Flinders was not freed until 1810, Banks retained his basic faith in French support for the ideal of a Republic of Letters which could foster international scientific exploration. In 1806 he assured a botanical collector destined for China that he should not fear that he would be kept prisoner if captured by the French since they always respected science and would recognise his project as one 'extremely interesting to the inhabitants of all Civilised nations'. Banks, however, did add with a pointed reference to Flinders's *bête noire*, the Governor of the Ile de France, that the only cause for concern was the remote eventuality that 'it should be your fortune to be the Prisoner of an ignorant & illiterate man'.[67] Flinders's continuing imprisonment he assumed, as he told the freed French explorer, Milius, in the same year, was not at the behest of Napoleon – whom Banks, for all his patriotic hostility to a foe of Britain, continued to respect as 'a determined friend to Science' – or, if so, it could only be because 'he must have been misled by false accusations'.[68]

THE LIMITS OF SCIENTIFIC COSMOPOLITANISM

While Banks in public utterances portrayed international exploration as an activity of such obvious benefit to all humanity as to warrant the support of all nations, he was in his actual practice rather ambivalent about the closely related pursuit of the collection of plants throughout the globe. Botanical collecting and the utilisation of its economic benefits were activities so much at the epicentre of Banks's activities that the claims of the Republic of Letters, though generally strong, did not always outweigh Banks's estimation of what was essential to British interests. At times, Banks could respond enthusiastically to the claims of scientific cosmopolitanism in the field of botany. Thus the plea for help by a French naturalist, who was sent in 1815 to collect natural history specimens in India and to establish a botanical garden at Pondicherry, appealed to Banks's conception of the Republic of Letters. Hence his description of the expedition as one 'pregnant with advantage to mankind' and 'of a nature that is incapable of being misused' when intervening with the Governor-General of Bengal to allow the Frenchman access to the botanical garden at Calcutta. It was, he assured the Governor-General in an uncharacteristically rhapsodic passage, a common practice to give away duplicate botanical specimens for it was like 'giving light from a lighted candle to a dark one, which confers a valuable benefit on the receiver without the smallest possible expense or diminution of the property'.[69]

But, as his last remarks suggested, Banks could be rather more cautious about extending such botanical advantages when there was a cost involved. For he was well aware that in the realm of imperial botany, as in other commercial areas, France and Britain were in competition. Indeed, fear of French superiority in the business of transplanting useful plants to the West Indies was part of the reason why Banks sponsored the famous *Bounty* breadfruit expedition for, as he wrote to Sir George Young, 'Our Politic Neighbours the French have preceded us several Years in the execution of similar Projects'.[70]

Such botanical competition became most evident when Banks felt the interests of that apple of his eye, the Royal Gardens at Kew, were at stake. Plants should only be exchanged, he instructed Kew collectors, when there was an advantage to be obtained. If it was politic to make such an exchange they should ensure that it detracted as little as possible from Kew's superiority by 'declining to write the names on the parcels' or by providing 'yourself where ever you can with a reserve of seeds of such Plants as are already in Kew Gardens or of the least curious & least beautiful Plants'.[71] Attempts to obtain from Banks specimens from Kew for foreign botanical gardens availed little: in 1814, for example, Banks largely stonewalled attempts to secure specimens for the war-ravaged botanical gardens of the University of Leyden.[72] Banks's jealousy was particularly provoked by any possibility that Kew might be outshone by a foreign garden. His main rival was the Imperial Gardens at Vienna – hence his determination in 1814, when the end of the long French War was in sight, to send new collectors abroad for he had heard that the Hapsburg Emperor had 'freighted ships at an immense expense, and sent well-educated botanists to collect for his Gardens at Schoenbrunn (the only rival to Kew that I have any fear about)'.[73] When Banks heard in 1817 that the French were sending an expedition to Australia he ordered the Sydney-based Kew collector, Allan Cunningham, to join a British hydrographic vessel so that he could collect 'plants, which could by no other means be obtained' thereby 'enriching the Royal Gardens at Kew with plants which otherwise would have been added to the Royal Gardens at Paris, & have tended to render their collection superior to ours'.[74]

But Kew Gardens could also play its part in furthering the scientific goodwill which undergirded the Republic of Letters and there was some truth in Banks's claim that 'Nothing is nearer my wishes than that a liberal Communication of Plants usefull to mankind should take Place between all Civilised nations'.[75] Perhaps because of the relatively under-developed nature of Russian science and botanical gardens Banks co-operated enthusiastically in the project of sending Catherine the Great 'as Compleat a Collection of Exotic Plants as can possibly be spared'[76] as part of more general diplomatic overtures to Russia from whence came much of Britain's vital naval stores.[77] Banks also accepted graciously requests for specimens from Kew from the Duke of Württemberg.[78] Banks was even involved in an exchange of seeds with his arch-rival, the Imperial Gardens at Vienna.[79]

In his dealings on behalf of Kew, then, the perennial tension between the claims of the Republic of Letters and patriotism was generally resolved in favour of British prestige as reflected in the superiority of its Royal Gardens. By contrast, the more remote claims of inter-national scientific good will between academies or in support of scientific exploration found Banks inclining more towards the claims of the Republic of Letters. But the balance was never totally inclined towards one or the other of these competing poles of nationalism versus cosmopolitanism. Even in an area so close to his heart as Kew, Banks could make some occasional concessions to international scientific diplomacy. On the other hand, when promoting such international ventures as Pacific exploration, Banks was – as his sponsorship of Flinders's expedition as a means of consolidating British control over the Australian landmass indicates – concerned to ensure that his advocacy of French scientific exploration did not result in any strategic disadvantage to Britain. In the end the Republic of Letters was too shadowy a homeland to accommodate fully one of Banks's girth and patriotic vigour.

Not surprisingly, Banks was particularly circumspect when it came to giving foreigners access to the industrial processes that were driving the incipient Industrial Revolution, but even in this sensitive area there were signs of ambivalent loyalties. Similarly the Society of Arts, of which Banks was an early member, could combine a determination to press British industrial and commercial advantage wherever possible with cosmopolitan aspirations of the sort embodied in its declaration that 'The surest method of improving Science is by a generous intercourse of the Learned in different Countries and a free Communication of Knowledge'.[80] Similarly, Banks cultivated some measure of international exchange in the currency of industrial processes while at the same time doing all he could to advance British superiority. He taxed his friendship with Matthew Boulton by asking him on a number of occasions to show European visitors around his works – a concession to the Baconian ideal that scientific and technological advance ought to be placed at the service of humanity as a whole.

Even after his bad experience with Baron Stein, who used such an inspection to steal the industrial secrets from which, as Banks wrote to Boulton, 'this nation derives its commercial importance',[81] Banks continued to persuade Boulton to allow foreign visitors to view those parts of his famous Soho works which 'strangers may with propriety be permitted to see'.[82] Banks was prompted in part by the hope of some reciprocal advantage; as he told Boulton when reflecting on the sorry saga of Stein: 'I was convinced he intended to serve us as we before had been served by his Countrymen'. He added, however, that hereafter he would have to be more conscious of his patriotic loyalties rather than his hopes of fostering technological exchange within the Republic of Letters: 'If I have anything to reproach myself of in respect to my conduct towards foreigners it is in having been too liberal & too unguarded in shewing those things which my duty to my country & to my self requird more reservation'.[83] And, of course, Banks the patriotic Englishman rejoiced to see Boulton or other English manufacturers outstripping their foreign rivals. He commended Boulton on his prudence in maintaining confidentiality about industrial processes 'which your Patriotism induces you to keep secret from Foreigners'.[84] He also complimented the porcelain manufacturer, Lewis Dillwyn, on his 'Patriotism in taking this infant manufactory under your protection' especially as he was likely to gain 'a superiority over the French'.[85] Banks, the promoter of the early Industrial Revolution, then, paid only very fleeting allegiance to the Republic of Letters.

Nonetheless, in his role as President of the Royal Society, Banks did acknowledge the claims of the Republic of Letters. The fact that such declarations of allegiance were more than lip-service was brought out in his attempts to bridge the gap between warring nations during the War of American Independence and, more significantly, during the Revolutionary Wars between Britain and France. True, there was always an element of calculation as Banks hoped to gain advantage for British science by keeping open the channels of communication with Europe and, in particular, France, the leading scientific power.[86] Nor did Banks ever deny an element of scientific competition with France: on a number of occasions he frankly acknowledged that they were 'by nature our rivals in science'.[87] He was, nevertheless, prepared to risk public and official displeasure at home in order to maintain his scientific ties with France at a time when it was regarded as a menacing foe. His glowing tributes to the ideal of a commonwealth of scientists which transcended national rivalries appear to have been more than rhetorical flourishes. In the end the Republic of Letters does seem to have been one of the peripatetic Banks's genuine homes – albeit one in which he only resided on particular occasions for limited periods.

CHAPTER SEVEN

The Expansion of Empire

THE CHARACTER OF THE SECOND BRITISH EMPIRE

Given that science in its modern form only emerged in the seventeenth century it is not altogether surprising that science in its national and, still more, in its international dimension found no obvious single resting place in the structures of the late eighteenth-century British State – hence the need for Banks to integrate scientific advice with the concerns of government through a complex range of bureaucratic channels. A more obvious indication of the underdeveloped character of the late eighteenth-century British State is that an activity which was much more central to its commercial and strategic concerns – the acquisition and continuing control of colonies – also was parcelled out among a number of departments. Only gradually, did a single department, the Colonial Office, develop to deal with the multiple concerns consequent on Britain's expanding imperial role.[1]

Faced with this bureaucratic vacuum, the policy-makers of the British State welcomed informal advice to deal with the growing volume of imperial problems. It was a mark of the understaffed nature of the administrative arm of the State intended to deal with Britain's colonies that this dependence on outside advisers continued into the nineteenth century. The illustrious career of Sir James Stephen, the chief architect of British imperial policy in the first half of the nineteenth century, began as a adviser before he finally abandoned his law practice and became an official of the Colonial Office in 1836.[2] In the late eighteenth century, before the formation of a Colonial Office, the need for such outside expertise was greater and among the more prominent advisers on imperial affairs was Sir Joseph Banks, together with his neo-mercantilist allies like Lord Sheffield.

This was a natural extension of Banks's role as science adviser to the British government since the promotion of science and the promotion of Empire were frequently complementary. Moreover, his activities in providing expert scientific advice to government meant he developed a natural familiarity with the procedures and personnel of the departments – notably the Committee for Trade, the Board of Control, the Home Office and, ultimately, the Colonial Office – on which the burden of maintaining the structures of Empire chiefly fell. Banks was also drawn into the role of an adviser on imperial matters because of his involvement in the early exploration and European settlement of Australia. Given that the early years of the colony of New South Wales corresponded to a long period when the concerns of government were focused on the French Wars, the role of spokesman for the infant colony in London largely fell to Banks.

The attitude of the late eighteenth-century British government to its colonial appendages was deeply coloured by the humiliating experiences of the American Revolution.[3] The American colonies had demonstrated the dangers of encouraging colonies of settlement – hence, as Harlow emphasised,[4] the second British Empire was, by and large, an empire of trading posts intended to facilitate the needs of commerce and war. Similarly, Manning describes the empire of the late eighteenth and early nineteenth centuries as the period of 'the strategic post' marking a transition from the 'the age of the self-sufficing empire' of the earlier eighteenth century to the 'age of systematic (and unsystematic) colonisation' in the later nineteenth century.[5] One of its major architects was Dundas, who used his considerable influence at the Board of Control to ensure that India remained a trading empire by actively discouraging British settlement there.[6] As always, there were exceptions: Canada continued to grow in population (largely thanks to the mass emigration of American Loyalists), thus creating problems about balancing the fear of another rebellion with the need to accommodate the traditional right of English colonists to be consulted about their government. The distant gaol of New South Wales also was to grow into a colony of settlement but that prospect seemed distant as the First Fleet and its human cargo of convicts arrived in 1788. Overall, however, the primary interest of British imperial policy makers was in securing colonies which could serve the commercial or strategic interests of the motherland.

Such a view of empire also suited the strident demands for cheap government which followed the American debacle, the American defeat being viewed in part as the outcome of a government which had become bloated, inefficient and given to political cronyism because there too many government posts to hand out to compliant clients. The abolition of the Board of Trade and Plantations (which had previously attempted to oversee American affairs) in 1782 was an indication of the strong political desire to mark a new beginning in the conduct of government which was to become leaner, more efficient and more responsive to the political nation. Ironically, within two years the Board was soon resuscitated in a new form, the Privy Council Committee for Trade – an indication of the ineluctable growth of the State and, with it, the need for a more complex bureaucratic apparatus to cope with the growing complexity of commercial, strategic and political developments in the age of the American, French and Industrial Revolutions.

But, though the Board of Trade was re-born under another name, it did not closely involve itself in the minutiae of imperial affairs. Under Jenkinson the task of the Committee for Trade was to promote forms of commerce which would serve his great, neo-mercantilist goal: the bolstering of British self-sufficiency in commerce and thus the better ensuring its strategic security. The business and cost of colonial admin-istration was left as far as possible to the colonies themselves or, if absolutely necessary, to existing departments of government – prin-cipally the Home Office. For the Home Secretary was, as George III described him, 'Secretary for the Home Department and British Settlements'.[7]

As the pace of colonial acquisition gathered pace in the French Revolutionary Wars this informal approach to the running of the Empire became more difficult to sustain and so in 1801 the colonies were trans-ferred to the Secretary for War. The creation of the Secretary for War in 1794 reflected the expansion of government under the pressure of war. Such a new position marked a return to a third secretaryship after the attempt in 1782 to reduce such posts to the traditional two by abolishing the special Secretaryship for the Colonies which had been established in 1768. But the military responsibilities of the Secretary for War meant that the colonies received scant attention until the threat of French domination abated. The appointment of that resolute administrator, the second Earl of Liverpool, in 1809 began a bureaucratic re-organisation which was carried further under Lord Bathurst, whose tenure of office from 1812 to 1827 largely created the Colonial Office as an effective arm of government. And, as so often with bureaucracies, the creation of one post laid the foundation for the creation of another, for the growing needs of the colonies led eventually to the establishment of an independent Colonial Office in 1854.

The period from the end of the American War in 1783 to the coming of Bathurst to the Colonial Office in 1812, then, was one when colonial issues lacked firm central direction. Such matters were dealt with on an ad hoc basis by an array of government departments and individuals. It is a phenomenon that gives point to Mackay's critique of Harlow's thesis about a basic policy shift promoting a 'Swing to the East' after the loss of the American colonies: for the structures of the British government did not lend themselves to any such fundamental policy position.[8] Only by around the 1830s, with the receding of the threat to both domestic and international order posed by the French Revolution and the develop-ment of more effective bureaucratic forms, was there the possibility of a more coherent examination of the direction of imperial policy and consideration of the ways in which the scattered threads of empire could be gathered together. The result, then, was that in the late eighteenth and early nineteenth centuries the British Empire was a coat of many colours as local traditions gave the forms of government in its different parts their own distinctive hues.

But, while the conduct of empire might have been managed in such an informal manner, the character of the second British Empire was shaped by more fundamental developments in this period. First and foremost it reflected the distrust of popular political movements which was a residue of the American Revolution and was heightened still further by the French Revolution. The demands of Ireland, Britain's first and most problematic colony, for greater self-government also strengthened wariness about creating colonial assemblies which might provide a platform for eventual demands for independence.[9] Whereas traditionally British colonies were ruled by a governor advised by a local assembly such representative forms were weakened in this period as the needs of war strengthened the military character of government. In its captured colonies, too, Britain often retained French, Dutch or Spanish forms of rule both for the sake of stability and because their more absolutist character suited the needs of a counter-revolutionary age.[10] In India, where there was little in the way of a British population to hinder such impulses, the impetus for centralisation was stronger. As Lord Stormont remarked of the machinery established by the India Act of 1784, which vested supreme power over Indian affairs in a governmental Board of Control, the goal was 'a strong government in India, subject to the check and control of a still stronger government at home'.[11] This insistence on maintaining British control over its colonies naturally meshed with the neo-mercantilist emphasis on ensuring that colonies served the interests of Britain itself.

IMPROVEMENT AND IMPERIALISM

Commercial policy was, then, largely shaped by the imperative of ensuring as far as possible British self-sufficiency using the techniques of improvement which, as Baily has emphasised, had served the British landed classes so well.[12] Both at the metropolitan level and through the local colonial elites the techniques of improvement offered the possibility of meshing the diverse fruits of empire into a web of trade with the mother-country at its centre. They also helped to bind together the scattered elements of Empire just as, within the British Isles, they had done much to weld together England and Scotland into a more effective greater Britain. The ideal of improvement not only offered the possibility of greater wealth and self-sufficiency for Britain but also provided some moral veneer to soften the crude realities of imperial expansion. Improvement, it could be argued, not only benefited the home country but also offered the indigenous people some hope of relief from the traditional scourges of disease and famine. Hence the claim of one of

Banks's obituarists that his actions, and those of his compatriots, were prompted by a desire

> to derive from an intercourse with unknown and ba[r]barous countries new materials
> for commercial activity, new facts of science, and new incentives to go forward in the
> duty of bestowing civilization to the whole human race.[13]

Such a view of the virtues of improvement as one of the fruits of British imperial expansion helped to justify conquest during the French Revolutionary Wars of former European colonies. This applied particularly to those of the Dutch where the colonial civilising mission had been undermined, in British eyes, by the lack of improving activity. Robert Percival, who had served in the British forces during the conquest of the Cape Colony, later justified such annexation in his *An account of the Cape of Good Hope* (1801). Thus he lamented 'how few improvements have been introduced into the colony' which he attributed to 'the want of energy, and the natural indolence of the Dutch at the Cape'.[14] According to the empire-builder, Thomas Raffles, British dominion over that jewel of the crown of the Dutch Empire, the East Indies, could be justified on the grounds that it brought with it

> the justice, humanity, and moderation of the British government, as much
> exemplified in fostering and leading on new races of subjects and allies in the career
> of improvement, as the undoubted courage and resolution of British soldiers in
> rescuing them from oppression.[15]

For Banks improvement of territories under British rule to advance the self-sufficiency of the motherland and, to a lesser extent, for their own benefit was the driving force behind his involvement in those instrumentalities of the British State which dealt with imperial policy – most notably the Privy Council Committee for Trade and the Board of Control. A similar outlook shaped his attitude to the development of territories which barely came under the direct supervision of a State, the bureaucratic machinery of which could not cope with the growing scale of empire. Hence its reliance on those, like Banks, who were linked informally with the affairs of government through the ties natural to a landowning oligarchy. This applied particularly in his role as 'a sort of Honorary Secretary of State for New Holland'[16] – a role of considerable importance at a time when that distant possession received scant attention from a government preoccupied by war.

Banks was convinced that a landmass the size of Australia must contain considerable resources of benefit to the Empire – hence his determination to foster exploration and agricultural experimentation in the hope that such activities would ultimately lead to improvement. As he wrote to John King, Under-secretary of State at the Home Office, in 1798 after expressing his mercantilist impatience that 'no one article has hitherto been discover'd by the importation of which the mother country can receive any degree of return for the cost of founding and hitherto maintaining the colony':

> It is impossible to conceive that such a body of land, as large as all Europe, does not produce vast rivers, capable of being navigated into the heart of the interior; or, if properly investigated, that such a country, situate in a most fruitful climate, should not produce some native raw material of importance to a manufacturing country as England is.[17]

For Australia was expected to play its part in the larger purposes of empire and dependence on the motherland was to be phased out as soon as possible. In his revealingly entitled 'Some Remarks on the Present State of the Colony of Sidney, in New South Wales, and on the means most likely to render it a productive, instead of an expensive, settlement' (1806), Banks emphasised the need for greater economic self-sufficiency for New South Wales by drawing an analogy between the developing colony and a growing child. While at the time of settlement the colony 'may not inaptly be compared to a new-born infant hanging at its mother's breast' it had now reached the status 'of a young lad beginning to attain some learning' but also 'gaining by his industry part of his necessary maintenance, and certain of soon becoming a blessing, instead of a burthen, to his family'. Some hopeful signs of such emerging economic independence were already evident: 'the seal fishery [which] open'd itself to view after the discovery of Basses Straits', 'the representation of Mr. McArthur respecting fine wool' and the beginnings of a trade with China in the sought-after marine delicacy, trepang or sea-slug.

However, such signs of healthy growth needed to be contained to ensure that Australia's economy continued to be tied to the needs of mother England. 'The whole benefit of the colony either in consumption or in produce', wrote Banks in a firmly mercantilist vein, 'should be secur'd, as far as possible, to the mother country'. But, in a more conciliatory spirit, he acknowledged that this would require some concessions. This applied particularly in relation to the monopoly rights that the East India Company claimed over all territory between the Cape of Good Hope and the Straits of Magellan. For if such rights were insisted on they 'will either drive him [the colony] into piratical enterprise or induce him to hazard a trade with other nations in preference to his mother country'.[18] Thanks largely to Banks's representations with the Committee for Trade it was proposed that the tariff restrictions imposed by the East India Company be largely removed in 1807 subject to a concession to the Company 'That the Trade should be confined to the Port of London for the first Five Years'.[19] But the Bill got lost in the political upheavals that followed and legislative protection for the colony did not come until the Company lost its monopoly on trade between England and India in 1813[20] – an instance of the way in which the great chartered company was becoming ever more answerable to the needs of the larger British State.

From the beginning of European settlement Banks was active in attempting to ensure that the territory of New South Wales would be improved both for the immediate benefit of the settlers and the longer-term advantage of Britain. As Frost has emphasised,[21] it was Banks who largely initiated the 'antipodean exchange' whereby the Australian continent was transformed by the introduction of European plants, to be grown chiefly for their economic benefit. However, to Banks's disappointment, the exchange yielded little in reverse, with Australia's ancient flora providing few specimens of advantage to Britain.

Not only did Banks supervise the transfer of plants on the First Fleet but, soon after its arrival, he attempted to supplement such botanical improvement with a range of new plants sent out in 1789 on the ill-fated *Guardian* which included a specially-built 'plant cabin' designed according to Banks's specifications. When the *Guardian* was wrecked Banks ensured that the successful *Gorgon* expedition was equipped to perform the same task when it sailed in 1791.[22] Despite the vicissitudes involved in transhipping plants across the globe, Banks could rejoice that his botanical endeavours literally bore fruit. By 1791 he was proudly displaying some 'very good ears of corn' grown in the new colony[23] and in 1797 he rejoiced with William Paterson, the former Administrator, on 'The prosperous state of your Colony' which gave him 'infinite satisfaction' and confirmed his long-held view that 'the Soil was good & the Climate excellent'.[24]

In the following year Banks organised another large consignment of 'plants for Botany Bay' based on the assumption that 'in a Climate similar to that of the South of France which Botany Bay Probably is the following vegetables ... will be highly usefull'.[25] The sending of such botanical specimens necessary to achieve this happy result required the co-operation of the Home Office which organised their dispatch. However, it is an indication of the flexible character of the British State that it was largely derived from the initiative of an outside expert without, at that time, any formal government office. Banks's position outside a particular department of government may indeed have been of advantage since he was better placed to co-ordinate the activities of several departments. When persuading government to mount the *Guardian* expedition, for example, we find him referring in a letter to Nepean at the Home Office of 'Conversations held with yourself & other Gentlemen in various departments of Government'.[26]

From the beginning of settlement, too, Banks encouraged the colony's Governors to be vigilant for what he later described (when introducing the botanical collector, George Caley, to Governor Hunter in 1798) as 'useful discoveries; I mean such as are likely to be useful to the Colony & the mother Countrey'.[27] In the very year of his arrival Governor Phillip was writing to Banks with specimens of what he hoped was a form of black lead as well as assuring Banks of his desire to initiate seed-collecting (preferably with the help of a trained botanist who 'would be a valuable acquisition to this Settlement'[28]). Predictably, Banks took a particular interest in the issue of flax with its possible naval uses. As early as 1795 Governor King of Norfolk Island was reporting to him that a sample of locally grown flax would be sent to the Calcutta Botanic Gardens – an instance of the way in which the botanical gardens assisted imperial botany on a global scale.[29]

Just as improvement at home embraced not only the better cultivation of the earth but also the better utilisation of the minerals under the earth (for example, the lead under Banks's property in Derbyshire) so, too, in the colonial setting Banks urged the need for developing mines. Hence his enthusiasm at the news in 1798 that coal had been discovered on the Hunter River in New South Wales. This was a development which, he, along with Dundas[30], hoped, would open up greater self-sufficiency not only for New South Wales but also for the Cape Colony which could now purchase coal more cheaply than from Britain.[31]

Banks was less than eager to support the plans of his opponent, John Macarthur, for obtaining large grants of land for raising merino sheep. Nonetheless, the promotion of fine wool was, for an improving sheep-owner like Banks, an example par excellence of the noble art of agricultural improvement. He therefore responded warmly to a proposed 'sheep adventure' by John Maitland, a London merchant, MP and Chairman of the Committee of the Wool Trade, since 'its success will be of infinite importance to the Manufacture of England' while 'its failure will not happen without much previous advantage to the infant Colony'.[32] When the Reverend Samuel Marsden, another early promoter of the New South Wales wool trade, sought to turn Banks against Major-General Lachlan Macquarie, Governor of New South Wales, 1809–21, he shrewdly chose to lament the want of 'a Civil Governor' urging the need for 'a Gentleman who had a taste for Agriculture and rural Improvements'.[33]

Colonial improvement was intended both to consolidate British possession of its territories and to make them more useful for the strategic and commercial needs of the motherland. In such a mercantilist view of empire the needs of war were an ever-present reality both in order to gain territory in the first place and to use it to best advantage in the face of a continuing great power struggle – chiefly with France, but also with Spain and the United Provinces. When Banks contemplated the future of Australia he was mindful that Britain's hold over the continent might take a more belligerent form than the spreading of sheep. In his advice to government on the future of the colony he was, then, content to envisage the prospect of other European countries settling there 'under a moral certainty of its getting into our hands in time of war'. The often aggressive character of mercantilist policy was evident, too, in his remark that there should be 'prevention of American intercourse with our infant colonies' and 'instructions should be sent to the Governor to enforce them with severity'.[34]

In a very different sphere of the world for which Banks also took a great deal of responsibility in the face of indifference by the British

government he also envisaged the advantages that Britain would gain by
the use of force. During the Napoleonic Wars Iceland, which Banks had
come to know on his visit there in 1772, became subject to the British
blockade as a dependency of Denmark which was allied with France. The
island's predicament prompted Banks to initiate a successful humanitarian campaign in 1807–8 to prevent the friendless islanders from
starvation. With his customary ability to straddle a number of different
departments he used as his main levers with government Lord Bathurst
at the Committee for Trade and Lord Castlereagh, an FRS and Secretary
for War.[35] This ultimately resulted in an Order-in-Council of 1810
declaring Iceland in a state of neutrality with Britain.

However, Banks also was active in attempting to interest the British
government in annexing Iceland – albeit in what he envisaged as a fairly
bloodless take-over of an island which, he considered, was anxious to
escape from Danish rule. He first drew up such a proposal in the form of
a memorandum to the Privy Council in 1801 following Denmark's entry
into the anti-British League of Armed Neutrality; he revived it again in
1807 following Denmark's forming an alliance with Napoleon.[36] After
upheavals in Iceland itself in 1809 he again repeated his view that 'it is
expedient Iceland should be annexed to the Crown of England & never
hereafter separated',[37] though by this time British rage with Denmark
had subsided and there was less official interest in annexing Iceland.
In urging arguments for Britain to proceed with the 'conquering' of
Iceland, as Banks bluntly put it, he advanced the familiar mercantilist
justifications that it would 'extend the commerce, add to the revenue,
and increase the nautical strength of the United Kingdom'. In particular,
it would gain for Britain 'the Iceland cod fishery', an important acquisition since, like the Newfoundland fishery for which Banks's ally, the

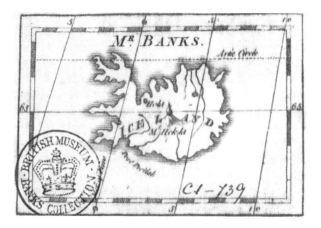

Banks's visiting card made after his return from Iceland.
(By courtesy of the British Library, British Museum Banks
Collection)

first Lord Liverpool, had fought so hard, it would increase the number of Britain's hardened sailors and thus its naval strength.[38]

To these arguments Banks added elsewhere a robustly nationalistic but geographically doubtful one based on the right of Britain to expand to its natural frontiers.[39] Interestingly this was also advanced in a letter to the Chief Justice of Iceland as part of a campaign to persuade the Icelanders that they belonged naturally under British rule for

> No one who looks upon the map of Europe can doubt that Iceland is by nature a part of the group of islands calld by the ancients "Britannia", and consequently that it ought to be a Part of the British Empire, which consists of every thing in Europe accessible only by seas; as such possessions can never be wrested from her by the powers of the combined world.[40]

When putting a variant of this view to the second Lord Hawkesbury (then Home Secretary) in 1807 he reinforced the point by adding that once Iceland was added to the group of islands constituted by Britain and its northern neighbours it would be eminently fitted for a 'naval empire'.[41]

Banks's determination to draw Australia and Iceland into Britain's larger imperial designs was consistent with his more general views about the importance of maintaining British control over as much useful territory as possible in order to ensure its strategic and commercial self-sufficiency. As the chief patron of British scientific exploration he assumed that exploration would bring in its train an enlargement of British imperial power. In 1788, the year of the foundation of the Association for Promoting the Discovery of the Interior Parts of Africa with Banks's active participation and of the First Fleet's arrival in Australia, he unblushingly told a French geographer that 'I certainly wish that my Countrymen should make discoveries of all kinds in preference to the inhabitants of other Kingdoms'[42] – for such discovery brought with it not only scientific kudos but also national advantage. As one of the officials of the Colonial Office admiringly commented he was 'the staunchest imperialist of the day'.[43]

However, Banks was discerning in his choice of areas for British imperial advantage. Thus he rejected the attempt by James Creassy, superintendent of the docks at Calcutta, to involve him in promoting an attack on Spanish territories in Central America in 1805. For Banks took the view, in a manner consistent with the emphasis on trade in the second British Empire, that it was better to leave 'Spain unmolested & to try to have a trade among them' – particularly since the Spanish colonists are 'now so much inclined to receive our goods'. Sooner or later he envisaged – with an entirely accurate prophecy – the Spanish colonies would obtain their independence 'when their trade will be a real & substantial benefit to this Country'. By not formally annexing such territories Britain could have the advantage of trade with that area of the globe without the cost of administering it, for 'this Country ... cannot now afford Population to put a western Empire in the same state of dependence as it has placed an Eastern one'.[44]

Part of the reason why Banks was asked to participate in such a plan was that his activities in the South Seas and involvement with the foundation of the colony of New South Wales made him appear one of the chief opponents of Spain's claim to dominance over the Pacific. As Creassy wrote to Banks's neo-mercantilist ally, Lord Sheffield, 'that great and useful Gentleman Sir Joseph Banks is better acquainted with the Spanish possessions, and all the South Seas, than any man now living'. In Creassy's view the British foothold in Australia provided a base for a more general attack on Spain's weakening hold on the Pacific – hence his suggestion that Botany Bay might send two ships for an attack on Panama.[45]

Banks, then, was not to be tempted into such aggressive designs on the Spanish possessions in the New World since he thought that, from the point of view of trade, they would fall into Britain's lap. However, he took a more assertive view about shoring up British dominance in the east, particularly in the lucrative East Indies. Banks was opposed to handing back to the Dutch British conquests made there during the Napoleonic Wars. He was urged on to take such a position by Henry Colebrooke, a former member of the Bengal Council now resident in Britain, who wrote to Banks in 1815 when the spoils of war were being divided. Maintaining control over Java , he argued, would bring with it 'a Mart for our Manufactures & an Emporium for our Trade'. Such imperialism was also given a moral gloss by envisaging how, under British protection, 'by the introduction of Arts & Education the people might be fitted to govern themselves'.[46]

Banks's interest in that part of the world was also stimulated by his correspondence with Thomas Raffles (the virtual administrator of Java from 1811 after it was captured by the British) who sent him material on its natural history. Raffles could also later assure Banks that, despite the revival of Dutch power after the end of the war, the British presence in the area was being consolidated by his founding of a British station at Singapore.[47] But generally Banks watched with dismay the return of Dutch possessions particularly the ceding of Java in return for concessions in Europe.[48] Hence he wrote in 1820 (the year of his death) that he opposed 'any design of giving up Bencoolen [Sumatra] to the dutch', particularly since 'we have already given up too much to that Government & they are now trying with no chance of success to exclude us from the Trading [in] th[at] Eastern archipelago'.[49] It was a vain hope for, though in British hands for over a century, Bencoolen was surrendered to the Dutch as the British concentrated their imperial energies on the Malay side of the Malacca Straits.[50]

But, though Banks had to bear the disappointment of seeing British territories in the East Indies returning to the Dutch, he could draw solace from the fact that the British retained Dutch territories in Ceylon and the Cape of Good Hope. The conquest of these colonies in 1795 had

been largely the initiative of Dundas since they formed a natural part of
his plans for creating a worldwide trading empire and for the shoring up
of British power in India. At a time when Dundas's power was in eclipse,
the Cape Colony was returned to the Dutch in 1802 but, in the face of a
possible threat by Napoleon to British communication to India, it was
permanently annexed in 1805.[51] In both of these colonial acquisitions
Banks was active in strengthening the British imperial hold by the
promotion of science as an ally of strategic or commercial advantage. In
Ceylon Banks prompted the formation of a botanical garden which was
intended, as he told its first superintendent, 'for the benefit of the
Commercial interests of the Island, and for the advancement of the
Science of Botany'.[52]

At the Cape, strategic concerns loomed larger for, as Dundas put it,
the Cape 'is really and truly the Key to India'.[53] As a consequence,
Banks's reponse to the request by Lord Glenbervie, the Governor-
designate in 1800 (though he did not ultimately take up the post), on
how best he might 'do service to science' paid particular attention to
ensuring a full maritime survey. Without the coast being thus 'accurately
& scientifically describd', he pointed out, the Cape would continue to
be a menace for shipping. But, of course, Banks could not let an
opportunity such as this go by without also arranging for a botanical
collector to send back specimens to Kew.[54] Banks was also consulted by

The Dutch colony at the Cape of Good Hope, 1762. Engraving by J. Rach,
Atlas van Stolk.

Dundas soon after the conquest of the Cape in 1795 about its economic possibilities. Banks suggested that the sheep industry might be developed further but disappointedly had to conclude that 'it is not likely that a Fishery of any extent on the New Foundland Plan could be establishd' – an important point since fisheries were the nurseries of seamen and hence of naval power.[55]

Dundas's enquiry probably also prompted a document entitled 'Observations political & Agricultural' in which Banks advocated a range of proposals well suited to Dundas's conception of the second British Empire as a collection of trading and strategic posts. 'The Cape in your hands', wrote Banks,

> ought to be not only a resting place for your ships, but 1) a support to your Indian territorial power, and 2) a colony by which to exonerate the mother country of part of its starving poor, to create there raw materials for your manufactures, and a market for your manufactured goods.

With a comment that underlines the extent to which the American debacle coloured the thinking of the architects of the second British Empire, Banks cautioned that 'You need not be afraid of colonies, if you do not furnish them with the elements of independence as you did with North America'. Predictably, Banks concluded by suggesting some possibilities for the agricultural improvement of the colony arguing that 'what chiefly would make it important would be the introduction of a new system of culture adapted to the climate'.[56]

For Banks, then, the guiding motif of British imperial policy should be the expansion of British commerce and hence national self-sufficiency whether this might be achieved by the force of arms or by what Montesquieu called 'soft commerce'. But to achieve such ends required action on the part of a State well used to the conduct of war but with little in the way of a bureaucratic apparatus appropriate to the consolidation of its imperial gains. The means by which Banks attempted to influence government and the channels through which he worked are the subject of the remainder of this chapter.

THE INFORMAL STRUCTURES OF EMPIRE

In a State like that of late eighteenth-century Britain Banks's endeavours for fostering the expansion of the Empire did not always flow smoothly through its often inadequate and convoluted bureaucratic channels. Hence the need to promote imperial ventures through other agencies which, although not a part of the formal state structures, were intertwined with the State through the informal ties natural to an oligarchy. The two most important of these agencies through which Banks worked to advance his imperial ends were the African Association, some of the leading members of which were influential in government circles, and the London Missionary Society which, although non-denominational, included representatives of the state church which brought with it some measure of state support.

The African Association

The African Association (or, to give it its full name, the Association for Promoting the Discovery of the Interior Parts of Africa) arose out of renewed interest in Africa, and especially its west coast, around the 1780s. A number of sites in Africa were considered for the penal colony which was ultimately established in New South Wales. This prompted an exploratory voyage along the African west coast in 1785 for which Banks provided a naturalist at the request of the Home Office.[57] Africa had also come increasingly under British gaze as a market for the growing volume of goods the Industrial Revolution made possible – particularly as the traditional pattern of trade based on slaves was under challenge with the growth of the anti-slavery movement. French exploration of Africa in the 1780s helped to give greater impetus to the establishment of the Association in 1788.[58]

The original membership indicates the diverse goals of the body. Prominent among its early members were agricultural improvers such as Banks, Sheffield and Sir John Sinclair – the experience of transforming waste or marginal lands into productive fields being conducive to the promotion of exploration to locate and exploit new territories. The goals of improvement were closely linked with the scientific interests of members such as Henry Cavendish and Bishop Watson (professor of chemistry at Cambridge, 1764 to 1771) – indeed, all save one of the original committee of the Association were Fellows of the Royal Society.[59] The link with the commercial imperatives of the early Industrial Revolution is evident in the membership of figures such as Wedgwood and Wilkinson while prominent anti-slavery campaigners such as Clarkson and Wilberforce plainly hoped that the Association would be a means of combating the slave-trade.[60] Underlying and, to some extent, justifying, these diverse impulses was an Enlightenment-tinged belief that it was intrinsically meritorious to bring the light of discovery to the dark corners of the world. As the original plan of the Association proclaimed: 'Certain however it is, that, while we continue ignorant of so large a portion of the globe, that ignorance must be considered as a degree of reproach upon the present age'.[61]

Though the founding president was Henry Beaufoy, 'the life and soul of the Association' (as Bryan Edwards, Secretary of the Association from 1795, put it[62]) was Banks, at whose home the original meeting to establish the Association was held. Much of Banks's importance in the Association's affairs rested on his contacts with government and ability to bring the Association within the penumbra of the British State. Within a month of the foundation of the Association Banks obtained the co-operation of Sir William Musgrave, a Treasury official and FRS, who replied that it was a 'particular pleasure to be of any service to Sir Jos. Banks whose endeavours are so laudably directed to the publick advantage'.[63] Soon afterwards Banks arranged with Lord Sydney, the Home Secretary, to secure the services of Simon Lucas, then an interpreter at the Court of St James.[64] Along with the Home Office Banks had allies who were willing to promote the Association's activities at the Admiralty and the office of the Secretary for War and Colonies.[65]

Some measure of state recognition of the Association came with the government's willingness to allow it to use the consular service and with the Association's role in suggesting consular positions. In 1793 Beaufoy reported to Banks that he had 'at last obtained a favourable opportunity of stating to Mr Dundas & Mr Pitt, the earnest wishes of the African Association for the appointment of a Consul to Snegahia'.[66] It was a matter that Dundas agreed to take up with the King – an indication of the high standing of the Association in government circles. Later, in 1804, Banks urged the second Lord Hawkesbury (then Foreign Secretary) to appoint a client as consul to Algiers since this would be 'a great advantage to the African Association, who have deservd something of the Public'.[67] Significantly, in 1815 the African traveller, Henry Salt, largely attributed his appointment as Consul-General for Egypt to Banks.[68]

To begin with Banks saw the aims of the Association as the fostering of exploration. However, as time went on and the conflict with the French became more acute, he became more inclined to link the Association's activities with more overtly imperialistic aims. In 1792 he responded to a proposal for an inland colony by stating that such a goal 'did not in my opinion coincide with the purpose of the association in its present state ... we hereafter might civilise & colonise but not at Present'.[69] By 1799 the increasing involvement of France in African affairs prompted Banks to use the Association as a spur to urge the British State to intervene more decisively in Africa. In mid-1799 he approached the government on behalf of the Association through the agency of his old ally, the Earl of Liverpool, President of the Committee for Trade,[70] to recommend the

secur[ing] to the British Throne, either by conquest or by Treaty, the whole of the coast of Africa from Auguin to Sierra Leone, or at least to procure the cession of the River Senegal, as that River will always afford an easy passage to any Rival Nation.

The aim of such a colony would be to exploit gold finds in that area and to conduct 'Trade with the Negroes for Manufactured Goods'. Such commercial motives could be softened by the argument that British rule would make the Africans 'more happy than they now are under the Tyranny of their arbitrary Princes'. The measure 'would become popular at home by converting them to the Christian Religion' and by bringing about some lessening of 'the Slavery of mankind upon the principles of natural justice & Commercial benefit'. Though Banks's ambitious plans were not realised – at least in the short term – his urgings may have had some effect on the British government for, in the following year, the British did establish a bridgehead in the area with the capture of the island of Goree.[71]

Renewed French interest in the area prompted Banks once again to attempt to jog the British government into action in 1802. By this time the linking of colonial affairs with the office of the Secretary for War in 1801 meant that he had a more natural bureaucratic base from which to work. Hence on 1 August 1802 he addressed to the Under-secretary of that department a long memorandum[72] intended to allow the British State to profit from 'the discoveries of the Emissaries of the African Association'. If the British allowed France to proceed with a colony in the area between the Senegal and Gambia Rivers, warned Banks, it would enable it 'to sell Colonial Product of all kinds in the European market at a Cheaper Price'. These imperial concerns prompted the dispatching of Mungo Park to West Africa in 1805 on his second and fatal voyage to the area. The expedition was organised by the African Association as before, but in consultation with the Secretary for War and Colonies – an indication of the increasing involvement of the British State in African affairs.[73] Indeed, the activities of the African Association were to wane as the role of the Colonial Office waxed. After 1815, when the distraction of war was removed from the concerns of the Secretary for War and Colonies, the role of the African Association dwindled until ultimately it was merged with the newly-founded Royal Geographical Society in 1831. The fortunes of the African Association, a voluntary body linked to the State by informal ties which laid the foundations for subsequent State-sponsored imperial activity, is, then, a cameo example of the changing character and boundaries of the British State in the Age of Revolution.

Closely related to Banks's work with the African Association was a more marginal involvement with the Sierra Leone Company. This was established in 1791 as a chartered company. However, its philanthropic character was reflected in the fact that there was no provision for either a territorial monopoly or payment to the State[74] for the main goal of the company was to provide a home for liberated slaves. The moving force behind it was Wilberforce and other members of the Evangelical Clapham Sect, some of whom were also members of the African Association. Banks's chief contribution was to advise Wilberforce on the choice of a botanist. In 1791, on Banks's recommendation, the post went to the Swedish botanist, Adam Afzelius, who, along with his work for the Company, sent home specimens to Banks for the gardens at Kew. When the Company criticised him for this Banks intervened on Afzelius's behalf, arguing that Banks had some claim on the Company since not only had he arranged the botanist's appointment but he also had equipped him. Nonetheless, added Banks more soothingly with a comment that underlined his imperial intent for Africa, 'I do not mean by this remonstrance in any degree to relax the wish I have always had to promote the great work of settling and cultivating a country that has hitherto produced no real advantage to Great Britain'.[75] In 1794

A West African village, engraving from a sketch by Mungo Park. The figure with the goatee beard is probably intended to represent Mungo Park himself.
(From M. Park, *Travels in the interior districts of Africa, performed under the direction and patronage of the African Association, in the years 1795–1797*, 1860 ed., facing p. 172)

Afzelius's collections were destroyed in a French raid, an event which must have strengthened Banks's suspicions about French intentions in West Africa and heightened his determination to persuade the British State to intervene.

With Afzelius's return to Europe in 1796 Banks's involvement with the Sierra Leone Company appears to have largely ceased. The Company itself increasingly found the maintenance of a colony beyond its slender resources and in 1808 it was taken over by the Crown – another small example of the expansion of the British State in the wake of a private initiative. With Sierra Leone a Crown colony there were renewed calls for it to act as a base for the expansion of British power. Banks, for example, was called on in 1809, now that the colony was 'in the hands of Government, and therefore ... extricated from the wretched system of fanaticism, and methodistical absurdity, which has hitherto characterized it', to aid in its utilisation for 'promoting civilization, and the consumption of the fabrics of England'[76] – an interesting summation of the goals of early nineteenth-century British imperialism.

The London Missionary Society

Despite Banks's involvement in the Sierra Leone Company, which was largely dominated by Evangelicals, his own religious beliefs – in so far as one can discern them in the fleeting references he made to a subject in which he appears to have had little interest – verged on deism.[77] Not surprisingly, then, he appears to have had little enthusiasm for the primary aims of missionary work. In a letter about a missionary in China he wrote that he was 'little inclined to Conversions'.[78] It is significant, too, that he made no real attempt to have Omai, the visiting Tahitian whom he took under his wing when he was in London between 1774 and 1776, instructed in the Christian faith.

Nonetheless, Banks was sympathetic to missionaries and used his influence with government to further their aims. His motives for doing so were mixed. From his mother who had been interested in the Moravian missionaries to Canada he perhaps derived a certain respect for their work and frequent heroism. Missionary activity, too, he saw as a source of education and civilising influences more generally. It also could be a channel for natural history specimens, as when Banks received about five hundred botanical specimens from Moravian missionaries in Tranquebar in India from 1775 to 1780.[79] But what appears to have been most important in Banks's eyes was that missionaries provided a cheap and effective means of extending British imperial influence. Appropriately, then, these informal agents of empire, as Banks's saw them, were given the ready support of Banks's informal links with government.

In the wake of the foundation of the London Missionary Society in 1795 Banks attempted to persuade government to aid their efforts to establish a mission in Tahiti and, to a lesser extent, was also involved in the establishment of missions in South Africa and Ceylon.[80] His main point of contact with the Society was the Anglican Evangelical clergyman, Thomas Haweis, who was prudent enough to draw Banks's attention to the possible imperial benefits that might arise from their partnership. In his first letter to Banks Haweis promised any help to the African Association that might 'in any wise contribute to their furtherance of their benevolent design'.[81] Thanks to the good offices of Sir Charles Middleton, the Evangelical reformer of the Naval Office, Haweis also gained access to Dundas, the chief architect of the second British Empire. He held out to him, too, a similar vista of a joint imperial-missionary venture when writing of the proposed plans for a mission in Tahiti: 'we are an english incipient Colony, & every Benefit resulting from the Civilization we hope to introduce must ultimately terminate in Britain'.[82]

With Banks and such major functionaries of the British State as Dundas and Middleton as allies Haweis hoped it would be possible to overawe the East India Company.[83] But the Company's traditional suspicion of missionary activity as an obstacle to commerce was not readily overcome, though Banks did what he could to persuade it to assist the London Missionary Society by such means as allowing the missionaries to travel on Company ships. When Banks was not able to intervene the Company proved unco-operative. As Haweis told Banks after he had been unavailable because of gout: 'We have felt probably the effects of your Indispositions, as the India company has refused every favor'.[84]

While the East India Company with its traditions of independence was not so ready to accommodate itself to the rising tide of Evangelicalism, instrumentalities which were more central to the British State proved more inclined to respond to Banks's approaches on behalf of his missionary allies. Thanks to Banks's representations the London Missionary Society was permitted by the War Office in 1799 to establish a post in the strategically sensitive Cape Colony.[85] It was a victory that prompted the Society to thank Banks for 'your efficacious interference ... on this and on former occasions'. The Society also prudently pointed out that the mission would not only assist the spread of Christianity but also 'the Interests of Science' since it would 'enlarge the Sphere of our acquaintance with the productions of nature, and ultimately extend the operations of Commerce'.[86] Banks also used his long acquaintance with Lord Liverpool at the Committee for Trade to advance the Society's plans for a mission to the Sandwich Islands. Banks reported to Haweis that Liverpool was well disposed, particularly since the interests of the missionaries and of British trade were in such happy accord since the Sandwich Islands 'lie exactly in the tract of the Furr Traders to the N.W. & may open a new source of whale Fishery in the Northern Pacific Ocean'.[87]

With the establishment of the Secretaryship for War and Colonies in 1801 the uses of missionary activity as an adjunct to empire had a more obvious bureaucratic advocate. Soon after the establishment of this office Banks wrote to the Under-secretary underlining the advantages to government of the work of the London Missionary Society 'who will in my opinion with a very Little assistance from Government Plant little Colonies in all Places in the South Sea where British ships may wish to touch'.[88] Soon afterwards the message was reinforced by Haweis who pointed out that 'nothing can tend to the prosperity of the Colonies of Port Jackson and Norfolk Island, as the Solid Establishment and enlargement of our Mission' on Tahiti. He also invoked the sanction of Joseph Banks by writing that he 'has known and been consulted in all our steps from the beginning'.[89] The outcome was that the British government did allow missionaries a passage to Tahiti – a bureaucratic success for which Haweis profusely thanked Banks while again alluding to the ultimate benefit Britain would obtain from the mission to Tahiti.[90]

This partnership between Banks and the London Missionary Society continued under the various changes of personnel at the office of the Secretary for War and the Colonies. Eventually, the link between missionary and empire was given a more permanent form under Lord Bathurst who largely created the nineteenth-century Colonial Office during his tenure of office from 1812 to 1827. As Banks reminded

Bathurst in 1815, the presence of missions 'advantages every ship that Touches in these remote Regions'[91] – hence his request for free passage for four missionaries and their wives to Sydney, a request to which Bathurst acceded.[92] And, in 1820, the year of his death, Banks could rejoice in a letter to the London Missionary Society that after its initial tribulations the mission in Tahiti was beginning to flourish.[93]

This unlikely alliance between the by no means orthodox Banks and the largely Evangelical London Missionary Society was, like the African Association, an instance of the way in which Banks was involved in using voluntary associations to assist the purposes of empire. The fact that Banks devoted so much attention to such bodies is an indication of the fact that the British State had, at that stage, not yet developed a large enough apparatus to promote its imperial reach through the direct agency of government. But, in a society such as late eighteenth- and early nineteenth-century Britain, the line between the central government and voluntary institutions was often an uncertain one. The ties that were a natural part of an interconnected oligarchy ensured that government was frequently drawn into the affairs of voluntary bodies – particularly those which impinged on imperial concerns. It was one of Banks's great abilities to operate on the uncertain boundaries of the State widening the scope of its activities by linking it with the voluntary bodies which he also helped to foster.

THE FORMAL STRUCTURES OF EMPIRE

The Home Office

It is, however, an indication of the increasing size and complexity of the British State that such informal methods of advancing empire became less significant. This is particularly noticeable in relation to the promotion of African exploration which from the end of the Napoleonic Wars became increasingly a direct concern of government led by a revitalised Colonial Office. In the late eighteenth century, however, imperial affairs had no clear bureaucratic home and were often untidily spread around a number of different departments. Banks's chief lever in attempting to move the formal apparatus of the British State was, as we saw in the Chapter Five, the Privy Council Committee for Trade and the Admiralty. In his imperial designs as in his scientific – for the two were inseparably intertwined – these were the principal formal departments of government through which he attempted to work. But in order to promote other imperial ventures and, in particular, to guard the interests of what he called his 'favourite colony' of New South Wales, where issues of science and trade were less to the fore, he needed to work with the Home Office. For it was the Home Office which dealt with colonial affairs and which (however perfunctorily) supervised the infant settlement of New South Wales until the Secretary for War became the Secretary for War and Colonies in 1801.

Banks appears to have had a fairly fruitful relationship with the Home Office in the 1780s when plans for the establishment of the Australian colony were being discussed and the First Fleet organised. This probably owed little to the undistinguished Lord Sydney, the Home Secretary from 1783 to 1789, but rather was the outcome of a very effective working relationship between Banks and the departmental Under-secretary, Evan Nepean. But Nepean was not a member of the Cabinet and his influence was therefore limited. Moreover, his poor health between 1789 and 1792 meant that his activities were also limited and indeed he was in Jamaica in late 1791 and early 1792.[94] From 1794 he left the Home Office becoming Secretary to the Admiralty in 1795.

With Nepean largely absent Banks faced a number of obstacles in dealing with the Home Office throughout the 1790s. First and foremost the British government was almost totally preoccupied with the threat of the French Revolution and, after 1793, with the war with France. As a consequence, even though his ally, Henry Dundas, was Home Secretary from 1791 to 1794 (following Lord Grenville who succeeded Lord Sydney) it availed Banks little since what time Dundas could spare from East India Company affairs was largely devoted to the increasingly menacing European sector. Second, while at the Committee for Trade Banks had a powerful ally in Hawkesbury and at the Board of Control he could call on the support of his close friend Lord Mulgrave and, to a lesser extent, Dundas, the Home Secretary from 1794 to 1801 was the Duke of Portland who had little interest in colonial ventures. Lastly, as the removal of colonial affairs to the office of the Secretary for War in 1801 indicates, the Home Office was simply too understaffed and too preoccupied with British domestic concerns to be able to devote much attention to imperial problems.

Banks's involvement with Australian issues up to 1801 is, then, an indication of the limits of the British State's mechanisms for dealing with its widening responsibilities. This meant the need for the increasing involvement of one such as Banks who held no official post (apart from that of Privy Councillor after 1797) but who was linked with those in power by the ties natural to an oligarchy. But, for all Banks's interest and enthusiasm for Australia, he was necessarily limited in what he could achieve both by the degree of influence he had with the Home Office or other departments and by the extent to which the British State could translate policy into action through formal bureaucratic processes.

The role Banks played as de facto head of Australian affairs was widely recognised: one of his protégés, the plant collector, George Suttor, stated it as a truth universally acknowledged that 'Sir Joseph was considered the Father and Founder of the Australian Colonies',[95] while Banks's colleague at the Royal Society, Viscount Valentia, remarked of New South Wales that 'I consider that settlement as particularly under your protection'.[96] Banks's evidence before the House of Commons committee on transportation in 1779 had initiated the British government's serious interest in New South Wales as a place for a penal settlement. Moreover, although the evidence is fragmentary, it would seem that he was involved in discussions in the mid 1780s which led to the First Fleet (which under Governor Phillip set up the penal colony in 1788). In 1783 Matra wrote to him of a rumour of a settlement at New South Wales 'to be immediately under Your direction, and in which Lords Sandwich [and] Mulgrave, Mr. Colman, & several others are to be concerned'.[97]

Evidently Matra discussed the matter with Banks for in his detailed submission to the Fox–North coalition on the possibility of such a colony Matra invoked Banks's sanction. Thus he commented that 'Sir Joseph Banks, highly approves of the Settlement, & is very ready to give his opinion of it, either to his Majesty's Ministry, or others, whenever they may please to require it'.[98] This proposal was placed on the Cabinet's agenda for December 1784 by Evan Nepean[99] and the matter was given renewed attention by the evidence of both Banks and Matra at another House of Commons committee on transportation in 1785. By 1786 Blagden could report to Banks's close friend, Lord Mulgrave, that he 'has been much consulted in the business of Botany Bay'[100] – the consultation being, no doubt, chiefly with Evan Nepean at the Home Office who was the chief advocate of the scheme within the government. Nepean's 'Heads of a Plan for effectually Disposing of Convicts' was the document which finally ensured Cabinet approval of the scheme in August 1786 and it was he who largely organised the First Fleet.[101]

Along with his crucial role in its foundation Banks continued to play a vital role in the colony's development. The succour of a colony that was something of a foundling among the British government's other multifarious concerns became a basic trust – so much so that he noted in February 1789 that 'I could not take office and do my duty to the colony. My successor would naturally oppose my wishes. I prefer, therefore, to be friendly with both sides'.[102] It was natural, then, that those interested in benefiting from the colony should seek to enlist Banks's support. Among those who sought his aid was William Richards who, having been the contractor for the generally successful First Fleet,[103] aspired to regain the contract to transport convicts after he had been outbid for the Second Fleet. Richards attempted to persuade Banks to grant his 'approbation' of a proposal he wished to make to the Treasury, thus avoiding 'a Competition at the Navy Board where it is the Custom to take the lowest offer – a proof of the impolicy of which has already been tryed', a reference to the disastrous Second Fleet which arrived in Sydney in mid-1790 with the loss of 267 of the 1,026 people who sailed from Britain.[104]

Appalled by the mismanagement of the Second Fleet, Banks saw merit in Richards' proposals and gave a very qualified assent to Richards' plea to use his influence in support, bidding him 'to make use of my name at the Treasury with the utmost caution Lest the gentlemen there should think that I mean to assume too great a influence in the business'.[105] It was a reminder that the path of the unofficial adviser was not always a

smooth one when it came to shaping policy – particularly in departments
such as the Treasury with which he had not been involved on any regular
basis. Even at the Home Office his sway was restricted after the departure
of his ally, Evan Nepean. As he remarked to Richards in December 1791:

> I really cannot inform you whether there is at present any immediate intention of
> sending out convicts or not, having since Mr. Nepean left the office of Under
> Secretary of state [for Jamaica] no acquaintance in that department. I cannot, I fear,
> unless I am consulted on the subject, be of any service to you.[106]

Banks's elevation to the dignity of a Privy Councillor in 1797 brought
with it, as he told Governor King on Norfolk Island, a greater opportunity 'to be of some service to you or your establishment'. He added
that 'I have for some time seen with regret that Ministers, fully occupied
with the business of carrying on a calamitous war, have to [sic] much
neglected the Interests of your Establishment, my favorite Colony'.[107] It
was a comment that underlined the marginal character of the colony
and its need, in default of government attention, for an unofficial
protector such as Banks. Two years later he made a similar comment to
Governor Hunter telling him to

> be assured that the situation of Europe is at present so critical, and his Majesty's
> Ministers so fully employed in business of the deepest importance, that it is scarce
> possible to gain a moment's audience on any subject but those which stand foremost
> in their minds, and colonies of all kinds, you may be assured, are now put into the
> background.

Nonetheless, he continued, 'Your colony is already a most valuable
appendage to Great Britain, and I flatter myself we shall before it is long
see her Ministers made sensible of its real value'.[108] Such hopes did
indeed come some way towards realisation once colonial affairs were
transferred from the Home Office after 1801 but, necessarily, up to 1815
the titanic struggle with France overshadowed all else.

Banks's involvement in the establishment of the penal colony of
New South Wales made him a natural target for proposals for another
penal colony on the other side of the Pacific, on the northwest coast of
America. The main figure in initiating such a venture was the fur trader,
Richard Etches, who had worked with Banks in promoting the exploration and exploitation of this area – activity which led to the
formation of the King George's Sound Company in 1785. Etches also
financed a reconnaissance of the area with a trading voyage from 1785 to
1788, and another from 1787 to 1797 which, at Banks's instigation,
included the botanist, Archibald Menzies.[109] In April 1788, some months
after the First Fleet had arrived at Botany Bay, Etches wrote to Banks
thanking him for 'The repeated acts of Friendship that I have experienced from You, particularly in our North west Expedition'. He also
proposed that 'Government having adopted the measure of Colonizing

with Convicts, I shou'd presume the same wou'd hold good with forming an establishment on the N.W. Continent of America or Islands, equally with New Holland'. Such a scheme would, of course, need an advocate with the State – hence Etches's request that after he had 'presented[ed] a memorial to Government' he 'sho'd hope for your *kind assistance* in carrying it *thro*'.[110]

It seems evident that Banks saw political difficulties with the project since, in the next letter later that month, Etches remarked how Banks had considered that there would be 'too *great expence* of the *Governmental* part of the Establishment'.[111] Nonetheless, it was a proposal that was taken seriously within Banks's circle. His old friend, the Scottish physician James Lind, wrote to him in November 1789 in support of a 'Plan for disposing of Convicts upon the NW coast of America' advanced by Patrick Wilson, a professor of astronomy in the University of Glasgow. He added that 'I shall be glad if it is carried into execution and proves useful either in a philosophical or political view'.[112] For Wilson such a plan fitted in well with the whole tenor of British imperial expansion with its possibilities 'for promoting Commerce or enlarging the Sphere of general Intercourse & Improvement'.[113]

But though Etches held out the glittering prospect of a fur trade with China which would provide an alternative way of paying for the expensive tea trade with what he called 'a drain to the nation of upwards of a Million and a half of specie annually'[114] his plan came to nothing. Perhaps government found the prospect of maintaining two distant convict settlements too unsettling to the Treasury or possibly the diplomatic problems of establishing a settlement in an area which Spain still claimed was an obstacle. In any case it is an episode that indicates the extent to which Banks was regarded as providing an *entrée* to government for imperial ventures (particularly those related to the Pacific). But it also indicates the limits of Banks's role: as someone who held no formal office he could suggest and encourage but ultimately he was dependent on the active support of those who were part of the political establishment.

Though the proposal for a convict settlement came to naught Banks's interest in the northwest of the American continent (an area brought into prominence by Cook's third great Pacific voyage of 1776 to 1779) remained strong. For, it was hoped, exploration of the northwest might eventually yield not only new resources such as the burgeoning fur trade but also the great holy grail of Pacific exploration: the Northwest Passage, and, with it, easy access for British ships to the lucrative markets of Japan and China. It was natural, then, that the Home Office involved Banks in 1790 in the fitting out of a proposed expedition, the principal aims of which were a thorough charting of that area and an assertion of British claims to the area in the face of Spanish attempts to assert its traditional claim to the western coast of the American continent. It was Banks to whom Lord Grenville, the Home Secretary, turned for re-assurance that the Spanish claim lacked substance.[115] Banks was later consulted, too, by Nepean on what goods should be taken in order to establish a settlement at Nootka Sound. This was a matter on which, in turn, Banks asked the advice of his botanical client, Archibald Menzies, who had recently returned from that part of the world.[116] Menzies' suggestions formed the basis of a document which Banks sent to the Home Office and was then forwarded on to the Admiralty by Lord Grenville.[117]

After various vicissitudes and complications caused by the threat of war in mid-1790 over the Spanish expulsion of a British settlement at Nootka Sound[118] the expedition to the northwest was placed under the command of George Vancouver at the end of 1790. A new plan for the voyage was drawn up by Nepean in consultation with Banks[119] and, needless to say, it was Banks who provided Menzies, the voyage's naturalist, with his extensive instructions for the marathon voyage which lasted from 1791 to 1795.[120] On the expedition's return Banks continued his involvement with the Home Office and his role as Menzies' patron. Thus he requested the then Home Secretary, the Duke of Portland, to grant the naturalist a continuation of his salary while he completed his journal and the cataloguing of the specimens from the voyage.[121]

Overall, then, the Vancouver expedition was a successful example of the way in which government and, in particular, the Home Office could draw on the expertise of an outsider like Banks to advance the cause of empire. Like the First Fleet and the breadfruit expedition it was also another instance of the fruitful working relationship built up between Banks and Nepean. However, with his departure from the Home Office in 1794 Banks's ties with that instrumentality of the State diminished considerably.

The Colonial Office

The transference of colonial affairs to the supervision of the third Secretary, whose title from 1801 became Secretary for War and Colonies, provided Banks with a more ready access to government particularly in dealing with the problems of New South Wales. It was a move that indicated the growing volume of colonial business as Britain's military and naval successes expanded the sphere of empire. It was also prompted by another sign of the expansion of the British State: the recognition that the Home Secretary had not the time to handle colonial as well as domestic affairs. This was particularly the case after the union with Ireland in 1801 which, as George III commented apropos this reshuffle of responsibilities, meant that there was now 'full employment for any man' on domestic affairs alone.[122]

Lord Hobart, who held the post of Secretary for War and Colonies from 1801 to 1804, appears to have been only too glad to allow Banks to assume unofficial responsibility for Australian affairs. The prominent colonist, D'Arcy Wentworth, was told by a former New South Wales surgeon in October 1804 that it was Banks 'under whose directions that Colony is now chiefly placed'.[123] Banks himself acknowledged his role as a voluntary agent for the new colony in a letter of March 1805 to his client, William Bligh, offering him the possibility of the Governor's post. 'I have always', wrote Banks alluding to the transfer of colonial affairs to its new bureaucratic resting place,

> since the institution of the new colony at New South Wales, taken a deep interest in its success, and have been constantly consulted by His Majesty's Ministers, through all the changes there have been in the department which directs it, relative to the more important concerns of the colonists.[124]

Indeed, Banks and Lord Hobart formed such an effective partnership that his departure from office in May 1804 to make way for Lord Camden (the incumbent from May 1804 to May 1805) prompted Banks to bemoan to Governor King that

> I had a great loss in Lord Hobart's going out of office; for I had just prevailed upon His Lordship and Mr. Sullivan, his Secretary, to understand the history of your colony, and was in hopes of going on better than I ever have done ... I have a new task to undertake, to bring Lord Camden and Mr. Cooke into the same happy disposition.[125]

Evidently, Banks managed to gain the confidence of Camden in his short tenure of office, since by April 1805 he reported that 'I have this morning Receivd a Letter from Lord Camden empowering me to offer the Government of N.S.Wales to Capt. Bligh'.[126]

After Camden the position briefly passed to Castlereagh, from June 1805 to February 1806, until he was replaced by an old opponent of Banks, William Windham. There was, initially, some coolness between the new Secretary and the unofficial adviser on Australian affairs. In a letter of March 1806 explaining the delay regarding a land grant near Sydney Banks rather primly explained that:

> The reason was that I have not yet ventured to present myself at the Office for the Colonies since it has been occupied by its new inhabitants nor probably shall, not till I have some good reason to give for intruding myself or till they manifest a wish to see me. To do otherwise might be very detrimental to my hopes of Establishing with Mr. Windham the same sort of confidence in me as Ld. Camden Ld.Castlereagh & their Predecessors have favord me with.[127]

But the two men were too useful to each other for this standoff to continue and the steady flow of material regarding the new colony between the Secretary for War and the Colonies and Banks soon resumed.[128] When in March 1807 Windham gave way to Castlereagh, who held a second term in the office until October 1809, Banks renewed his good working relationship with that powerful politician and FRS to advance the cause of his accident-prone client, Bligh, who had been deposed in the Rum Rebellion of 1808. Banks attempted to reassure the anxious Bligh (who understandably feared for his career after having

A view of Sydney Cove–Port Jackson 7 March 1792, ink and watercolour by 'The Port Jackson Painter'.
(By courtesy of the Natural History Museum, London, Watling Collection, Drawing 21)

been the subject of two major mutinies) by writing to him that 'All I hear in Lord Castlereagh's office, however, is in your favour'.[129] But even Banks's advocacy could not persuade Castlereagh to keep as Governor someone as manifestly out of sympathy with the colonists as Bligh. No doubt, too, Banks's role in making such a disastrous appointment accounts for the fact that, in contrast to the previous governors, Bligh's replacement, Lachlan Macquarie (Governor from 1809 to 1821), was not a client of Banks. The new Governor was also the first army rather than naval officer, which also reflects the fact that Banks had considerable contacts with the Admiralty but few with the Army.

As always, then, Banks's influence depended on the extent to which the political power-brokers of the day were willing to take his advice. In general in Australian affairs he enjoyed considerable sway both because of his expertise and because the Secretaries of State for War and the Colonies were far more concerned with prosecuting the war against Napoleon than with colonial matters – particularly those that concerned the distant gaol of New South Wales which had little or no strategic significance. But Banks could not assume the co-operation of the Secretaries and each change of office necessitated a delicate minuet as Banks established his credentials. Banks, too, had to be prepared to accept with patience the fact that politicians were not always as readily available as he might have wished. When his wayward botanical collector, George Caley, complained in 1804 about being kept waiting by the Governor of New South Wales Banks drew on his own experience in urging greater stoicism:

> Be comforted, if it is a comfort for you to know that when I have occasion to wait upon the Secretary of State or the Treasury, merely to offer my services to do what they want to have done for your colony and others, my waiting is at least as long and as tedious as yours. We must all make up our minds to wait the leisure of those above us.[130]

With the coming to office of Banks's former colleague from the Privy Council Committee for Trade and fellow sheep-breeder, Lord Bathurst, in June 1812 colonial affairs were placed on a more secure bureaucratic footing and, as a consequence, the British State became less dependent on Banks's role as an unofficial adviser on colonial affairs. For Bathurst, who held the post of Secretary for War and the Colonies from 1812 to 1827, brought greater permanence and stability to the position. The fact that most of Bathurst's tenure of office was held in peacetime meant that he could properly devote himself to the colonial part of his portfolio rather then concentrate, as his predecessors had, on the problems of war.

This created the conditions for Bathurst – together with his energetic parliamentary Under-secretary, Henry Goulburn (who also had a long tenure of office from 1812 to 1821) – effectively to create the nineteenth-century Colonial Office. For they brought to bear on its concerns the administrative rejuvenation which had been gradually seeping through the British State since the financial reforms initiated in 1780 by the bitter experience of defeat in the American Revolution.[131] One telling index of the increase in the level of the Colonial Office's activity is the sharp rise in the number of pages dispatched: from 922 in 1806, to 2,957 in 1816 and 5,257 in 1824.[132] After 1824 the increase was even more evident largely due to the appointment of a permanent Under-secretary. They are figures which underline the extent of change in the Colonial Office under Bathurst and are indicative of the increasing growth of the British State more generally.

Bathurst was an administrative reformer but he was a man of the British *old regime*, suspicious of radical change and committed to maintaining the traditional political pre-eminence of the landed classes in the age of revolution. He shared with Banks, too, an essentially mercantilist conception of empire viewing it largely in commercial and strategic terms – which was of a piece with his support for a system of Corn Laws (though he acknowledged the need for some flexibility in framing and adapting them).[133] His lieutenant, Henry Goulburn, was of like mind regarding the colonies as 'one of the greatest sources of our glory, and one of the great supports of our power, affording resources in war, and increasing our commerce in peace'.[134] Banks and Bathurst, then, shared a similar philosophy of empire and they also shared a similar drive for greater efficiency.

However, the greater professionalism that was being developed in the Colonial Office meant that the need to consult an expert outsider was diminishing. This, together with his advancing years and declining health, helps to explain why Banks appears to have been called on less for advice on Australian matters. In the year after Bathurst assumed office Banks attempted to persuade him of the injustice meted out to Bligh but concluded that 'tho always kind to me [he] does not seem to think of the Admiral's services and of the privations he has endured and the sacrifices he has made as I do'.[135] Nonetheless, Banks's influence still carried considerable weight. When there was a possibility of Macquarie being recalled as Governor of New South Wales Banks, as he told his client, the soldier and astronomer, Sir Thomas Brisbane, 'went to Lord Bathurst to Remind his Lordship' of Brisbane's claims. Brisbane's appointment, Banks endeavoured to persuade Bathurst, 'would not only profit the Cause of Science' but also would 'be able to bring about the Reform intended in the Constitution of the Colony'.[136] Though Macquarie was not recalled at that stage Banks continued to work for Brisbane's appointment telling Blagden in 1819 that he was hopeful that Brisbane would become Governor and that there would also be an opportunity to erect an astronomical observatory and to appoint an observer.[137] And, indeed, Brisbane did ultimately succeed Macquarie in 1821, no doubt largely thanks to Banks's earlier support.

Though Bathurst relied less than some of his predecessors on Banks's routine advice, particularly on Australian affairs, he was well disposed towards those projects of Banks's which he considered relevant to the goals of his department. Banks, for example, had Bathurst's support in facilitating the work of his worldwide network of scientific correspondents. Thus Bathurst enthusiastically supported Banks's suggestion that Allan Cunningham, a former Kew gardener sent by Banks to New South Wales as a botanical collector, should join the expedition to the western plains led by Lieutenant John Oxley.[138]

Bathurst's ability to over-awe unco-operative colonial governors could also prove useful. Thus Banks invoked Bathurst's name when he found Governor Macquarie of New South Wales unwilling to provide the assistance that his counterpart at the Cape Colony had provided Cunningham's former colleague at Kew, James Bowie, at Bathurst's prompting.[139] Banks drove home the message by pointing out to Macquarie that any 'countenance to scientific pursuits' he might provide 'will be brought into Notice'.[140] Macquarie took the hint and provided Bathurst with collections of botanical specimens some of which Bathurst sent on to Banks.[141] Bathurst, too, looked to Banks for advice on appointments to colonial botanical gardens as, for example, the post of superintendent of the Ceylon garden which became vacant in 1818.[142] Another area where the Colonial Office called on Banks's scientific expertise was in providing a suitably qualified person to assist with settling the boundary line between the United States and Canada in 1817.[143]

The revitalisation of the Colonial Office under Bathurst is evident in the response to one of Banks's longstanding interests, the exploration of Africa. Previously government had largely left this field to the initiative of the African Association, a body which, though essentially private, was linked to government by the involvement of a number of well-connected individuals, as we have seen. When the Mungo Park expedition was being planned in 1804 the then Secretary of State for War and Colonies, Lord Camden, gave it his official blessing. However, he commented that since it was an expedition for discovery rather than for military ends it would be best if Banks drew up Park's instructions.[144] By contrast, with the end of the Napoleonic Wars in 1815, the Colonial Office was directly involved in two ambitious expeditions to Africa. The first of these sought to use the coastal region of Senegambia as a base from which to reach the Niger. However, this goal was not achieved, despite the involvement of some one hundred individuals between 1815 and 1821, because of the hostility of rulers on the Upper Senegal.[145] The second expedition attempted to sail up the Congo River.

Whereas previously planning for such expeditions had largely fallen to the African Association it was the State itself which now took responsibility. But an outside expert, like Banks, was not excluded from the planning for the expedition up the Congo. Thus Banks was asked for advice, 'as nothing can be done without your assistance', as to a 'proper person as a Naturalist'.[146] Banks secured for the voyage (at government expense) the service of Christen Smith, a Danish professor of botany, together with a gardener from Kew. In commenting on plans for the voyage Banks explicitly drew on the experience of the *Endeavour* and breadfruit expeditions in suggesting that 'in all matters of Naval Equipment it is better to adopt a Plan of sufficient extent at first than to do it after a failure which if attributable to parsimony will in a country like this meet with censure'.[147] Though the voyage ended disastrously at the rapids which blocked the Congo River two hundred miles from the sea, the botanical specimens largely survived and were returned to Banks's house-cum-research institute at Soho Square.[148]

Despite this setback Bathurst continued to look to Banks for advice on matters connected with African exploration. In 1817 Bathurst gave his enthusiastic support to Banks's plan for Burckhardt to travel to Timbuctoo and authorised the purchase of presents for the local ruler[149] (though, in the event, Burckhardt died before he could complete the journey). And in 1819 the Colonial Office's support for a proposed expedition to the interior of Madagascar was deferred until Bathurst received from Banks his assurance that the goals of the expedition were worthwhile and 'that we are not under the plea of promoting science creating an unnecessary appointment'.[150]

Just as projects initiated by the Committee for Trade had necessarily involved the co-operation of the Admiralty so, too, as the Colonial Office became more active it also came to rely more heavily on that most basic instrument of British power, the Navy, and its bureaucratic counterpart, the Admiralty. The Congo expedition of 1815, for example, was formally authorised by Bathurst but much of its execution was left to the Admiralty[151] and, in particular, to John Barrow, second Secretary of the Admiralty, 1804–6 and 1807–45 – which accounts for Banks's close involvement in the planning for this expedition. The extent to which he shared Banks's interests is evident in his comment to Banks about the 1815 expedition that even 'if it should fail in obtaining much geographical Learning we may at least extend the practical knowledge of African botany'.[152] Barrow's enthusiasm for the expansion of empire through exploration stirred the aging Banks to

> renewed vigour. If anything will cure the gout it must be the pleasure I derive from finding our Ministers mindful of the credit we have obtained from Discovery, and willing to continue and to increase and enlarge the only splendid source of Honour which Peace allows of.[153]

After Banks's death in 1820, Barrow assumed his role as the promoter of British scientific-cum-imperial exploration[154] – an indication of Banks's success in institutionalising his drive for imperial expansion through the medium of scientific exploration. The growing size and sophistication of the British State were evident, however, in the fact that under Barrow such activities were increasingly accommodated within the formal structures of government rather than being dependent on the initiatives of an informal adviser like Banks. Nonetheless, the voluntary traditions of the African Association were continued under its successor organisation, the Royal Geographical Society, of which Barrow was one of the founders in 1830. The ideology which underlined Barrow's promotion of scientific exploration was one that Banks would largely have shared: that such undertakings were 'the means of extending the sphere of human knowledge' and that such knowledge would be of benefit to the nation sponsoring them and, indeed, all of humanity. As Barrow put it in the familiar Baconian vein ' "knowledge is power"; and we may safely commit to the stream of time the beneficial results of its irresistible influence'.[155]

The very extent of Banks's activities as a promoter of empire were, then, an indication of the limitations of the British State which, as a consequence of its own bureaucratic limitations, became dependent on an outside expert such as Banks. As the Colonial Office and other agencies of government expanded their role so did the significance of Banks in initiating new imperial ventures diminish, though he continued to be called on to provide expert advice. Banks, then, lived through a period when the role of the State was expanding under the pressure of war, colonial conquest and rapid economic growth. Nonetheless, conservatism and the deeply-rooted fear of the English landed classes of the central government meant that the State, where possible, continued to rely on the voluntary traditions of that landed elite.

Sir John Barrow. Painting by John Jackson c.1810.
(By courtesy of the National Portrait Gallery, London)

This applied most obviously at the level of local government where the unpaid Justice of the Peace remained the foundation of civil order but it applied, too, in other spheres of public life including that of science. Hence Banks's role as a de facto adviser to government on scientific issues was never really challenged by the growth of a formal department of government and the use of the Royal Society as an informal sounding board for government policy remained significant as late as World War Two.[156] Indeed, it was not until 1916 that a specific department to deal with scientific issues – the Department of Scientific and Industrial Research – was established. By contrast, by Banks's death, imperial affairs had a well-established place at the centre of the State with the re-invigorated Colonial Office which continued to grow in size and significance throughout the nineteenth century. Not surprisingly in a State still largely governed by a landowning elite that proudly traced back its origins to a medieval warrior caste, imperial concerns more naturally formed part of the central definition of the State than did scientific ones.

The growing significance of the Colonial Office reflects, too, another increasingly important feature of the British State: the extent to which its priorities were shaped by commercial concerns. For it was one of the successes of such neo-mercantilist architects of the second British Empire as Dundas, Hawkesbury, Sheffield and Banks to link closely the cause of empire with that of trade and with the maintenance of naval power. Such assumptions were to come under challenge from the largely middle-class proponents of free trade for whom empire was more of a burden than a source of wealth. Such agitation, however, never completely undermined the association between empire and British economic and strategic self-sufficiency. It also led to increased work for the Colonial Office as it was called on to re-shape an empire built in wartime conditions on authoritarian principles to one which better accorded with English traditions of representative government and the rule of law. Such developments indicated the extent to which it was now assumed that government should act in the imperial sphere even at the cost of expanding the administrative machinery of the State. Such a view contrasted markedly with the attempt in the aftermath of the American Revolution to reduce as much as possible the sway of the State and the size of its bureaucratic agencies.

It was an attempt that was undermined by the need for government action in the face of fundamental economic, political and military changes, which demanded action on the part of the central government. However, during the period from the end of the American Revolution to the end of the Napoleonic Wars with the attempt at constraining the growth of the bureaucracy, there was also a niche for outside experts such as Banks to help shape scientific or imperial policy. Such informal methods helped to develop the character of the second British Empire in the decades before it was brought back more firmly under the sway of the formal apparatus of the State.

Epilogue

At the end of his life in 1820 Banks represented a splendid anachronism that was increasingly at variance with the movements of the age. As President of the Royal Society he stood for an Enlightenment view of science as part of general polite culture and as a stimulus for improving the lot of humanity. The increasing specialisation and professionalisation of science he regarded as weakening its civic functions and the founding of new professional bodies such as the Geological or the Astronomical Societies devoted to particular disciplines was in his eyes a threat to the traditional pre-eminence of the Royal Society. While Banks had gone a long way in his journey from a young *virtuoso* to a systematic natural historian in the Linnaean mould, elements of the gentlemanly ethos of the collector were still a part of him, putting him at variance with his younger contemporaries for whom their disciplinary identity was primary.

In the political realm, too, Banks's career marked a transition from a State which could still use the services of an outside gentleman expert to one which increasingly relied on professional civil servants. Though from a relatively *nouveau* gentry family, Banks identified closely with the oligarchic ethos of the landed class for whom power was linked with patronage and personal loyalties. Part of the reason that Banks was able to achieve so much in his manipulation of the apparatus of the British State to accomplish his scientific and imperial ends was that the formal structures of government were still sufficiently malleable and unsystematic – in certain ways 'irrational' – to accommodate the intervention of an outsider such as himself. By temperament Banks identified with ministers like Hawkesbury and government officials like Nepean, Stevens or Barrow, who embodied the more efficient and reforming aspects of the State bureaucracy. Though a beneficiary in terms of his access to the power of 'Old Corruption', he did not gain personal wealth from his service to the State embodying the service ethic that was one of the reasons for the long tenure of power of the English landed classes. By contrast, his lifelong friend, Lord Auckland, made sure that his political service was rewarded with some of the riper fruits of the old unreformed constitution, a reminder of the prevalence of the ethos of 'Old Corruption' in the midst of Pitt's attempts at making the State a more efficient instrument of public duty. That record of the excesses of 'Old Corruption', Wade's *Black Book*, noted that Auckland received £1,400 p.a as Vendue-Master at Demarara 'where he had never been' and £1,900 p.a. as Auditor at Greenwich Hospital 'for doing nothing' since he never conducted an audit.[1]

But, though Banks was – by the standards of some of his contemporaries – austere in his willingness to perform public duties without seeking a financial reward, in another sense he embodied aspects of the world of 'Old Corruption': for his *modus operandi* was based on a merging of the public and the private. Personal connections including the favour of the King – for in some ways Banks was a traditional courtier even, to a degree, a royal favourite – were Banks's means of access into the inner recesses of power. On the whole Banks used such political leverage for publicly beneficial ends, or at least for ends that suited the interests of his fellow landowners. But if the ends were 'rational' the means were those of a more traditional State in which government officials had not yet been fully transformed into civil servants, whose first loyalty was to the public sphere. As the formal apparatus of government grew over the course of the nineteenth century, making the border between the State and voluntary action more exact and recognisable, the opportunity to play the Banksian role of an outside expert with access to the apparatus of the State diminished. The sharpening of the divide between the public and the private was also accompanied by a weakening of the elaborate network of influence and connection which had ensured that the same oligarchic elite controlled most major institutions whether or not they were formally a part of the State.

Nonetheless, the mantle of Banks as a promoter of scientific exploration and promoter of schemes to link science with imperial expansion did fall on others, notably Sir John Barrow and Sir Roderick Murchison. Though both these figures continued in the Banksian vein to use voluntary associations, notably the Royal Geographical Society, in the service of the State, it was significant that, in contrast to Banks, both were formally members of the bureaucracy: Barrow being a Secretary of the Admiralty and Murchison Director-General of the Geological Survey. Moreover, Murchison who, as Stafford shows, came closest to a re-incarnation of Banks as a promoter of imperial science was one of a group of civil-servant scientists such as the Hookers at Kew, Beaufort at the Hydrographical Department of the Admiralty and Sabine at the Kew Observatory.[2]

Furthermore, Murchison and, to a lesser extent, Barrow, were also part of a state apparatus that had been hardened by the long experience of war with the French and by the long assault of opponents of 'Old Corruption'. In many ways, too, the seeds planted by Pitt and his fellow reformers in the aftermath of the American debacle had come to maturity in the decades after Banks's death. Though the level of state expenditure dropped after victory over France brought with it the luxury of being able to dispense with a large military establishment, the experience of a long war had accustomed the British public to a larger governmental apparatus than their eighteenth-century forebears had known. The number of government officials in 1827 was, for example, some forty percent higher than in 1797.[3] Though public spending fell by twenty-five percent in the two decades after Waterloo,[4] this drop was from a level that because of the war had been raised to heights that horrified contemporaries.

By Continental standards the apparatus of the British State remained small[5] and frugal and there was considerable reluctance to re-allocate the funds once spent on war to the needs of peace. But it was increasingly a bureaucracy which was cleansed of the wasteful sinecures which had generated the crusade against 'Old Corruption' – a crusade which, tellingly, began to die away in the 1830s as the public came to be convinced that genuine reform had been instituted.[6] The officials of the British State also drew on the ethic of both the Evangelicals and the Utilitarians in developing a stronger sense of their duty to the public and their need to combine economy with efficiency. Due bureaucratic process became more important and, as a consequence, Banks's way of doing things through personal contacts became less acceptable. Banks's skilful exploitation of the uncertain boundary between the public and the private by linking nominally private associations like the Royal Society, the Royal Institution, the African Association or the Society of Arts with government purposes also became more difficult to practice as the British State and its servants demanded more formal control over public ventures.

The boundary between public and private was drawn even more clearly between royal possessions and those held by the State – one instance of this being the way in which Kew Gardens, after a period of decline following Banks's death, became formally subject to state control in 1840. It was an instance of the way in which the imperial scientific venture which Banks did so much to launch and which Barrow and Murchison were to help to sustain was being drawn more directly into the orbit of the State. Symptomatic, too, was the way in which Banks's vast collections were, after his death, placed in the public domain in the British Museum and eventually served as the nucleus of the British Museum of Natural History.

For state direction of such collections or of the botanical transplantations facilitated by Kew brought with it greater control over an empire which, in the scientific realm, as in other respects, was gradually being more closely integrated with the apparatus of central government.[7]

Where Banks had to employ his own private collectors or work with the fluctuating favours of ministers, colonial governors or East India Company officials, imperial science gradually became more directly the responsibility of a State that, largely thanks to Banks, had become conscious of its imperial and economic benefits. Amassing scientific collections based on systematic principles was the scientific equivalent of mapping the world, making its products available in the imperial centre in a form which was readily accessible and exploitable. For 'empire' is, in part, a mental construction – a way of conceiving the world which gives privileged status to the forms of knowledge and canons of rationality that predominate in the metropolitan power.

Given the parsimonious character of the nineteenth-century British State some of the Banksian-pioneered methods of sponsoring science at low cost continued: the practice, for example, of taking along a scientist on a naval voyage or of using private initiatives for imperial ends in the manner which Murchison so successfully fostered in relation to the Royal Geographical Society. But, though the frugality of the British State meant that science remained in the private as well as the public sphere, the age of great individual collectors like Banks had passed as imperial science more and more became something that belonged to the public sphere to be utilised, when necessary, by the State. For it was a State which, after the turmoil of the Napoleonic Wars had subsided, had become more conscious of both the duties and benefits occasioned by many of the imperial possessions which it had acquired at a time when a distracted and inadequately-staffed government left much of their care to interested outsiders like Banks. The very word 'empire' which for much of the eighteenth century still referred to 'the British Empire in Europe', the three traditional kingdoms of England, Scotland and Wales, had begun by 1815 to acquire the larger sense of all territories under British control around the globe.[8]

Part of the reason why the State needed its own apparatus to deal with imperial issues and its own imperially-derived scientific collections was that it could no longer rely on the cosy arrangement between government and prominent members of the landowning elite whereby government officials could call on the expertise or personal resources of a prominent individual like Banks. In the first place this was an offence to the *amour-propre* of an increasingly professionalised civil service. But, more fundamentally, it represented a change in the relationship between the State and the landowning classes. For much of the eighteenth century the landowning classes had been allowed to hold the reins of power with little complaint from other elements of society, both because of long-engrained habits of deference and because it was considered that, by and large, their policies were in the interests of the country as a whole.

The beginnings of a crack in this consensus were evident in the way in which Banks and his fellow defenders of the landed interest had to make concessions over the export of unprocessed wool and, more tellingly, over the Corn Laws. This rift, of course, widened to the point where in 1846 the Corn Laws were repealed – the ultimate symbol of the new political power of the middle classes and the consequent diminution of the status of the landed interest. Government had increasingly, then, to hold the ring by balancing a number of different interest groups of which the landed interest was but one. As a consequence it could no longer assume that the landed classes would be so ready to serve a State, the interests of which did not always equate with their own.

Moreover, the protectionist apparatus of which the Corn Laws was the peak came to seem less and less necessary to a State that had been persuaded by the experience of the French Wars that the key to victory had been its commercial buoyancy which was best advanced by free trade.[9] As early as 1799 Pitt's lieutenant, George Rose, used statistical evidence to support the proposition that 'Great Britain ... draws her means for carrying on the war, from the increasing manufactures and trade of her people'.[10] The neo-mercantilism of Banks and his allies had been based on the view that the strategic interests of Britain could be combined with the advancement of agrarian improvement through state direction of commerce and imperial policy. But the need for such government action seemed less persuasive in a century when Britain had subdued its traditional rival, France, and had a clear mastery of the seas. Ironically, the victory of free trade in the nineteenth century was made possible by the more mercantilist-inclined policies of the eighteenth century which had helped to ensure British naval supremacy.[11]

As such a supremacy began to seem less secure towards the end of the nineteenth century so, too, the State began to become more interventionist and, as Drayton points out, to become more inclined to foster a form of neo-mercantilism in regards to science through such imperial centres as Kew Gardens.[12] But there was a fundamental difference between the scientific neo-mercantilism of the late eighteenth century and that of the late nineteenth century. Where Banks worked as a private individual who had to woo political support, by the late nineteenth century scientific initiatives emerged from the apparatus of the State itself – a State that was being transformed from the night-watchman State of the mid-nineteenth century to one that could properly grapple not only with strategic concerns but also with long-neglected domestic concerns such as mass education and public health.[13]

What makes Banks of greater than biographical interest, then, is the way in which his life embodied some of the larger movements of an age which had to grapple with the consequences of political and economic revolution. In science he marked the transformation from *virtuoso* to scientist while, in his guise as an adviser to government, his activities also corresponded to a period when greater professionalisation was weakening the position of the gentlemanly amateur. For, though Banks was able to play an active role in government, largely because of his connections as a gentleman scholar and landowner, by the time of his death in 1820 the British State was beginning to become more reliant on professional expertise and was less inclined to allow its affairs to be handled by those who did not hold formal office. The price of an effective State was the growth of the professional civil servant and, however reluctantly and grudgingly, it was one that those who held power in nineteenth-century Britain ultimately paid.

Notes

INTRODUCTION

1 Brewer, *The sinews of power*. This draws on such earlier studies of the eighteenth-century British fiscal system as Mathias and Brown, 'Taxation in England and France 1715–1810' and O'Brien, 'The political economy of British taxation'. For recent discussion of the issues raised in Brewer's book see Jupp, 'Landed elite and political authority in Britain c.1760–1850', Harling and Mander, 'From "fiscal-military" state to laissez-faire state 1760–1850' and Stone, *An imperial state at war* and O'Brien and Hunt, 'The rise of a fiscal state'
2 Rose, *A brief examination*, p. 1
3 G. N. Clark, 'The birth', pp. 118–9
4 Dowell, 'The word "State"', p. 22
5 Definitions of Lasswell and Kaplan, and MacIver and Page listed in Kolb, 'State', p. 690
6 Paine, *Rights*, p. 184
7 Kolb, 'State', p. 691
8 Innes, 'Parliament'
9 Langford, *Public life*, p. 586
10 Wilson, *The sense of the people*; Colley, *Britons*. See also Eastwood, 'Patriotism and the British State'
11 As Aylmer writes: 'the prevailing impression of eighteenth-century administraion is one of an extraordinary patchwork of old and new, useless and efficient, corrupt and honest – mixed together', 'From office-holding', p. 106
12 Harling, *The waning*, p. 12
13 Baker, 'Changing perspectives' and Mackay, *In the wake of Cook*, p. 23
14 Crone, 'Richard Price'
15 Stewart, *The rise of public science*
16 HMC, Fortescue, II, Auckland to Lord Grenville, 6 Nov. 1791
17 Mackay, *In the wake of Cook*

CHAPTER ONE   AN EXPANDING STATE

1 Christie, *Wars and revolutions*, p. 137
2 Stone, *An imperial state*, p. 6
3 Tilly, 'Reflections', p. 42
4 Mann, *States, war and capitalism*, p. 106. Graph reproduced by kind permission of the publishers, Basil Blackwells
5 House of Commons, Parliamentary Papers, 1830–1: 7 (no. 92), p. 300, 'Return of the number of persons employed and of the pay or salaries granted to such persons in all public offices or departments . . .'
6 Baker, 'Changing attitudes'
7 Halévy, *England in 1815*, p. 17. See also Keir, 'Economical reform'
8 Torrance, 'Social class and bureaucratic innovation'
9 Eastwood, 'Amplifying the province of the legislature', p. 284; Brewer, *Sinews of war*, p. 87 and Durey, 'Radical critique of "Old Corruption"'. For a survey of the

changing character of the institutions of government during this period see Chester, *The English administrative system.*

10 Finer, 'Patronage and the public service', p. 353

11 Ehrman, *The younger Pitt,* I, p. 90 and Baker, 'Changing attitudes', p. 216

12 Finer, 'Patronage and the public service', p. 352

13 Foord, 'Waning'

14 Parris, *Constitutional bureaucracy,* p. 49

15 Christie, *Wars and revolutions,* p. 186

16 Atkinson, 'State and empire and convict transportation', p. 35

17 Brewer, *Sinews of power,* passim and Torrance, 'Social class and bureaucratic innovation', p. 66

18 Bentham, *Introduction,* p. 200

19 Eastwood, 'Amplifying the province of the legislature', p. 293

20 Steven, *Trade, tactics and territory,* p. 11

21 Baker, 'Changing attitudes towards government', pp. 216–7

22 HyC, IV: 24G, *Aiton, 29 Aug. 1785

23 Carter, *Sheep and wool correspondence,* p. 108, *Eden, 20 Mar. 1787

24 HMC, Fortescue, II, Auckland to Lord Grenville, 6 Nov. 1791

25 BUL, Withering 5/170, *C. Wilkins, 2 Dec. 1794 (copy at DTC, 9: 130–1)

26 Dupree, *Sir Joseph Banks*

CHAPTER TWO   THE ROYAL SOCIETY AND THE EMERGENCE OF SCIENCE AS AN INSTRUMENT OF STATE POLICY

1 Bacon, *The new organon* . . .

2 Rossi, *Francis Bacon,* pp. 26–8

3 Martin, *Francis Bacon,* pp. 164–5

4 Hill, *Intellectual origins,* p. 99

5 Webster, *The Great Instauration*

6 Jones, *Country and court,* p. 57

7 Hunter, *Science and society,* pp. 71, 130 and Hunter, 'The Crown, the public and the new science, 1689–1702'

8 Tomlinson, 'Financial and administrative developments'

9 On whom see Willmoth, *Sir Jonas Moore*

10 Hunter, *Science and society,* pp. 94, 97–8 and 'Espinasse, 'The decline and fall', p. 350

11 Houghton, 'The English virtuoso', p. 54

12 McClellan, *Science reorganized,* p. 26

13 Hahn, *The anatomy,* pp. 66–7 and Gillispie, *Science and polity,* p. 340

14 Hunter, *Science and society,* pp. 128–9, 190

15 Westfall, *Never at rest,* pp. 834–5

16 Williams, *The Whig supremacy,* p. 381

17 BL, Add. 38223: 273–4, *C. Jenkinson, 18 Nov. 1788; Mackay, 'A presiding genius of exploration', p. 37

18 Salomon, *Science and politics,* p. 8

19 Y, *[Lord Macartney], 22 Jan. 1792

20 Dupree, 'Nationalism and science'

21 'His Majesty's Ministre des Affaires Philosophiques' was Auckland's facetious term, HMC Fortescue, II, p. 225, Lord Auckland to Lord Grenville, 6 Nov. 1791

22 Carter, *Sir Joseph Banks,* p. 538

23 Beaglehole, *Journals of Captain James Cook,* I, p. cclxxxii

24 Woolf, *The transits of Venus,* pp. 83, 166

25 RS, CMO VI: 189, John Boddington, Office of Ordnance, to Dr Matthew Maty, Secretary of the Royal Society, 24 Aug. 1773; RS, CMO VI: 144

26 Lyte, *Sir Joseph Banks,* pp. 202–3

27 McClellan, *Science reorganized,* pp. 30–1

28 On which see Widmalm, 'Accuracy, rhetoric, and technology: the Paris–Greenwich triangulation, 1784–88'

29 Carter, *Sir Joseph Banks*, pp. 203–4, 133

30 Roy, 'An account of the measurement of a base line on Hounslow Heath', p. 385. See also Roy, 'An account of the trigonometrical operation', for a further description of this project

31 Miller, 'The revival', p. 116

32 Close, *The early years of the Ordnance Survey*, pp. 32–43, 62–3

33 RS, CMO IX: 54–66, 24 Feb. 1814

34 BL, Add. 56298: 3, Lennox, 4 Jan. 1783; RS, Misc. MS 4: 30, 34–6 and RS, CMO VIII: 190, 218–9, 224–6

35 Blagden, 'Report on the best method of proportioning the excise upon spiritous liquors', p. 321

36 SL, SC 1: 41, Ramsden, 14 Nov. 1792; SC 1: 55, T. Barton (Excise Office), 1 Apr. 1794 and SC 1: 65, T. Barton, 20 Jan. 1797

37 SL, SC 1: 19, *Victualling Office, 29 Mar. 1809

38 Its chief advocate within the Society was Daines Barrington RS, CMO, VI: 212, 17 Feb. 1774. ESRO, E2/22/1, Barrington to Ashby, 25 Jul. 1774. On which see Fry, *Alexander Dalrymple*, pp. 188–9

39 ML, MSS 743/3, *Blagden, 2 Apr. 1818 and Y, *Blagden, 25 Apr. 1818

40 RS, CMO IX: 139, 141, Admiralty, 20 Nov. 1817. On the expedition of 1773 which was also largely prompted by Barrington see RS, CMO 6: 158, 19 Jan. 1773. Also Williams, *The British search*, pp. 164–5

41 SL, WM 1: 14, Lord Sidmouth, 22 Mar. 1817

42 See, for example, Banks's notes from 1792 on the different systems of English measures LAO, Cragg 2/30: 34–6. A pamphlet from the same period, entitled *An attempt to establish throughout His Majesty's domains an universal weight and measure* (1794) by William Martin, remarks in its preface that 'The difficulties and perplexities which continually arise to men of Trade and Commerce, from the variety of Weights and Measures used in different parts of England, are so well known from experience, that little apology is required for attempting to remove them' (p. iv)

43 BL, Add. 8099: 140 v, A. S. Leblond, 30 Jan. 1802

44 As expressed in his 'Advantages of decimal arithmetic', ML 80/2: 319ff (Copy at DTC, 15: 331–7)

45 BL, Add. 33981: 22, C. Grant, 19 Apr. 1802

46 Y, *Blagden, 31 Mar. [1817]

47 Banks et al., 'First report of the commissioners to consider the subjects of weights and measures', p. 316

48 Connor, *The weights and measures of England*, p. 256 and Hoppit, 'Reforming Britain's weights and measures, 1660–1824', p. 104

49 Zupko, *Revolution in measurement*, p. 178

50 See, for example, a letter to this effect from Boddington of the Board of Ordnance to Maty, Secretary of the Royal Society, RS, Misc. 4/86, 19 Jan. 1774. Banks made similar points about the role of the Board of Longitude in RGO, 35, 66, *Maskelyne, [3 May 1797]

51 Fitz, Blagden, [27 Dec. 1783]. In this letter Blagden informed Banks that 'Maskelyne also has been canvassing against you as President'.

52 [Gregory], 'A review of some leading points', p. 246

53 Hall, *All scientists now*, p. 10

54 BL, 52281: 102, Perceval, 10 Feb. 1811

55 RS, CMO IX: 117, 7 Nov. 1816

56 Y, Blagden, Mar. 1818. On the significance of the act see Miller, 'The Royal Society of London 1800–1835', p. 313

57 Barrow, *Sketches of the Royal Society*, p. 62

58 McClellan, *Science reorganized*, p. 34

59 Kew, BC 3.3, *Graf von Josef Windisch-Gratz, 2 Jun. 1785
60 Home, *Hunterian oration*, p. 32
61 RS, B. 68, *Blagden, 29 May 1818
62 ANL, MS 9(101), Kirwan, 9 Apr. 1797 (Copy at DTC, 10(1): 119–21)
63 BL, Warren Dawson MS 2: 23, *?, c.1781
64 RS, CMO IX: 331–2, 28 Mar. 1822, Council of the Royal Society to Lords Commissioners of the Treasury
65 Alter, *The reluctant patron*, p. 208
66 Gillispie, *Science and polity*, p. x
67 Rappaport, 'Government patronage of science'
68 DTC, 11: 17–8, *Dupont de Nemours, 18 Jul. [1798]

CHAPTER THREE   THE LEVERS OF POWER

1   HMC Fortescue, II, p. 225, Lord Auckland to Lord Grenville, 6 Nov. 1791
2   Duncan, *A short account*, p. 9
3   NMM. 41/80, * Sandwich, 1 Sep. 1775
4   Cannon, *The letters*, I, p. 338, W. Jones to Viscount Althorp, 13 Jan. 1780
5   Rodgers, *The insatiable earl*, pp. 126–93
6   Brougham, *Lives of the philosophers*, II, p. 345 and Barrow, *Sketches*, p. 18
7   Anon, 'The Right Honourable Sir Joseph Banks', p. 99
8   Fortescue, *Correspondence of George III*, II, p. 351
9   *ibid.*, p. 348, Sandwich to Lord North, 8 Jun. 1772
10 Beaglehole, *Endeavour journal of Banks*, II, p. 335
11 *ibid.*, II, p. 355, Sandwich's draft reply to Banks submitted to the George III, 22 Jun. [1772]
12 Rodgers, *The insatiable earl*, p. 92 and Sutherland, *The East India Company*, p. 124
13 Rauschenberg, 'Banks's voyage to Iceland', p. 197
14 Cuvier, 'Historical éloge', p. 4
15 Fortescue, *Correspondence of George III*, IV, p. 119, Sandwich to George III, 16 Jul. 1774
16 Ellis, *A description of the mangostan and the breadfruit*, p. iii
17 YB: OS, C. Burney to Sandwich, 22 Nov. 1778
18 DTC, 1: 236, Sandwich, 3 Dec. 1778
19 Cust, *History of the Society of Dilettanti*, p. 35
20 Sprigge, *Correspondence*, II, p. 244, Jeremy to Samuel Bentham, 2 Mar. 1779
21 BL, Add. 33977: 103v, Matra, 3 Jul. 1779
22 NMM, F14: 65, *Sandwich, 18 May 1778
23 APL, *Kippis, 15 Aug. 1795 (Copy at DTC, 9: 282–3)
24 DTC, 1: 300, Sandwich, 10 Oct. 1780
25 ANL, MS 7218/1, Hawkesworth to Sandwich, 19 Nov. 1771
26 DTC, 2: 188–9, Sandwich, 21 Sep. 1782
27 Kippis, *A narrative of the voyages*, p. ix
28 RS, CMO VI: 191, 11 Nov. 1773
29 *HRNSW*, II, p. 9
30 Listed in the *DNB* as 'Yonge'
31 Atkinson, 'Whigs and Tories and Botany Bay', p. 294
32 Namier, *The structure of politics*, pp. 286–7
33 Fortescue, *The correspondence of George III*, IV, p. 433, George III to Sandwich, 13 Sep. 1779
34 Rodgers, *The insatiable earl*, pp. 292, 297–9
35 ANL, 7218: 2, Barrington to Sandwich, 13 Dec. 1779
36 See correspondence between Sandwich and Barrington on this subject calendared in *National Register of Archives Report* 5472, p. 36
37 Farnsworth, 'A history of Revesby Abbey', pp. 111–2
38 Y, Stephenson, 21 Mar. 1768

39 Y, Phipps, 21 Mar. 1768
40 Phipps, *A letter*, p. 3
41 Namier and Brooke, *House of Commons*, II, p. 277
42 *ibid.*
43 Banks later wrote of Blagden that he 'quitted me for some time & attached himself more to Ld M[ulgrave] whom he met at my house, than to me'. BL Add. 33272: 80, *Blagden, 15 Apr. 1790
44 RS, Blagden Corr., Box M–P. no. 27, Phipps to Blagden, 28 Sep. 1774
45 NMM, 41/79, *Sandwich, 25 Aug. 1775
46 NMM, 41/80, *Sandwich, 1 Sep. 1775
47 NMM, 41/84, *Sandwich, 19 Sep. 1775
48 SGC, 6/5, Memorandum by Banks on the Boston election of 1784 and *ibid.*, *?, 3 Jul. [17]84
49 Namier and Brooke, *House of Commons*, II, pp. 227–8 and Wheatley, *Historical . . . memoirs of Sir N. W. Wraxall*, II, p. 173
50 Phipps, *A voyage*, p. 12
51 Mackay, *In the wake of Cook*, p. 62
52 PRO, HO 42/11: 210, *Phipps, 30 Mar. 1787
53 Steven, *Trade, tactics and territory*, p. 114
54 DTC, 7: 169, Phipps, 19 Oct. 1790
55 NMM, Petrie MS no. 13, *Mrs Flinders, 19 Jul. 1808
56 DTC, 17: 211, *Bligh, 25 Aug. 1808
57 RS, Misc MS, 1.37, Banks's notes on disputes within the Royal Society about Dr Hutton, 8 Jan. 1784
58 [Gregory], 'A review', p. 172
59 BL, Add. 52281: 135, *Reeves, 7 Dec. 1814
60 Brougham, *Lives of the philosophers*, II, pp. 374–5
61 Bladon, *Diaries of . . . Robert Fulke Greville*, p. 72
62 Lubbock, *Herschel chronicle*, pp. 112–3, 120–1
63 RAS, MSS Herschel, W.1/13.B.5, *Herschel, 28 Aug. 1782
64 Banks, 'A speech delivered to the Royal Society', p. 4
65 BL, Egerton MS 2641: 145–6. *Hamilton, 28 Nov. 1788
66 Bladon, *Diaries . . . of Robert Fulke Greville*, p. 209
67 Y, Young, 1 Jul. 1799
68 Aspinall, *Later correspondence of George III*, III, p. 306, George III, 25 Dec. 1799
69 Roth., S192.27, *R. Jenkinson, 13 Sept. 1802 (DTC, 13: 252–3)
70 BL, Add. 33981: 104, *East India Company [John Roberts, Chairman], 28 Apr. 1803
71 Lodge, *Portraits of illustrious personages*, 'Sir Joseph Banks', XII, p. 9
72 BL, Add. 33981: 124–5, R. Pearson, 8 Aug. 1803
73 BL, Add. 42072: 73–3, *Greville, 13 Aug. 1805
74 Y, *Sheffield, 14 Sep. 1806
75 Carter, *Sheep and wool*, p. 443, *Greville, 20 Aug. 1805
76 DTC, 20: 36–7, *Home, 24 Sep. 1817
77 DTC, 16: 299, *East India Company, 2 Aug. 1806
78 Beaglehole, *Endeavour journal of Banks*, I, p. 3
79 Lysaght, *Joseph Banks in Newfoundland*, p. 265
80 DTC, 2: 97, *Hasted, [Feb. 1782]
81 Farnsworth, 'A history of Revesby Abbey', pp. 114, 116–7
82 BM (NH), Entymological Library, Dru Drury Letterbook, Drury to Pallas, 11 Apr. 1768
83 Y: OF, Banks's speech on accepting the presidency of the Royal Society, 12 Dec. 1778
84 De Beer, *The sciences*, p. 28
85 *HRNSW*, I, ii, p. 239
86 LAO, Hawley 6/3/2, *Henry Hawley, 9 Oct. 1794
87 ANL, MS 9/128, *J. B. Perrin, 23 Aug. 1798
88 DTC, 11: 17–8. *Dupont de Nemours, 18 Jul. [1798]

89   YB: OF, *Dundas, 5 Apr. 1794
90   Carter, 'Sir Joseph Banks and the plant collection', p. 303, *Hawley, 6 Jul. 1795
91   NYPL, MS Division, Myers Coll. 2285, *Brougham, 21 Jul. [1799]
92   RS, B: 20, *Blagden, 15 Oct. 1783
93   Farnsworth, 'A history of Revesby Abbey', p. 295, *Bertier, 17 Jun. 1788
94   Carter, 'Sir Joseph Banks and the plant collection', p. 347
95   BL, Add. 38233: 273–4, *Jenkinson, 18 Nov. 1788
96   YB: OF, *?, 18 Jan. 1814
97   Hunter, *Science and society*, p. 135
98   Pares, *King George III and the politicians*, p. 173
99   SGC, 6/5, *?, [1784]
100 NMM, GAB 2 (MS 9997), *?, 20 Nov. 1788
101 Farnsworth, 'A history of Revesby Abbey', p. 133
102 Well., MS 5215: 6, * Rose, 11 Feb. 1794
103 BL, Egerton MS 2641: 153–4, *Hamilton, 10 Aug. 1794
104 YB: OF, *Dundas, 5 Apr. 1794
105 Thorne, *House of Commons*, II, p. 243
106 Farnsworth, 'A history of Revesby Abbey', p. 123
107 Banks, 'Instruction', p. 490
108 SL, Co 6: 31, *Liverpool, 10 Jun. 1798
109 Kew BC, 2: 191, Hawkesbury, 22 Feb. 1798 (Also at DTC, 10(2): 226–7)
110 BAO, 84, *Boulton, 2 Dec. 1799
111 BL, Add. 38234: 97–8, *Jenkinson, 6 Jul. 1800
112 ML, Banks MSS, Vol. 16: 214–6
113 Y, *Parkinson, [16 Feb.] 1801
114 BAO, 119, *Boulton, 1 May 1804
115 YB: OF, 10/20, *Jenkinson, 20 May 1804
116 Roth., S192.7.25 LS, Jenkinson [2 Jun. 1804]
117 BAO, 136, *Boulton, 12 Apr. 1805 (Also at DTC, 15: 271–3)
118 NLW, MS 12415.F.57, *Lloyd, 30 Apr. 1807
119 HRO, *Knight, 9 May 1807
120 *HRNSW*, VI, p. 187, *King, 20 Sep. 1806
121 LAO, Hill MS 22/8/8/1, *Heron, 17 Dec. 1806
122 PRO, HO 42/118: 118–9, *?, 25 Dec. 1811
123 Y, Banks Papers 58, ser. 1, Box 14, *Sheffield, 13 Mar. [1815]
124 Farnsworth, 'A history of Revesby Abbey', p. 127
125 DTC, 20: 102–4, *Knight, 30 Jun. 1818 (Original at HRO)
126 DTC, 20: 99–101, *Knight, 20 Jun. 1818 (Original at HRO)
127 RS, B: 85, *Blagden, 7 Dec. 1819
128 RS, B: 86, *Blagden, 20 Dec. 1819
129 C[harles] H[atchett], Banksiana written at the Request of my friend Dawson Turner
     Esq of great Yarmouth (copy in Banks Archives Office, BM(NH))
130 DTC, 20: 98, *Dillwyn, 6 May 1818
131 Brougham, *Lives of the philosophers*, p. 368
132 Gee, 'Charles Jenkinson as Secretary at War', p. 70
133 Brooke, 'Charles Jenkinson' in Namier and Brooke, *House of Commons 1754–90*, II,
     p. 675
134 Wickwire, 'King's friends'; Sutherland, *The East India Company*, p. 238 and Ehrman,
     British goverment and commercial negotiations, pp. 35–6
135 Cawthorne, *An hasty sketch*, p. 8
136 Ehrman, *The younger Pitt*, I, p. 41
137 Jenkinson to Mackay, 5 Feb. 1780, Gee, 'Charles Jenkinson as Secretary at War',
     p. 84
138 Gee, 'The British War Office', p. 124
139 O'Gorman, *The rise of party*, p. 618 and Pares, *George III and the politicians*, p. 172
140 Sutherland, *The East India Company*, p. 137

141 Ehrman, *The younger Pitt*, I, p. 332
142 Black, *British foreign policy*, p. 478, Mitchell to Hawkesbury, 1 Jan. 1791
143 Aspinall, *Later correspondence of George III*, V, p. 160, George III to Lord Hawkesbury, [18 Dec. 1808]
144 SL, CL 2: 87, *Hawkesbury, 21 May 1790
145 DTC, 5: 139–42, *Hawkesbury, 30 Mar. 1787 and Mackay, *In the wake of Cook*, pp. 172–3
146 RS, Misc. MSS, 6: 60, *Hawkesbury, 30 Mar. 1787
147 BL, Add. 33980: 185, *Haweis, 6 May 1799
148 Dawson, *The Banks letters*, pp. 450–626
149 BL, Add. 38310: 43, *Hawkesbury, 3 Oct. 1789
150 PRO, BT 6/246, *Hawkesbury, 16 Nov. 1789
151 BL, Add. 38324: 97–8, *Liverpool, 6 Jul. 1800
152 Roth., S192.7.27 LD, *Hawkesbury, 18 May 1804
153 DTC, 14: 274–5, *Liverpool, 2 Jun. 1804
154 BL, Add. 38255: 372–3, *Liverpool (second Earl), 14 Jan. 1814

CHAPTER FOUR   NEO-MERCANTILISM AND THE LANDED INTEREST

1 The literature on the eighteenth-century aristocracy is extensive. For a recent synthesis see Cannon, *Aristocratic century*.
2 Cain and Hopkins, 'Gentlemanly capitalism and British expansion overseas', p. 510
3 Gascoigne, *Joseph Banks and the English Enlightenment*, pp. 185–236
4 Gilpin, *France in the age of the scientific state*, p. 441
5 Judge, 'The idea', p. 45. For a critique of Judge and a defense of the view of mercantilism as a continuing tradition preceding the *Wealth of nations* for some one and a half centuries, see Rashid, 'Economics'.
6 Heckscher, *Mercantilism*, I, p. 21
7 Schaeffer, 'The entelechies', p. 83
8 Coleman, *Revisions in mercantilism*, p. 5
9 Gay, *The Enlightenment*, II, p. 347
10 Crowley, 'Neo-mercantilism and the *Wealth of nations*'
11 CL, Shelburne 48: 17 (p. 193), 'A short discourse on the present state of the colonies in America with respect to the interest of Great Britain'
12 Black, *The Association*
13 Brewer, *Sinews*, p. 200
14 Carter, *Sheep and wool*, pp. 60–1, Stephenson, 28 Jan. 1782
15 Garnier, *History of the English landed interest*, p. 191
16 Wilson, 'Newspapers and industry', p. 83
17 Perkins, *Sheep farming*, pp. 6, 22–3
18 Anon., *[Printed resolutions of] The committee of the County of Lincoln in pursuance of their instructions and from the sd co. at a public meeting holden at Lincoln . . . October 1781*, nos. 5 and 9
19 *ibid.*, no. 8
20 [Pacey], *Considerations . . .*, pp. 29, 38
21 Wilson, 'Newspapers and industry', p. 90
22 Carter, *Sheep and wool*, p. 46, Chaplin, 15 Dec. 1781
23 *ibid.*, p. 74, Chaplin, 13 Apr. [1782]
24 On the divisions within the embryonic 'landed interest' see Langford, *Public life*, p. 326
25 Black, *The Association*
26 Carter, *Sheep and wool*, p. 66, Chaplin, 7 Feb. 1782
27 Wilson, 'Newspapers and industry', p. 100
28 Young, 'On the necessity', pp. 402–3, 405
29 Gazley, *Arthur Young*, p. 217, BL, Add. 35126: 418, *Young, 13 May 1788

30 Betham-Edwards, *Autobiography of Arthur Young*, p. 163
31 Carter, *Sheep and wool*, p. 95, Young, 7 Dec. 1786
32 *ibid.*, p. 88, Sheffield, 8 Oct. 1786
33 Y, Sheffield, 28 Nov. 1786
34 Carter, *Sheep and wool*, p. 94, Sheffield, 1 Dec. 1786
35 BL, Add. 35126: 405, Sheffield to Young, 9 Oct. 1787
36 Carter, *Sheep and wool*, p. 143, Young, 22 Feb. [1788]
37 LAO, Tyr 4/1/139, John Bourne to ?, 28 Oct. 1786
38 Carter, *Sheep and wool*, p. 112, Sheffield, 8 Jun. 1787
39 J[oseph] B[anks], 'Instructions given to the Council [Counsel] against the Wool Bill'
40 Carter, *Sheep and wool*, p. 154, *Hawkesbury, 21 Jun. 1788
41 Y, Shepherd, 20 Jun. 1788
42 Langford, *Public life*, p. 326
43 Y, Shepherd, 20 Jun. 1788
44 Y, Stephenson, 5 May 1788
45 Carter, *His Majesty's Spanish flock*, p. 43
46 Though probably written by G. Chalmers in association with him. Carter, *Banks. A guide*, p. 133
47 Carter, *Sheep and wool*, p. 58, Pacey, 21 Jan. 1782
48 Smith, *Wealth of nations*, pp. 281–2
49 Young, 'On the necessity', pp. 402–3
50 Gazley, *Arthur Young*, p. 164
51 Wilson, 'Newspapers and industry', p. 88
52 Holroyd (Lord Sheffield), 'On the trade in wool', p. 389
53 Langford, *Polite and commercial people*, p. 446
54 Barnes, *History of the English Corn Laws*, pp. 60, 55
55 Gazley, *Arthur Young*, p. 264
56 *ibid.*, pp. 262
57 SL, CL 1: 18, Notes on the 'Structure of the present Corn Laws'
58 SL, CL 1: 38, Linton, *Linton, 21 Nov. 1789
59 SL, CL 2: 64, Sheffield, 3 Apr. 1790
60 LUL, AL 60/3, Sheffield, 16 Apr. 1790
61 Holroyd, *Remarks on the Bill*, pp. 4, 78
62 SL, CL 2: 86, Linton, 26 Feb.1791
63 SL, CL 2: 87, *Liverpool, 21 May 1790
64 BL, Add. 35127: 80–1, *Young, 15 Jan. 1791
65 Sinclair, *Address . . . on the Corn Bill*, p. 4
66 Barnes, *History of the English Corn Laws*, pp. 61, 93
67 Carter, *Sheep and wool*, p. 202, Sinclair, 16 May 1791
68 NLS, Adv. MS 21.1.12: 5, *Chalmers, 18 May 1791
69 Roth., S192.7.12, *Liverpool, 27 Feb. 1799
70 Holroyd (Lord Sheffield), *Remarks on the deficiency of grain*, p. 151
71 Roth., S192.7.14, Liverpool, 7 Sep. 1800
72 Roth., S192.6, *Carrington, 3 Feb. 1801
73 Banks, 'Communications on spring wheat', pp. 342–2
74 WSRO, Petworth House Archives, 69, Sheffield to George, third Earl of Egremont, 29 Dec. 1813
75 BL, Add. 35132: 7–8, Sheffield to Young, 20 Jun. 1814
76 Holroyd (Lord Sheffield), *A letter*, pp. 53–4
77 Sinclair, *Thoughts*, p. 13
78 LUL, [355], *Second Earl of Liverpool, 10 Feb. 1815
79 LS, Smith MSS 1.158, *J. E. Smith, 18 Mar. 1815
80 BL, Add. 33982: 160, *T. Banks, 9 Sep. 1818
81 BL, Add. 35133: 467, Sheffield to Young, 28 Dec. 1819
82 WSRO, Petworth Ho. 69, Sheffield to George, third Earl of Egremont, 2 Feb. 1820

83 Smith, *Wealth of nations*, pp. 192–3, 196–7
84 *ibid.*, pp. 196–7
85 DTC, 6: 280–1, Smith, 18 Dec. 1789
86 Gazley, *Arthur Young*, p. 165
87 Smith, *Wealth of nations*, p. 196
88 BL, Add. 56,299: 66, Banks, Memorandum on the economic condition of the country, 1799
89 Crowley, 'Neo-mercantilism', p. 357
90 Roth., S192.7.114, Liverpool, 7 Sep. 1800
91 BL, Add. 38234: 164, *Liverpool, 28 Sep. [1800]
92 [Dalrymple], *Thoughts*, p. 4
93 Heron, *Sketch*, pp. 7, 9
94 [Young], *An examination*, p. 18
95 Roth., S192.7.17, Liverpool, 5 Oct. 1800
96 DTC, 18: 53, *?, 12 Aug. 1810
97 Bayly, *Imperial meridian*, p. 80
98 *ibid.*
99 Harlow, *The founding*, I, p. 4
100 *ibid.*, II, p. 792
101 In his recent work, *The privileges of independence. Neomercantilism and the American Revolution* (1993), Crowley emphasises the importance of Sheffield and Jenkinson in shaping imperial policy in the aftermath of the American Revolution. He characterises their outlook as 'neomercantilists who combined economic liberalism with economic nationalism' (p. 77). Though this is not altogether inconsistent with my analysis – since where possible such neo-mercantilists paid at least lip-service to economic liberalism – I would argue that in economic matters their nationalism very much overshadowed their liberalism.
102 Fergusson, 'The colonial policy', p. 412
103 Graham, *British policy and Canada*, p. 61
104 Harlow, *The founding*, I, pp. 440–1
105 Graham, *British policy and Canada*, p. 59
106 Holroyd (Lord Sheffield), *Observations on the commerce*, p. 1
107 Holroyd (Lord Sheffield), *Observations on the manufactures*, p. 86
108 Carter, *Sheep and wool*, p. 83, Holroyd, 6 Nov. 1785
109 Holroyd (Lord Sheffield), *Strictures*, p. [i]
110 Crowley, 'Neo-mercantilism and the *Wealth of nations*', p. 347
111 Holroyd (Lord Sheffield), *Strictures*, p. 230
112 *ibid.*, p. 61
113 Ehrman, *Commerical negotiations*, p. 184
114 Holroyd (Lord Sheffield), *Strictures*, p. 3
115 *ibid.*, p. vii
116 Holroyd (Lord Sheffield), *Remarks on the bill*, p. 61
117 *ibid.*, p. 59
118 Holroyd (Lord Sheffield), *Remarks on the deficiency of grain*, pp. 151–2
119 BL, Add. 33,030: 464–5, Lord Sheffield, 'Memorial regarding the West Indies' [?1802]
120 For Banks's views on slavery see Gascoigne, *Banks and the English Enlightenment*, pp. 39–44
121 CL, Sheffield Papers, 4 Mar. 1807, R. Millington to Sheffield
122 Fergusson, 'The colonial policy', pp. 68–9
123 Fieldhouse, 'British imperialism', p. 41
124 Bellot, *William Knox*, p. 193
125 CL, Knox 7: 8, Sheffield to [W. Knox], 3 Jul. 1783
126 Fieldhouse, 'British imperialism', pp. 41–2
127 Ragatz, *The fall of the planter class*, p. 178
128 Gazley, *Arthur Young*, pp. 79–80

129 *ibid.*, p. 165
130 Davidson, 'England's commercial policy', p. 39
131 Bell, 'British commercial policy', p. 436
132 Cobbett, *Parliamentary history*, XXIII, cols 602, 604
133 Harlow, *The founding*, I, p. 599
134 Ritcheson, *Aftermath of revolution*, p. 75
135 Henderson, 'The Anglo-French commercial treaty'
136 Crowley, 'Neo-mercantilism and the *Wealth of Nations*', p. 355
137 BL, Add. 33453, Sheffield to Auckland, 17 Aug. 1794
138 Ehrman, *The younger Pitt*, I, p. 336
139 Wheatley, *The . . . memoirs of Sir N. W. Wraxall*, IV, p. 307
140 Crowley, 'Neo-mercantilism and the *Wealth of Nations*', p. 351
141 Harlow, *The founding*, I, pp. 482–3
142 Mackay, *In the wake of Cook*, pp. 57–120
143 Crowley, 'Neo-mercantilism and the *Wealth of Nations*', p. 351
144 Jenkinson, *A collection of all the treaties of peace, alliance and commerce*, I, p. iii
145 Ehrman, *The younger Pitt*, I, p. 340
146 Harlow, *The founding*, II, pp. 266–8, 273
147 Cobbett, *Parliamentary history*, XXV, col. 1373
148 Hiller, 'The Newfoundland fisheries', p. 15
149 It was a policy for which he had the strong support of George Chalmers, American loyalist and clerk at the Committee for Trade. Cockcroft, *George Chalmers*, pp. 93–94
150 Madden, *Imperial reconstruction*, p. 354
151 Hyam and Martin, *Reappraisals*, p. 57
152 Fergusson, 'The colonial policy', pp. 43–4
153 BL, Add. 38219: 289, Sheffield to Hawkesbury, 27 Jul. 1786
154 Fergusson, 'The colonial policy', p. 445
155 Holroyd (Lord Sheffield), *Strictures on the necessity*, p. [1], 3
156 Ehrman, *The younger Pitt*, II, p. 513 and Mackay, 'Direction and purpose', p. 499
157 BL, Add. 38230: 308v, Sheffield to Hawkesbury, 13 Sep. 1795
158 Fergusson, 'The colonial policy', p. 75
159 Ehrman, *The younger Pitt*, I, p. 441
160 CL, Melville papers, *Considerations on the Subject of a Treaty*, Oct. 1787
161 *ibid.*, p. 227
162 BL, Add. 38311: 84, Liverpool to Dundas, 11 Oct. 1800
163 SL, CL 2: 62, Hawkesbury, 19 May 1790 (Copy at BL, Add. 38310: 53)
164 SL, Ag 1: 100, Hawkesbury, 11 Sep. 1795
165 BL, Add. 38234: 16v, *Liverpool, 28 Sep. [1800]
166 Carter, *Sheep and wool*, p. 166, *Mar., 30 Sep. 1788
167 BL, Add. 34424: 105–6, *Eden, 25 Feb. 1787
168 Carter, *Joseph Banks*, p. 262
169 Carter, *Sheep and wool*, p. 176, Sheffield, 17 Oct. 1789
170 BL, 34435: 259–60, *Auckland, 26 Jan. 1791
171 ATL, MS 155/21, Auckland, 29 Dec. 1790
172 Holroyd (Lord Sheffield), *Strictures on the necessity of inviolably maintaining the navigation and colonial system of Great Britain*
173 Well., Banks autogr. letters, *Sheffield, 12 Mar. 1804
174 SL, NF 1: 3, Notes on Newfoundland, April 1807. See also NF 1: 4 'Crops & sowing methods best suited for Newfoundland'
175 Marshall, 'First and second British Empires', p. 23
176 Coleman, 'Adam Smith, businessmen and the mercantile system'
177 Ehrman, *The British government and commercial negotiations*, p. 180
178 Fergusson, 'The colonial policy', p. 206, Liverpool to Hobart, 15 May 1802
179 *ibid.*, p. 453
180 Harlow, *The founding*, II, pp. 1 and 792
181 Cock, *An answer to Lord Sheffield's pamphlet*, p. 29

182 Cookson, 'Political arithmetic', p. 51
183 Eastwood, *Governing rural England*

CHAPTER FIVE SCIENCE IN THE SERVICE OF THE STATE

1 ANL, MS 9 (Banks MSS), Kirwan, 9 Apr. 1797
2 BL, Add. 33,980: 185, *Haweis, 6 May 1799
3 For a detailed account of which see Mackay, *In the wake of Cook*, pp. 123–143
4 PRO, BT 6/246, *Jenkinson, 25 Aug. 1787; Y, William Frodsham to William Fawkener (Clerk to the Board), 20 Sep. 1787
5 Y, Frodsham to Banks, 20 Oct. 1787
6 Well., MS 5219, Fawkener to Hove, 2 Apr. 1787
7 BL, Add. 38,310: 43, Jenkinson, 3 Oct. 1789. For a detailed account of Hove's expedition and Banks's involvement with the growing of cotton see Mackay, *In the wake of Cook*, pp. 144–167
8 Edwards, *The growth*, p. 79
9 Mackay, *In the wake of Cook*, p. 164
10 SL, Tea 1: 2, Jenkinson, 1788
11 SL, Tea 1: 10, Jul. 1789, figures on teas imports 'as Ld. Sheffield informs me'
12 DTC, 6: 103–11, *Devaynes (Chairman, EIC), 27 Dec. 1788; Carter, *Joseph Banks*, pp. 171–3; Mackay, *In the wake of Cook*, pp. 181–2
13 SL, Tea 1: 2, *Jenkinson, 1788; BL, Add. 38223: 201–2, *Jenkinson, 29 Sep. 1788
14 Banks, 'Proceedings', pp. 406–613 and Lambert, *House of Commons sessional papers*, Vol. 75, pp. 1–61
15 BL, Add. 38224: 33–36, *Jenkinson, 2 Mar. 1789
16 SL, Ag 1: 80, Fawkener (Clerk to the PC), 29 Jan. 1795
17 SL, Ag 1: 86, 'The crop of 1794 . . .', ?2 Feb. 1795
18 Stearn, 'The bread crisis', p. 181
19 SL, Ag 1: 95, Jenkinson, 20 Aug. 1795
20 SL, Ag 1: 97, *Jenkinson, Aug. 1795 (draft)
21 SL, Ag 1: 100, Jenkinson, 11 Sep. 1795
22 Aspinall, *The later correspondence of George III*, II, pp. 399–400, Duke of Portland to George III, 3 Sep. 1795, George III to Duke of Portland, 4 Sep. 1795
23 Barnes, *History of the Corn Laws*, p. 74
24 CLL, Hill Coll. 6: 3, Jenkinson, 12 Aug. 1804 (Copy at DTC, 6: 3)
25 BL, Add. 38234: 130–1, *Jenkinson, 15 Aug. 1800
26 SL, Ag 3: 70, Banks, 'Notes on the effects of manufacturing interests on the price of corn during times of short supplyes'
27 *Y, Sheffield, 13 Mar. [1815]
28 DTC, 9: 4, *Jenkinson, 13 Feb. 1794
29 ML, MS 743/2, *Jenkinson, 17 Mar. 1795 (Copy at DTC, 9: 5–6)
30 BL, Add. 33,980: 5–8, Blagden to Jenkinson, 20 Mar. 1795
31 Farnsworth, 'A history of Revesby Abbey', p. 199
32 PRO, Adm. 1.4377, *Naval Commissioners, 31 Jan. 1801
33 Kumar, 'The evolution of colonial science in India', p. 55
34 PRO, BT 5/12: 131–2, 14 Jan. 1801
35 PRO, BT 5/12: 148, 21 Mar. 1801
36 BL, Add. 33980: 308, Helenus Scott (physician in employ of the EIC), 15 Aug. 1801
37 Kew, BC 4: 58–60, *Court of Directors, Jan. 1803. This report was then transmitted to Bengal with the annotation 'We transmit Copy of a Letter from the Right Honorable Sir Joseph Banks Bar. on the cultivation of hemp', IO, Home Misc Ser., Vol. 375: 633, 22 Apr. 1803
38 PRO, BT 5/13: 153, 31 Jan. 1803
39 Frost, *Matra*, p. 111
40 Frost, *Dreams of a Pacific empire*, p. 12

41 PRO, BT 5/16: 80, 21 May 1806

42 Carter, *Sheep and wool*, p. 404, *Fawkener (Clerk to the Privy Council), [Sep. 1803]

43 PRO, BT 5/14: 113, 19 Mar. 1804

44 *HRNSW*, 6: 187, *King, 20 Sep. 1806

45 Carter, *Joseph Banks*, pp. 488–9

46 Carter, *Sheep and wool*, p. 306, *Bathurst, 20 Aug. 1798

47 DTC, 17: 306–10, Bathurst, 30 May 1809, Jun. 1809, *Bathurst, 10 Jun. 1809

48 On which see below Chapter 7

49 PRO, BT 5/19: 311, 20 Nov. 1809

50 Jenkinson, *The coins of the realm* (1805)

51 SL, PC 1: 2, 29 Mar. 1797

52 Craig, *The mint*, pp. 226–7

53 Roth., S192.7.2, *Jenkinson, 26 Aug.–3 Sep. 1797

54 Craig, *The mint*, pp. 263–4

55 DTC, 6: 209–12, Boulton, 26 Jun. 1789

56 BL, Add. MS 38421: 265–6, *Jenkinson, 27 Jun. 1788

57 SL, Co 5: 48–49, Cavendish, 23 Jul., 6 Aug. 1798; Weeks, 'Chemical contribution of Charles Hatchett'

58 DTC, 13: 281–83, Hatchett, 24 Oct. 1802; SL, Hp 1: 50, Jenkinson, 12 May 1801. Hatchett's paper entitled 'Experiments and observations on the various alloys, on the specific gravity, and on the comparative wear of gold. Being the substance of a report made to the Right Honourable Lords of the Committee of the Privy Council, appointed to take into consideration the state of the coins of the Kingdom, and the present establishment and constitution of His Majesty's Mint' appeared in the Royal Society's *Philosophical Transactions* in 1803 (vol. 93, pp. 43–194)

59 Craig, *Red tape*, pp. 44, 46

60 *ibid.*, p. 266

61 DTC, 11: 338, Boulton to Thomas Lack, 4 Dec. 1799

62 DTC, 10(2): 300–1, Bathurst, 24 Jun. 1798

63 Dyer and Gaspar, 'Reform, the new technology and Tower Hill', p. 472

64 DTC, 18: 199, Banks, 'Some observations relative to the present state of H. M. New Mint on Tower Hill', 7 Jan. 1813

65 RM, Record Book 20: 123, *Wellesley Pole, 21 Aug. 1818

66 SL, SS1: 1b, Nepean to Stevens, 30 Jan. 1789

67 Mackay, *In the wake of Cook*, p. 106

68 Carter, 'Joseph Banks as the Father of Australia', p. 23

69 DTC, 19: 7–15, 50–1, Nepean, 8 Apr., 10 Apr., 2 Aug. 1814

70 Thus one of the proposals for the scheme was sent by Banks to the Home Office through the good offices of his old friend, Lord Mulgrave. PRO, HO 42: 210, *Constantine Phipps, Lord Mulgrave, 30 Mar. 1787. There is also another copy at HO 42/11

71 ML, A78/4,*[Lord Chatham], 1 Sep. 1793

72 Carter, *Joseph Banks*, p. 216

73 Manning, *British colonial government*, p. 84

74 RS, Misc MSS 7: 56A, H. Parker, 22 Nov. 1786

75 Frost, 'The antipodean exchange', p. 59 and Frost, *Sir Joseph Banks and the transfer of plants*

76 *HRNSW*, 4: 348, Nepean, 28 Apr. 1801

77 PRO, Adm. 1/1800, Flinders to Nepean, 15 Mar. 1801

78 PRO, Adm. 1/9800, Lords of Admiralty instructions to Flinders, 1801

79 eg, see DTC 15: 290–1, *Marsden, 21 Feb. 1805 in which Banks queries deduction made from the salaries of the crew of the *Investigator* or RS, Misc MSS 6: 71, *Marsden, 20 Oct. 1810 which endorses Flinders's promotion

80 DTC, 1: 300, Sandwich, 10 Oct. 1780

81 Christie, *Wars and revolutions*, p. 220

82   cf their correspondence from 1809–1811 on merinos listed in Carter, *Sheep and wool*, p. 34

83   PRO, Adm. 1: 4377, *Spencer, Jan. 1801

84   SL, A 5: 32, *Glenbervie, 22 Dec. 1800

85   DTC, 9: 332, *Spencer, 11 Dec. 1795

86   BL, Add. 33,981: 271, *Navy Board, May 1808

87   Carter, *Joseph Banks*, p. 447

88   Barrow, *Sketches of the Royal Society*, p. 6

89   On the Royal Society's role in promoting and equipping this expedition see RS, CMO, IX: 145–156

90   DTC, 2: 97, Hasted, [Feb.1782]

91   DTC, 1: 304, King, [Oct. 1780]

92   Allan, 'The Society of Arts and government', p. 451

93   For more on the foundation of the Board of Agriculture and Banks's involvement therein see Gascoigne, *Banks and the English Enlightenment*, pp. 188–96

94   Mitchison, 'The old Board of Agriculture', pp. 64, 68

95   SL, CL 2: 94, Jenkinson, 16 Aug. 1800

96   Roth., S192.5, Banks to Committe of Trade, n.d.

97   For more on the foundation of the Royal Institution and Banks's involvement therein see Gascoigne, *Banks and the English Enlightenment*, pp. 216–24

98   Y, Spencer to Banks, 3 Mar. 1799

99   Berman, *The Royal Institution*, pp. xxiii–iv

100 Mitchinson, 'The old Board of Agriculture', p. 65

101 Berman, *The Royal Institution*, p. 53

102 Brockway, *Science and colonial expansion*, p. 111

103 Banks, however, never held any formal postion at Kew. Desmond, 'Transformation of the Royal Gardens', p. 106

104 SL, J 1: 22, *Dancer, 17 Dec. 1794

105 Cannon, *Letters of Sir William Jones*, II, p. 775, Jones to Russell, 22 Sep. 1787. On the early history of the gardens see Banks, 'Some hints submitted to Dr Alexander Anderson towards aiding him in his plan of giving an account of the rise & progress of the Botanical Gardens at St Vincent, 16 Oct. 1798', RS, Misc. MSS, 6: 65 (Also at DTC, 11: 104–9)

106 PRO, WO 40/4, Bundle 2, Anderson to Yonge, 30 May 1785

107 SL, BG 2: 48, Lockhead, 15 Dec. 1812

108 SL, BG 2: 55, Palmerston, 13 Jun. 1813

109 SL, BG 2: 49, Lockhead, 2 Mar. 1813

110 SL, WI: 9, Palmerston, 2 Sep. 1815

111 DTC, 19: 318, Caley, 9 Nov. 1816

112 Kew, Kew Collectors. Caley 1799–1810: 61, Palmerston, 5 Dec. 1817

113 *ibid.*: 62, *Palmerston, [Dec. 1817]

114 L. Guilding, *An account of the botanic garden in the island of St Vincent*, pp. 22–3

115 SL, Bo 1: 37, Robert Jenkinson, 9 May 1811

116 SL, Bo 1: 39, Banks, 'A project for the establishment of a botanic garden in the Island of Ceylon ... with a view to an increase of the resources of that colony & an improvement of the science of botany in Europe'

117 SL, Bo 1: 41, [Note on the Ceylon Botanic Garden plan]

118 SL, Bo 1: 42, Banks, 'Proposed instructions for the Resident Superintendent & Chief Gardener of HM Royal Botanic Garden in the Island of Ceylon'

119 Desmond, *Kew*, p. 102

120 SL, BG 2: 26, Anderson, 21 Jul. 1792

121 SL, BG 1: 5, ' Sir Joseph Banks's Report on the difficulty of protecting the exotic plants cultivated in the Royal Botanical Garden at Kew' n.d.

122 G ..., *A letter to Sir Humphrey Davy*, pp. 19–20

123 DTC, 19: 56–63, *G. Harrison (assis. sec to Treasury), 1 Sep. 1814; Thiselton-Dyer, 'Historical account of Kew to 1841', p. 308, Harrison, 13 Sep. 1814

124 Carter, *Joseph Banks*, p. 476
125 SL, BG 1: 64, *Bowie, 24 Sep. 1818
126 Kew, Kew Collectors, 7: 33, Macquarie, 18 Dec. 1817; SL, BG 1: 48, *Macquarie, Jul. 1818
127 BL, Add. 56299: 35–6, *MacLean, 22 Jun. 1798
128 DTC, 19: 40–1, *Aiton, 7 Jun. 1814
129 Marshall, *Eighteenth century England*, p. 257
130 Sutherland, *The East India Company*, p. 137
131 Marshall, *Problems of empire*, p. 47
132 Christie, *Wars and revolutions*, p. 191
133 Carter, *Sheep and wool*, pp. 230, 214–5
134 Ehrman, *The younger Pitt*, I, p. 456
135 Philips, *The East India Company*, p. 5
136 Steven, *Trade, tactics and territory*, p. 11
137 *ibid.*, p. 114
138 PRO (Chatham Papers), 30/8, no. 361/93, *Dundas, 15 Jun. 1787. Also at Y and DTC, 5: 184–91 (where it is wrongly described as written to Sir George Young)
139 Parry, *Trade and dominion*, p. 401
140 SL, BG 1: 26 Apr. 1786, 'Extract by Lieutenant-Colonel Robert Kyd'
141 IO, Home Misc. Ser. MS 799: 29, Kyd to Court of Directors, 13 Apr. 1786 (copy at DTC, 5: 529–32)
142 SL, BG 2: 1, [Board of Control], Extract consultation, 16 Jun. 1786
143 PRO, Cornwallis MSS, 30/11/13, *Young, 11 Jan. 1787
144 Archer, 'India and natural history'
145 IO, E/1/86: 57a–c, *Morton, 17 Jan. 1791
146 RASB, Letters and memoranda concerning the foundation and early history of the Royal Botanic Gardens, Calcutta, *East India Company, 2 Aug. 1816
147 Desmond, *European discovery*, p. 233 and Kumar, *Science and the Raj*, p. 41
148 Anderson, *Narrative of the British embassy*, p. iii
149 Ehrman, *The younger Pitt*, I, pp. 418, 421
150 Pritchard, 'The instructions of the East India Company to Lord Macartney', pp. 391–2, Lord Macartney's First report to the East India Company, 23 Dec. 1793
151 SL, C 1: 33, 11 Dec 1815, T. Reid to [Dr Wells], 11 Dec. 1815; 27 Dec. 1815
152 SL, C 1: 34, Amherst, 11 Dec. 1815
153 ML, MSS 743/2: 210, *Amherst, 9 Dec. 1815
154 Clarke, *Narrative of a journey in the interior of China*, p. vi.
155 Atkinson, 'Whigs and Tories', p. 292
156 BL, Add. 33,978: 9, Morton, 13 Apr. 1785
157 SL, Hp 1: 46, Roxburgh, 26 Dec. 1803
158 SL, Hp 1: 30, *EIC, 20 Nov. 1810; Hp 1: 33 William Ramsey, 21 Mar. 1811
159 IO, E1/180, *EIC, 22 Feb. 1787 (also at Y)
160 DTC, 6: 103–11, *Devaynes (Chairman of the EIC), 27 Dec. 1788
161 Kew, BC 1: 343, N. Smith, 27 Apr. 1789
162 Parry, *Trade and dominion*, p. 382
163 BL, Add. 33,980: 159–60, *Roxburgh, 9 Aug. 1798
164 IO, Misc. Lett. Rec. 86: 200–200a, *[Thomas Martin], 28 Feb. 1791
165 SL, EI, 1: 2, Kyd, 9 Feb. 1792
166 Anderson, *Letters to Sir Joseph Banks*, p. 28, John Cox to James Anderson (Physician-General at Madras), 27 Nov. 1787
167 Carter, *Joseph Banks*, p. 274
168 Kew, BC 1: 321, Young, 18 Sep. 1788
169 Carter, *Joseph Banks*, p. 275
170 Anderson, *Letters to Sir Joseph Banks*, p. 2, East India Company, 10 Apr. 1788
171 SL, En 1: 61, 'Private memorandum' re cochineal, 1792; SL, En 1: 60, *?, 21 Aug. 1792
172 SL, En 1: 14, *Ingles, 18 Aug. 1796

173 Berman, *The Royal Institution*, p. 88. On this episode see also Gascoigne, *Banks and the English Enlightenment*, pp. 220–21
174 SL, Bo 1: 13, *F. Robson, 25 May 1796
175 Philips, *The East India Company*, p. 80
176 SL, Co 5: 55, Jenkinson, 1 Sep. 1798
177 Archer, 'India and natural history'; Mackay, *In the wake of Cook*, pp. 176–89
178 SL, LMS 1: 19, Haweis, 3 Mar. 1800
179 ML, A79/4: 187, *Flinders, 1 May 1801
180 BL, Add. 33.981: 91, *Bosanquet (Director of the EIC), 8 Apr. 1803; Carter, *Joseph Banks*, p. 406
181 Woodward, *The age of reform*, p. 388; Keay, *The Honourable Company*, p. 393

CHAPTER SIX   SCIENCE IN THE SERVICE OF THE REPUBLIC OF LETTERS

1   Brougham, *Lives of the philosophers*, II, p. 378
2   DTC, 15: 338, *Chenevix , 22 Mar. 1805
3   Carter, *Sheep and wool*, p. 147, *Eden, 11 May 1787
4   BL, Add. 56301(1), Van Marum, 5 May 1789
5   BL, Add. 8099: 395, Van Beeck Calkuen, Feb. 1801
6   Barnes, *Le Clerc et la République des Lettres*
7   Daston, 'Nationalism and scientific neutrality', p. 108
8   Schlereth, *Cosmopolitan ideal*, p. xi; Venturi, *Italy and the Enlightenment*, pp. 18–9
9   Hampson, *The Enlightenment*, p. 155
10 Goldgar, *Impolite learning*, p. 239
11 Anon., 'Memoir of Sir Joseph Banks', p. 193
12 Anon., 'Obituary. Sir Joseph Banks', p. 90
13 Goodman, *The Republic of Letters*, p. 21
14 Schlereth, *Cosmopolitan ideal*, pp. 47–8.
15 Daston, 'Ideal and reality in the Republic of Letters', p. 380
16 *ibid.*, p. 367
17 Carter, *Sir Joseph Banks*, pp. 585–6
18 Hindle, *Pursuit of science*, p. 220
19 Cohen, *Franklin and Newton*, p. 108
20 BL, Add. 8095: 81, Franklin, 9 Sep. 1782
21 BL, Add. 8095: 176, Franklin, 27 Jul. 1783
22 Dupree, 'Nationalism and science', p. 38
23 Gillispie, *Science and polity*, p. x
24 Fitz., Blagden, 18 Jul. 1783
25 Fitz, Blagden, 1 Jul. 1783
26 YB: OS, Blagden to M. Le Roy, 2 Nov. 1784
27 BL, Add. 8096: 502–3, Leroy, 14 Aug. 1787. On the relations between the Royal Society and the Académie des Sciences during the eighteenth century see Bernal, 'Les rapports scientifiques'
28 DTC, 5: 27, *Condorcet, [15 Mar. 1786]
29 On which see above, pp. 24–5
30 BL, Add. 33272: 28, Blagden, 2 Jun. 1787
31 RS, CMO IX: 277, 17 Jul. 1821
32 BL, Add. 8097: 326–7, Lavoisier, 24 Jul. 1790 [French]
33 BL, Add. 8097: 432v, Tatin, Jul. 1791
34 SL, France, 1: 17, *Gallois, 3? Mar. 1793
35 PRO, Chatham 30/8, Vol. 111: 127–8, *Pitt, 17 Mar. 1797 (Printed in De Beer, 'The relations between fellows of the Royal Society and French men of science', p. 259)
36 De Beer, 'The relations between Fellows of the Royal Society and French men of science', p. 260, [*Charretié], 18 Mar. 1797
37 De Beer, *The sciences*, p. 73, Bracy Clark to James Edward Smith, 4 Dec. 1797

38 On which see Gascoigne, *Banks and the English Enlightenment*, pp. 204–5

39 Baron, *Jenner*, II, p. 167, *Jenner, 14 Dec. 1811

40 De Beer, *The sciences*, p. 242, Dolomieu, [30 Apr. 1801] [French]

41 De Beer, p. 103, *Dolomieu, 16 Jul. 1801

42 SL, France 1: 28, *Otto, 26 Jan. 1802?

43 BL, Add. 8099: 245, Faujas de St. Fond, Oct. 1802 [French]

44 Kew BC 2: 274, De Beer, 'The relations between Fellows of the Royal Society and French men of science', p. 281, [Fourcroy], 4 May 1803

45 De Beer, *The sciences*, p. 141, Milius, 3 Sep. 1804

46 Pinkerton, *Literary correspondence*, II, pp. 359–60, *Pinkerton, 5 Jun. 1807

47 Y, *Blagden, 11 May 1818

48 Dupree, *Sir Joseph Banks*

49 Kippis, *A narrative*, p. 365

50 Porter, *Gibbon*, p. 150

51 B. Franklin, Plenipotentiary for the Congress of the United States to the Court of France to all Captains and Commanders of armed Ships acting by Commission from the Congress of the United States of America, now in war with Great Britain, 10 Mar. 1779, De Beer, *The sciences*, p. 26

52 APS, *Franklin, 29 Mar. 1780

53 Weld, *A history of the Royal Society*, II, p. 141, *Franklin, 13 Aug. 1784

54 BL, Add. 8097: 216–7, Malaspina, 20 Jan. 1789 [French]

55 BL, Add. 8097: 221–2, Malaspina, 13 Jul. 1789 [French]

56 Cook, *Flood tide of empire*, pp. 118, 528

57 Kew, BC 2: 52, *Labillardière, 22 Aug. 1791

58 ATL, MS Papers 155: 19 (copy of original in NMM), *Labillardière, 9 Jun. 1796

59 Kew, BC 2: 140, *Lord Grenville, 20 Jul. 1796 (printed in De Beer, *The sciences*, p. 58–9)

60 De Beer, *The sciences*, p. 90, De Jussieu, 16 May 1800 [French]

61 De Beer, 'The relations between Fellows of the Royal Society and French men of science', p. 271, *Otto, 13 Jun. 1800

62 PRO, Adm 7/708, Flinders to Minister of the Marine of the Colonies of France, 12 Apr. 1800

63 *HRNSW*, V: 397, Flinders, 12 Jul. 1804

64 DTC, 15: 56–7, *Institut National, 22 Aug. 1804

65 Daston, 'Nationalism and scientific neutrality', p. 111

66 KAO, U951/232/46, Delambre, 5 Mar. 1805

67 De Beer, *The sciences*, p. 148, *Manning, 20 Apr. 1806

68 DL, MS Q158: 97, *Milius, 24 May 1806

69 DTC, 19: 117–8, *Hastings, 11 Jan. 1815

70 PRO, 30/11/13, *Young, 11 Jan. 1787

71 SL, BG 1: 19, *Bowie and Cunningham, 10 Jun. 1815

72 SL, Bo 1: 49, *Hamilton, 22 Apr. 1814 and Forbes, *Martinus Van Marum*, p. 146–7

73 DTC, 19: 40–1, *Aiton, 7 Jun. 1814

74 DTC, 20: 17–9, * Cunningham, 20 Feb. 1817; cited in Desmond, *Kew*, p. 102

75 ML, A82: 143, *[Roxburgh], 4 Dec. 1801

76 ATL, *Burgess, 6 May 1795

77 Carter, 'Banks and the plant collection from Kew', pp. 284–7

78 BL, Add. 33980: 148–9, *Graf von Zeppelin, 18 May 1798 and Aspinall, *Later correspondence of George III*, III: 552, Duchess of Württemberg to the King, 9 Jun. 1801

79 Princeton, General MSS (Misc), John, Archduke of Austria, 1 Dec. 1807; SL, BG 2: 76, Bathurst, 17 Jan. 1820

80 Allan, 'Notions of economic policy', p. 217

81 BCL: 15, *Boulton, [16 Feb. 1787]

82 BCL: 16, *Boulton, 10 Jun. 1787

83 BCL: 12, *Boulton, 13 Feb. 1787

84 BAO: 39, *Boulton, 20 Oct. 1795

85 DTC, 19: 85, *Dillwyn, 9 Oct. 1814
86 Dupree, 'Nationalism and science', p. 50
87 KAO, U951/Z34: 75, 'Collections on the subject of old china'; similarly BM(NH), BC: 118–9, *Manning, 25 Apr. 1810 where Banks talks of science and 'our Rivals the French'

CHAPTER SEVEN   THE EXPANSION OF EMPIRE

1 For an overview of the character of the British Empire from 1776 to 1832 see Gascoigne, 'Empire', on which some of this section draws
2 Manning, *British colonial government*, p. 484
3 On the conservative reaction generated by the American Revolution see Gould, 'American independence and Britain's counter-revolution' and Wilson, *The sense of the people*, p. 277
4 Harlow, *The founding of the Second British Empire*, I, p. 4
5 Manning, *British colonial government*, p. 289
6 Fry, *The Dundas despotism*, p. 199
7 Ehrmann, *The younger Pitt*, I, p. 329
8 Mackay, 'Direction and purpose', p. 501
9 Morton, 'The local executive', p. 441
10 Manning, *British colonial government*, p. 392
11 Harlow, 'The new imperial system', p. 142
12 Bayly, *Imperial meridian*, p. 78–81
13 Anon, 'Obituary. Sir Joseph Banks', p. 87
14 Percival, *An account*, pp. 229, 247
15 Bennett, *The concept of empire*, pp. 67–8, Raffles dispatch to Lord Minto, 10 Jun. 1811
16 Maiden, *Sir Joseph Banks*, p. 187
17 *HRNSW*, III, pp. 382–3, * King, 15 May 1798
18 *HRNSW*, VI, p. 90, pp. 86–7
19 PRO, BT 5/17: 58, PC Committee for Trade minutes for 2 Mar. 1807
20 Steven, *Trade, tactics and territory*, pp. 101–5, 128
21 Frost, 'The antipodean exchange'
22 Frost, *Sir Joseph Banks and the transfer of plants*; Frost, *Botany Bay mirages*, pp. 144–58
23 *HRNSW*, II, p. 725, Butler to Southwell, 30 Jan. 1791
24 DTC, 10(2): 96–97, *Paterson, 31 Mar. 1797
25 SL, SS 1: 48, Banks, 'Scheme of plants for Botany Bay', 1798
26 PRO, HO 28/6: 231, *[Nepean], 7 Jun. 1789 (also at SL, G1: 11)
27 DTC, 11: 120–1, *Hunter, 13 Dec. 1798
28 ML, C213, Phillip, 17 Nov. 1788
29 DTC 9: 244–5, P. G. King, 31 Jul. 1795
30 Fry, *The Dundas despotism*, p. 199
31 *HRNSW*, VI, p. 90, Banks, 'Some remarks'. After the discovery of coal in 1797 the Home Secretary, the Duke of Portland, had written to Governor Hunter urging the same trade to the Cape, no doubt at Banks's urging. *HRA*, Ser. 1, II, p. 241, Duke of Portland to Governor Hunter, 4 Jul. 1799
32 Carter, *Sheep and wool correspondence*, p. 415, *Maitland, 31 Mar. 1804
33 Carter, *Sheep and wool correspondence*, p. 509, Marsden, 25 Nov. 1811
34 *HRNSW*, VI, pp. 107–8, Banks, 'Some observations on a bill for admitting the produce of New South Wales to entry at the Customs-house of the United Kingdom', 7 Jul. 1806
35 SL, PR 1: 10–11, *Bathurst, 14 Jun. 1807 and Bathurst, 16 Jun. [1807]; DTC, 17: 90, *Castlereagh, 2 Jan. 1808 and RS, Misc MS, 6: 29, *Castlereagh, 24 Feb. 1808
36 Agnarsdottir, 'Raoageroir' ['Plans for a British annexation'], pp. 57–8; McKay, 'Great Britain and Iceland'
37 BM (NH), BC: 42–3, *Pole (Secretary to the Admiralty), 16 Apr. 1809

38 Hermannsson, 'Sir Joseph Banks and Iceland', p. 30
39 RGSA, MS6.c, 'Notes on Iceland', 2
40 Hermannsson, 'Sir Joseph Banks and Iceland', p. 31, *Stephensen, [1801] (DTC, 12: 167–70)
41 Hermannsson, 'Sir Joseph Banks and Iceland', p. 31, *R. Jenkinson, 30 Dec. 1807
42 DTC, 6: 89–90, * Buache de la Neuville, 20 Nov. 1788
43 Desmond, *Kew*, p. 123
44 DTC, 15: 280, *Creassy, 8 Feb. 1805. On which see Kinnaird, 'Creassy's plan' and Thomas, 'Creassy's plan'
45 SL, P1: 1, Creassy to Sheffield, 8 Nov. 1804
46 Y, Colebrooke, 4 Aug. 1815
47 DTC, 20: 168–69, Raffles, 4 Mar. 1819
48 James, *The rise and fall*, p. 165
49 RS, B: 87, *Blagden, 1 Jan. 1820
50 Lloyd, *The British Empire*, p. 120
51 L. Turner, 'Cape of Good Hope'; Manning, *British colonial government*, pp. 394–405
52 DTC, 18: 45–46, *Kerr, 30 Jun. 1810
53 CL, Melville MSS, 'Considerations on the Subject of a Treaty between Great Britain and Holland relative to their Interests in India'
54 SL, A5: 32, *Glenbervie, 22 Dec. 1800
55 SL, A3: 18, John Bruce (India Office), 2 Dec. 1795 in which he writes 'Mr. Dundas begs his thanks to You, and requests your good offices upon a Subject, respecting which, he wishes to proceed, upon the fullest evidence'. SL, A3: 19–20 is a detailed memorandum on the Cape with Banks's comments in the margin
56 A5: 31, Banks, 'Observations political & Agricultural by a Friend'
57 Hy C, *Aiton, 29 Aug. 1785; Mackay, *In the wake of Cook*, pp. 128–9
58 Drayton, 'Imperial science', p. 98
59 Rutherforth, 'Sir Joseph Banks', p. 168
60 Plumb, 'The discovery of western Africa', p. 172
61 African Association, *Proceedings*, I, p. 7
62   Hallett, *Records*, p. 17
63 SL, A1: 12, Musgrave, 18 Jul. 1788
64 Hallett, *Records*, p. 49; Carter, *Joseph Banks*, p. 242
65 Rutherforth, 'Sir Joseph Banks', p. 205
66 SL, A2: 49, [?Beaufoy], 27 Jun. 1793
67 SL, A5: 23, * Robert Jenkinson, 29 Jun. 1804
68 Farington, *Diary*, VIII: 11
69 SL, A2: 28, *Gilbert, 18 Aug. 1792
70 BL, Add. 38233: 94–5, *Jenkinson, 8 Jun. 1799. It was also possibly sent to the Earl of Chatham, President of the Council, who may have been the 'My Lord' to whom the copy at PRO, CO 2/1: 9 is addressed.
71 Hallett, *Penetration of Africa*, p. 322
72 PRO, CO 2/1: 7, *John Sullivan, 1 Aug. 1802
73 DTC, 15: 140–41, 171, Lord Camden, 28 Sep. 1804, 8 Nov. 1804
74 Ehrman, *The younger Pitt*, I, p. 403
75 DTC, 8: 196–97, *Wilberforce, 8 Apr. 1793
76 SL, A5: 39, Corry, 17 May 1809
77 Gascoigne, *Banks and the English Enlightenment*, pp. 41–55. Consistent with his vaguely Deistic and anticlerical stance Banks was sympathetic to Freemasonry. His interest did not, however, extend to a willingness to accept the post of Grand Master of the Witham Lodge, Lincoln, when offered to him in 1801. He did, however, respond that 'He sincerely wishes that God may preserve the long established Institution', *The New South Wales Freemason*, 1 May 1952, p. 185, *Thorold, 30 Mar. 1801 (I owe this reference to Dr James Franklin)
78 DTC, 16: 267, *Staunton, 7 May 1806
79 UCLA, Webster Coll., Solander, 22 Aug. 1775; Maiden, *Sir Joseph Banks*, p. 52

80 Strauss, 'Sir Joseph Banks', p. 249
81 SL, LMS 1: 3, Haweis, 14 Jun. 1796
82 Gunson, 'Co-operation without paradox', p. 527, Haweis to Dundas, 22 Jul. 1796
83 IO, E1/95: 24, Haweis to EIC, 1796(2)
84 SL, LMS 1: 19, Haweis, 3 Mar. 1800
85 SL, LMS 1: 49, Haweis, 5 Mar. 1799
86 SL, LMS 1: 50, Hardcastle, 7 Mar. 1799
87 BL, Add. 33980: 185, *Haweis, 6 May 1799
88 PRO, CO 201/24: 39, *Sullivan, 24 Jul. 1802
89 PRO, CO 201/24: 101, Haweis to Sullivan, 6 Sep. 1802
90 ATL, Haweis, 30 Jan. 1803
91 PRO, CO 201/79: 162, *[Bathurst], 10 Jul. 1815
92 SL, LMS 1: 16, Bathurst, 12 Jul. 1818
93 ML, MSS 743/3, *[London Missionary Society], 10 Jan. [18]20
94 Nelson, *The Home Office, 1782–1801*, p. 30
95 ML, M5 A3072, Suttor, 'Memoirs', p. 14
96 SL, Wo, 2: 98, Valentia, 4 Sep. 1802
97 Frost, *Matra*, p. 100
98 *ibid.*, p. 113
99 *ibid.*, p. 103
100 YB: OS, Blagden to Mulgrave. 9 Dec. 1796
101 Carter, *Sir Joseph Banks*, pp. 215–16; Frost, *Botany Bay mirages*, pp. 110–43
102 *HRNSW*, I, ii, p. 229
103 Frost, *Botany Bay mirages*, p. 112
104 Clark, *A history of Australia*, I, p. 123
105 DL, MS Q 161: 39, Richards, 29 Jul. 1791, *Richards, 4 Aug. 1791. Richards also
    wrote a series of letters to Pitt on the same subject, PRO, 30/8 (Chatham Papers),
    160: 22–3, Richards to Pitt, 8 Jan. 1791; *ibid.*, 25 Oct. 1792 in which he (quite rightly)
    pointed out the superior conveyance and provisioning of the First Fleet.
106 *HRNSW*, I, ii: 580, * Richards, 31 Dec. 1791
107 DTC, 10 (2): 75–6, *King, 30 Mar. 1797
108 *HRNSW*, III: 532, *Hunter, 1 Feb. 1799
109 Mackay, *In the wake of Cook*, p. 62
110 Haway, *Four letters*, p. 132, Etches, 17 Jul. 1788
111 *ibid.*, p. 130, Etches, 20 Jul. 1788
112 Fitz., Lind, 17 Nov. 1789
113 Dillon, 'Convict colonies', p. 99, Wilson to Lind, 28 Nov. 1789
114 Haway, *Four letters*, p. 139, Etches, 19 May 1792
115 PRO, HO 42/16, *Nepean, 15 Feb. 1790 cited in Mackay, *In the wake of Cook*, p. 87
116 SL, PN 1: 17, Menzies, 4 Apr. 1790 contains his list of suggestions
117 Mackay, *In the wake of Cook*, p. 91
118 On the Nootka Sound Crisis see Norris, 'Policy of the British cabinet' and, from the
    Spanish side, Cook, *Flood tide of empire*, chs 5 and 6
119 Mackay, *In the wake of Cook*, p. 96
120 BL, Add. 33979: 75–78, *Menzies, 22 Feb.1791
121 DTC, 10 (1): 15–16, * Duke of Portland, 3 Feb. 1796
122 Aspinall, *The later correspondence of George III*, p. 591, George III to Lord Pelham,
    7 Aug. 1801
123 ML, Wentworth MSS, A 754/2: 173, D. Considen to Wentworth, 9 Oct. 1804
124 ML, Doc. 1612 (typescript), *Bligh, 15 Mar. 1805
125 *HRNSW*, V: 457–58, *King, 29 Aug. 1804
126 PRO, CO 201/38: 100, *John King, 19 Apr. 1805
127 Carter, *Joseph Banks*, p. 432, *William Kent, 12 Mar. 1806
128 *ibid.*
129 *HRNSW*, VI: 706, *Bligh, 25 Aug. 1808
130 *HRNSW*, V: 461, *Caley, 30 Aug. 1804

131 Woods, ' Lord Bathurst's policy', p. 38
132 Young, *The Colonial Office*, pp. 282–83
133 *ibid.*, pp. 17–18 and McLachlan, 'Bathurst at the Colonial Office', p. 481. See also Beaglehole, 'The Colonial Office'
134 Jenkins, *Henry Goulburn*, p. 70
135 SL, SS 1: 13, *[? Liverpool]
136 ML, Doc. 1967, *Brisbane, [1817+]
137 Y, *Blagden, 24 Feb. 1819
138 ANL, MS 9 (Banks MSS), Goulburn, 4 Feb. 1817 (copy at DTC, 20: 14)
139 Carter, *Joseph Banks*, p. 476
140 SL, BG 1: 48, *Macquarie, Jul. 1818
141 SL, BG 2: 76, Bathurst, 17 Jan. 1820
142 SL, LMS 1: 16, Bathurst, 12 Jul. 1818
143 SL, HB 1: 5, Goulburn, 19 Feb. 1817
144 BL, Add. 37232: 54–55, Lord Camden, 28 Sep. 1804
145 Hallett, *Records*, p. 231
146 DTC, 19: 167–68, Barrow, 29 Jul. 1815
147 LUL, MS 355, *Barrow, 12 Aug. 1815
148 Carter, *Joseph Banks*, p. 502
149 DTC, 20: 51, Goulburn to Barrow, 23 Sep. 1817
150 SL, A5: 99, Goulburn to Everard Home, 17 Dec. 1819
151 Tuckey, *Narrative*, p. xxx
152 SL, A5: 75A, Barrow, 6 Dec. 1815
153 Lloyd, *Mr. Barrow*, p. 114
154 Young, *The Colonial Office*, p. 86
155 quoted, Fara, *Sympathetic attractions*, p. 212
156 McGucken, 'The central organisation'

EPILOGUE

1 Rubinstein, 'The end of "Old Corruption"', p. 66
2 Stafford, *Scientist of empire*, p. 193
3 ie, a change from 16,267 to 22,912. House of Commons, Parliamentary Papers, 1830–1: 7 (no. 92), p. 300, 'Return of the number of persons employed and of the pay or salaries granted to such persons in all public offices or departments ...'
4 Harling, *The waning*, p. 177
5 As early as the end of the eighteenth century, for example, Prussia had about double the number of public servants of Great Britain, Fischer and Lundgreen, 'The recruitment', p. 462
6 Harling, *The waning* and 'Rethinking "Old Corruption"'
7 Miller, 'Joseph Banks, empire and "centers of calculation"', p. 33
8 Ehrman, *The younger Pitt*, III, p. 423
9 Cookson, 'Political arithmetic and war', p. 51
10 Rose, *A brief examination*, p. 39
11 O'Brien, *Power with profit*, p. 33
12 Drayton, 'Imperial science', p. 283
13 Harling, *The waning*, p. 12. State expenditure increased from 7% to 16% of GNP from 1792 to 1873 and reached 37% in 1913. Schremmer, 'Taxation and public finance', p. 356

List of Abbreviations

*	Letter from Banks (name of correspondent without an asterisk or recipient signifies letter to Banks)
ANL	Australian National Library, Canberra
APL	Auckland Public Library
APS	American Philosophical Society
ATL	Alexander Turnbull Library
BAO	Birmingham Assay Office MSS, Boulton Correspondence, Birmingham Central Library
BL, Add.	British Library, Additional MSS
BM(NH)	British Museum of Natural History
BCL	Birmingham Central Library
BUL	Birmingham University Library
CL	William Clements Library, University of Michigan, Ann Arbor
CLL	Central Library, Lincoln
DL	Dixson Library (State Library of New South Wales), Sydney
DNB	*Dictionary of National Biography* eds S. Lee and L. Stephen, 22 vols, Smith Elder and Co., 1908–9
DTC	Dawson Turner Copies, Banks Correspondence (20 vols in 21), Botany Library, British Museum of Natural History
Fitz.	Fitzwilliam Museum, Cambridge, Perceval Collection MS 215
HMC	Historical Manuscripts Commission
HRA	*Historical Records of Australia*
HRNSW	*Historical Records of New South Wales,* ed. F. Bladen, 8 vols, Sydney, 1892–1901
HRO	Herefordshire Record Office, Thomas Andrew Knight Correspondence, Hereford
HyC	Hyde Collection, Sommerville, NJ, USA
IO	India Office
KAO	Kent Archives Office, Canterbury
Kew BC	Royal Botanic Gardens Library, Kew, Banks Correspondence
LAO	Lincolnshire Archives Office, Lincoln
LS	Linnean Society
LUL	London University Library
ML	Mitchell Library (State Library of New South Wales, Sydney)
NLS	National Library of Scotland
NLW	National Library of Wales, John Lloyd Correspondence
NMM	National Maritime Museum, Greenwich
NYPL	New York Public Library
Princeton	Firestone Library, Princeton University (Manuscripts Department)
PRO	Public Records Office
RAS	Royal Astronomical Society
RASB	Royal Asiatic Society of Bengal
RGO	Royal Greenwich Observatory
RGSA	Royal Geographical Society of Australasia (South Australian Branch)
RM	Royal Mint
Roth.	Rothampstead Agricultural Research Station, Hertfordshire

RS   Royal Society
RS, CMO   RS, Council Minutes
SGC   Spalding Gentlemen's Society
SL   Sutro Library, San Francisco
UCLA   Library of University of California at Los Angeles (Manuscripts
            Department)
Well.   Wellcome Institute for the History of Medicine, London
WSRO   West Sussex Records Office
Y   Yale University, Manuscripts and Archives, Banks Correspondence
            (arranged in chronological sequence)
YB: OF   Yale University, Beinecke Rare Book and Manuscript Library, The James
            Marshall and Marie Louise Osborn Collection Files
YB: OS   *ibid.,* Osborn Shelves

Bibliography

MANUSCRIPT SOURCES

The Libraries which hold the MS sources are listed in the List of Abbreviations.

PRINTED SOURCES

(**Note:** Place of publication is London unless otherwise specified)

Abel, C. *Narrative of a journey in the interior of China . . .*, 1818.

African Association *Proceedings of the Association for Promoting the Discovery of the Interior Parts of Africa*, 2 vols, 1790.

Agnarsdottir, A.'Raoageroir um innlimum Islands i Bretaveldi a arunum 1785–1815', *Serprentun ur Sögu, timariti Sögufelagsins*, 17 (1979), 1–58 ['Plans for a British annexation of Iceland, 1785–1815', includes an English summary]

Allan, D. G. C. 'Notions of economic policy expressed by the Society's correspondents and its publications, 1754-1847: (iii) Internationalism, scientific 'improvement' and humanitarianism', *Journal of the Royal Society of Arts*, 107 (1959), 217–9.

—— . 'Society of Arts and government, 1754–1800. Public encouragement of arts, manufactures, and commerce in eighteenth-century England', *Eighteenth Century Studies*, 7 (1973), 434–52.

Alter, P. *The reluctant patron. Science and the state in Britain 1850–1920*, Oxford: Berg, 1987.

Anderson, A. *Narrative of the British embassy to China in the years 1792,1793 and 1794*, 1796.

Anderson, J. *Letters to Sir Joseph Banks . . .on the subject of cochineal insects, discovered at Madras*, Madras, 1788.

Anon. 'Memoir of Sir Joseph Banks', *New Monthly Magazine*, 14 (1820), 185–94.

Anon. 'Obituary. Sir Joseph Banks', *Gentleman's Magazine*, 89 (1820), I, 534, 637–38; II, 86–89.

Anon. 'The Right Honourable Sir Joseph Banks', *Annual Biography and Obituary*, 5 (1821), 97–120.

Archer, M. 'India and natural history: the role of the East India Company 1785–1858', *History Today*, 9 (1959), 736–43.

Aspinall, A. *The later correspondence of George III*, Cambridge: Cambridge University Press, 1966–70, 5 vols.

Atkinson, A. 'State and empire and convict transportation, 1718–1812' in C. Bridge (ed.), *New perspectives in Australian History*, (Occasional Seminar Papers No. 5 of the Sir Robert Menzies Centre for Australian Studies, Institute of Commonwealth Studies, University of London), 1990, pp. 25–38.

—— . 'Whigs and Tories and Botany Bay', *Journal of the Royal Australian Historical Society*, 61 (1975), 289–310.

Aylmer, G. 'From office-holding to civil-service: the genesis of modern bureaucracy', *Transactions of the Royal Historical Society*, fifth series, 30 (1980), 91–108.

Bacon, F. *The new organon and related writings*, F. Anderson (ed.), Indianapolis: Bobbs-Merrill, 1960.

Baker, N. 'Changing attitudes towards government in eighteenth-century Britain' in A. Whiteman, J. S. Bromley and P. G. M. Dickson (eds), *Statesmen, scholars and merchants*, Oxford: Clarendon Press, 1973, pp. 202–219.

Banks, J. 'Communications on spring wheat', *Communications to the Board of Agriculture*, 5(1806), 181–5.

——. 'Instruction given to the Council [=Counsel], against the Wool Bill', *Annals of Agriculture*, 9 (1788), 479–506.

——. 'Proceedings of His Majesty's Most Honourable Privy Council, and information received respecting an insect supposed to infest the wheat of the territories of the United States of America', *Annals of Agriculture*, 11 (1789), 406–613.

——. 'A speech delivered to the Royal Society on Wednesday November 30, 1780, being their anniversary', *Philosophical Transactions of the Royal Society*, 71 (1781), 1–7.

Banks, J. et al. 'First report of the commissioners appointed to consider the subjects of weights and measures', *Annual Reports*, 61 (1819), 315–9.

Barnes, A. *Jean le Clerc (1657–1736) et la République des Lettres*, Paris: Librairie Droz, 1938.

Barnes, D. *History of the English Corn Laws*, Routledge, 1930.

Baron, J. *The life of Edward Jenner*, 1827.

Barrow, J. *Sketches of the Royal Society and the Royal Society Club*, 1849.

Bayly, C. *Imperial meridian. The British Empire and the world, 1780–1830*, Longman, 1989.

Beaglehole, J. C. 'The Colonial Office 1782–1854', *Historical Studies, Australia and New Zealand*, 1 (1941), pp. 170–89.

—— (ed.) *Journals of Captain James Cook on his voyages of discovery*, 3 vols in 4, Cambridge: Cambridge University Press (for the Hakluyt Society), 1955–74.

——. *The Endeavour journal of Joseph Banks 1768–1771*, 2 vols, Sydney: Trustees of the Public Library of New South Wales in association with Angus and Robertson, 1962.

Bell, H. C. 'British commercial policy in the West Indies, 1783–1793', *English Historical Review*, 21 (1916), 429–41.

Bellot, L. *William Knox: the life and thought of an eighteenth-century imperialist*, Austin, Texas: University of Texas Press, 1977.

Bennett, G. (ed.) *The concept of empire. Burke to Atlee 1774–1947*, A. and C. Black, 1953.

Bentham, J. *Introduction to the principles of morals and legislation*, J. H. Burns and H. L. Hart (ed.), Athlone, 1970.

Berman, M. *Social change and scientific organization. The Royal Institution 1799–1844*, Heinemann, 1978.

Bernal, J. D. 'Les rapports scientifiques entre la Grande-Bretagne et la France au XVIIIe siècle', *Revue d'histoire des sciences*, 9 (1956), pp. 289–300.

Betham-Edwards, M. *The autobiography of Arthur Young: with selections from his correspondence*, 1898.

Black, E. C. *The Association, 1769–1793*, Cambridge, Mass.: Harvard University Press, 1963.

Black, J. *British foreign policy in an age of revolutions, 1783–1793*, Cambridge: Cambridge University Press, 1994.

Bladon, F. M. *The diaries of Colonel the Honourable Robert Fulke Greville, equerry to His Majesty King George III*, Bodley Head, 1930.

Blagden, C. 'Report on the best method of proportioning the excise upon spirituous liquors', *Philosophical Transactions*, 80 (1791), 321–2.

Breihan, J. R. 'William Pitt and the commission on fees, 1785–1800', *Historical Journal*, 37 (1984), 59–81.

Brewer, J. *The sinews of power. War, money and the English state, 1688–1783*, Unwin Hyman, 1989.

Brockway, L. *Science and colonial expansion: the role of the Royal Botanic Gardens*, New York: Academic Press, 1979.

Brougham, H. *Lives of the philosophers of the time of George III*, 1855.

Cain, P. J. and Hopkins A. G. 'Gentlemanly capitalism and British expansion overseas, 1: the Old Colonial System, 1688–1850', *Economic History Review*, 2nd ser., 39 (1986), 501–25.

Cameron, H. C. *Sir Joseph Banks*, Sydney: Angus and Robertson, 1966.

Cannon, G. (ed.) *The letters of Sir William Jones*, 2 vols, Oxford: Clarendon Press, 1970.

Cannon, J. *Aristocratic century: the peerage of eighteenth century England*, Cambridge: Cambridge University Press, 1984.

Carter, H. B. *His Majesty's Spanish flock*, Sydney: Angus and Robertson, 1964.

——. 'Joseph Banks as the Father of Australia' in P. Gilbert (ed.), *Banks–Cook portfolio*, Melbourne: Hill House 1990, 23–56.

——. 'Sir Joseph Banks and the plant collection from Kew sent to the Empress Catherine II of Russia 1795', *Bulletin of the British Museum (Natural History) Historical Series*, 4 (1974), 283–385.

——. *Sir Joseph Banks 1743–1820. A guide to biographical and bibliographical sources*, Winchester: St Paul Bibliographies in association with the British Museum (Natural History), 1987.

——. *The sheep and wool correspondence of Sir Joseph Banks 1781–1820*, Sydney: Library Council of New South Wales, 1979.

Cawthorne, J. *An hasty sketch of Mr. Pitt's celebrated administration: most respectfully inscribed to the right honourable Lord Auckland*, 1800.

Chester, N. *The English administrative system 1780–1870*, Oxford: Clarendon Press, 1981.

Christie, I. R. *Wars and revolutions. Britain 1760–1815*, Edward Arnold, 1982.

Clark, C. M. H. *A history of Australia*, Vol. 1, *From the earliest times to the age of Macquarie*, Melbourne: Melbourne University Press, 1962.

Clark, G.'The birth of the Dutch Republic' in L. Sutherland (ed.), *Studies in history*, Oxford: Oxford University Press, pp. 112–144.

Clarke, A. *Narrative of a journey in the interior of China*, 1818.

Close, C. *The early years of the Ordnance Survey*, Newton Abbott: David and Charles, 1969.

Cobbett, W. *Parliamentary history of England*, 36 vols, 1806–20.

Cock, S. *An answer to Lord Sheffield's pamphlet on the subject of the navigation system . . .*, 1804.

Cockcroft, G. *The public life of George Chalmers*, New York: Columbia University Press, 1939.

Cohen, I. B. *Franklin and Newton*, Philadeplphia: American Philosophical Society, 1956.

Coleman, D. C. 'Adam Smith, businessmen, and the mercantile system in England', *History of European Ideas*, 9 (1988), 161–70.

——. *Revisions in mercantilism*, Methuen, 1969.

Colley, L. *Britons. Forging the nation 1707–1837*, New Haven: Yale University Press, 1992.

Connor, R. D. *The weights and measures of England*, HMSO, 1987.

Cook, W. L. *Flood tide of empire. Spain and the Pacific North-west, 1543–1819*, New Haven: Yale University Press, 1973.

Cookson, J.'Political arithmetic and war in Britain, 1793-1815', *War and Society*, 1 (1983), 37–60.

Craig, J. *A history of red tape. An account of the origin and development of the Civil Service*, Macdonald and Evans, 1955.

——. *The Mint. A history of the London Mint from AD 287 to 1948*, Cambridge: Cambridge University Press, 1953.

Crone, C. 'Richard Price and Pitt's Sinking Fund of 1786', *Economic History Review*, second ser., 4 (1952), 243–9.

Crowley, J. 'Neo-mercantalism and the *Wealth of Nations*; British commercial policy after the American Revolution', *Historical Journal*, 33 (1990), 339–60.

——. *The privileges of independence. Neomercantilism and the American Revolution*, Baltimore: Johns Hopkins Press, 1993.

Cust, L. *History of the Society of Dilettanti*, 1898.

Cuvier, G. 'Historical éloge of the late Sir Joseph Banks', *Edinburgh New Philosophical Journal*, 2 (1827), 4.

[Dalrymple, A.] *Thoughts of an old man, of independent mind, though dependent fortune, on the present high price of corn*, 1800.

Daston, L. 'The ideal and reality of the Republic of Letters in the Enlightenment', *Science in Context*, 4 (1991), 367–86.

———— . 'Nationalism and scientific neutrality under Napoleon' in T. Frängsmyr, J. L. Heilbron and R. E. Rider (eds), *The quantifying spirit in the eighteenth century*, Canton, MA: Science History Publications, 1990, pp. 179–206.

Davidson, J. 'England's commercial policy towards her colonies since the Treaty of Paris', *Political Science Quarterly*, 14 (1899), 39–68.

Dawson, W. *The Banks letters. A calendar of the manuscript correspondence of Sir Joseph Banks preserved in the British Museum, the British Museum (Natural History) and other collections in Great Britain*, Trustees of the British Museum, 1958.

De Beer, G. 'The relations between Fellows of the Royal Society and French men of science when France and Britain were at war', *Notes and Records of the Royal Society*, 9 (1951–2), 244–99.

———— . *The sciences were never at war*, Edinburgh: Nelson, 1960.

Desmond, A. *The European discovery of the Indian flora*, Oxford: Oxford University Press, 1992.

———— . *Kew: The history of the Royal Botanic Gardens*, Harvill Press with the Royal Botanic Gardens, Kew, 1995.

———— . 'Transformation of the Royal Gardens at Kew' in R. Banks, B. Elliott, J. Hawkes, D. King-Hele and G. Lucas (eds), *Sir Joseph Banks. A global perspective*, Royal Botanic Gardens, Kew, 1994, pp. 105–16.

Dillon, R. 'Convict colonies for the Pacific Northwest', *The British Columbia Historical Quarterly*, 19 (1955), 93–102.

Dowell, H. 'The word "State"', *Law Quarterly Review*, 39 (1923), 98–125.

Drayton, R. 'Imperial science and a scientific empire: Kew Gardens and the uses of nature, 1772–1903', unpublished PhD thesis, Yale University, 1993.

Duncan, A. *A short account of the life of the Right Honourable Sir Joseph Banks KB, President of the Royal Society of London*, Edinburgh, 1821.

Dupree, A. H. 'Nationalism and science – Sir Joseph Banks and the wars with France' in D. Pinkney and T. Ropp (eds), *A festschrift for Frederick B. Artz*, Durham N. C.: University of North Carolina Press, 1964, pp. 37–51.

———— . *Sir Joseph Banks and the origins of science policy*, Minneapolis: Associates of the James Ford Bell Library, 1984.

Durey, M. 'The radical critique of "Old Corruption" and the beginnings of public service reform in late eighteenth-century Scotland. The Edinburgh Sasine Office as a case study', *Scottish Tradition*, 16 (1990/1), 33–55.

Dyer, G. and Gaspar, P. 'Reform, the new technology and Tower Hill, 1700–1966' in C. E. Challis (ed.), *A new history of the Royal Mint*, Cambridge: Cambridge University Press, 1992, pp. 398–492.

Eastwood, D. ' "Amplifying the province of the legislature": the flow of information and the English state in the nineteenth century', *Historical Research*, 62 (1989), 276–94.

———— . *Governing rural England. Tradition and transformation in local government 1780–1840*, Oxford: Clarendon Press, 1994.

———— . 'Patriotism and the English state in the 1790s' in M. Philp (ed.), *The French Revolution and British popular politics*, Cambridge: Cambridge University Press, 1991, pp. 146–68.

Eden, R. *Journals and corresponence of William, Lord Auckland*, 4 vols, 1860–2.

Edwards, M. *The growth of the British cotton trade*, Manchester: Manchester University Press, 1967.

Ehrman, J. *The British government and commercial negotiations with Europe 1783–1793*, Cambridge: Cambridge University Press, 1962.

———— . *The younger Pitt*, 3 vols, Constable, 1969–96.

Ellis, J. *A description of the mangostan and the breadfruit*, 1775.

'Espinasse, M. 'The decline and fall of Restoration science', *Past and Present*, 14 (1958), 71–89.

Fara, P. *Sympathetic attractions. Magnetic practices, beliefs, and symbolism in eighteenth-century England*, Princeton: Princeton University Press, 1996.

Farington, J. *The Farington diary*, J. Greig (ed.), 7 vols, Hutchinson, 1923–28.

Farnsworth, J. R. 'A history of Revesby Abbey', unpublished PhD thesis, Yale University, 1955.

Fergusson, C. B. 'The colonial policy of the first Earl of Liverpool as President of the Committee for Trade, 1786–1804', unpublished PhD thesis, Oxford University, 1952.

Fieldhouse, D. 'British imperialism in the late eighteenth century' in W. K. Robinson and F. Madden (eds), *Essays in imperial government presented to Margery Perham*, Oxford: Basil Blackwell, 1963, pp. 23–46.

Finer, S. E. 'Patronage and the public service', *Public Administration*, 30 (1952), 329–60.

Fischer, W. and Lundgreen, P. 'The recruitment and training of administrative and technical personnel', in C. Tilly (ed.), *The formation of the nation state*, Princeton: Princeton University Press, 1975, pp. 256–561.

Foord, A. 'The waning of the "Influence of the Crown"', *English Historical Review*, 62 (1947), 484–507.

Forbes, R. J. (ed.) *Martinus Van Marum. Life and work*, Vol. III, Haarlem: H. D. Tjeenk Willink & Zoon, 1971.

Fortescue, J. (ed.) *The correspondence of King George the Third from 1760* ..., 6 vols., Macmillan, 1927–8.

Frost, A. 'The antipodean exchange: European horticulture and imperial designs' in D. Miller and P. Reill (eds), *Visions of empire. Voyages, botany, and representations of nature*, Cambridge: Cambridge University Press, 1996, pp. 58–79.

——— . *Botany Bay mirages. Illusions of Australia's convict beginnings*, Melbourne: Melbourne University Press, 1994.

——— . *Dreams of a Pacific empire. Sir George Young's proposal for a colonization of New South Wales (1784–5)*, Sydney: Resolution Press, 1980.

——— . *Sir Joseph Banks and the transfer of plants to and from the South Pacific 1786-1798*, Melbourne: Colony Press, 1993.

——— . *The precarious life of James Mario Matra voyager with Cook, American loyalist, servant of empire*, Melbourne: Miegunyah Press, 1995.

Fry, H. *Alexander Dalrymple (1737–1808) and the expansion of British trade*, Toronto: University of Toronto Press, 1970.

Fry, M. *The Dundas despotism*, Edinburgh: Edinburgh University Press, 1992.

G ..., J. W. L. *A letter to Sir Humphrey Davy, Bart. on his being elected President of the Royal Society...*, 1821.

Garnier, R. *History of the English landed interest; its customs, laws and agriculture*, 2nd ed., 2 vols, Sonnenschein, 1908.

Gascoigne, J. 'Empire' in I. McCalman (ed.), *The Age of Romanticism and Revolution: An Oxford companion to British culture*, Oxford: Oxford University Press, forthcoming.

——— . *Joseph Banks and the English Enlightenment. Useful knowledge and polite culture*, Cambridge: Cambridge University Press, 1994.

Gay, P. *The Enlightenment*, 2 vols, Wildwood House, 1973.

Gazley, J. G. *Life of Arthur Young, 1741–1820*, Philadelphia: American Philosophical Society, 1973.

Gee, O. 'The British War Office in the later years of the American War of Independence', *Journal of Modern History*, 26 (1954), 123–36.

——— . 'Charles Jenkinson as Secretary at War, with special reference to the period from the general election of September 1789 to the fall of North's administration in March 1782', unpublished B.Litt thesis, Oxford University, 1949.

Gillispie, C. *Science and polity in France at the end of the old regime*, Princeton: Princeton University Press, 1980.

Gilpin, R. *France in the age of the scientific state*, Princeton: Princeton University Press, 1968.

Goldgar, A. *Impolite learning. Conduct and community in the Republic of Letters*, New Haven: Yale University Press, 1995.

Goodman, D. *The Republic of Letters. A cultural history of the French Enlightenment*, Ithaca, NY: Cornell University Press, 1994.

Gould, E. 'American independence and Britain's counter-revolution', *Past and Present*, no. 154 (1997), 107–41.

Graham, G. S. *British policy and Canada 1774–91: A study in eighteenth-century trade policy*, Longmans Green, 1930.

[Gregory, O.] 'A review of some leading points in the official character and proceedings of the late President of the Royal Society', *London and Edinburgh Philosophical Magazine*, 56 (1820), 161–74, 241–57.

Guilding, L. *An account of the Botanic Garden in the Island of St. Vincent, from its first establishment to the present time*, Glasgow, 1825.

Gunson, W. 'Co-operation without paradox: a reply to Dr. Strauss', *Historical Studies*, 11 (1965), 513–34.

Hahn, R. *The anatomy of a scientific institution: The Paris Academy of Sciences, 1666–1803*, Berkeley: University of California Press, 1971.

Halévy, E. *England in 1815*, Ernest Benn, 1961.

Hall, M. B. *All scientists now. The Royal Society in the nineteenth century*, Cambridge: Cambridge University Press, 1984.

Hallett, R. *The penetration of Africa: European enterprise and exploration principally in Northern and Western Africa up to 1830. Vol.1 to 1815*, Routledge & Kegan Paul, 1965.

—— . (ed.) *The records of the African Association 1788–1831*, T. Nelson, 1964.

Hampson, N. *The Enlightenment*, Harmondsworth: Penguin, 1981.

Harling, P. and Mander, P. 'From "fiscal-military" state to laissez-faire state, 1760–1850', *Journal of British Studies*, 32 (1993), 44–70.

Harling, P. 'Rethinking "Old Corruption"', *Past and Present*, no. 147 (1995), 127–58.

—— . *The waning of 'Old Corruption'. The politics of economical reform in Britain, 1779–1846*, Oxford: Clarendon Press, 1996.

Harlow, V. T. *The founding of the Second British Empire, 1763–1793*, 2 vols, Longmans, 1952 and 1964.

—— . 'The new imperial system, 1783–1815' in J. Holland Rose, A. Newton and E. A. Benians (eds), *The Cambridge History of the British Empire*, Vol. 2, *The growth of the new empire 1783–1870*, Cambridge: Cambridge University Press, 1961, pp. 131–88.

Haway, F. 'Four letters from Richard Cadman Etches to Sir Joseph Banks, 1788–92', *British Columbia History Quarterly*, 6 (1942), 125–40.

Heckscher, E. *Mercantilism*, George Allen and Unwin, 2 vols, 1955.

Henderson, W. O. 'The Anglo-French commercial treaty of 1786', *Economic History Review*, 2nd ser., 10 (1957), 104–14.

Hermannsson, H. 'Sir Joseph Banks and Iceland', *Islandica. An annual relating to Iceland and the Fiske Icelandic Collection in Cornell University Library*, 18 (1928).

Heron, R. *Sketch of a plan for the perpetual prevention of dearth and scarcity of provisions in Great Britain and Ireland: in a letter to the Right Honourable Henry Addington*, ?1802.

Hill, C. *Intellectual origins of the English Revolution*, New York: Panther, 1972.

Hiller, J. 'The Newfoundland fisheries issue in Anglo-French treaties, 1713–1904', *Journal of Imperial and Commonwealth History*, 24 (1996), 1–23.

Hindle, B. *The pursuit of science in Revolutionary America 1735–1789*, Chapel Hill: University of North Carolina Press, 1956.

Historical Manuscripts Commission, *Fourteenth Report, Appendix, Part V, Manuscripts of J. B. Fortescue preserved at Dropmore*, vol. II, 1894.

Holroyd, J. B. (Lord Sheffield), *A letter on the Corn Laws: and on the means of obviating the mischiefs and distress, which are rapidly increasing*, 1813.

—— . *Observations on the commerce of the American states*, Dublin, 1784.

—— . *Observations on the manufactures, trade and present state of Ireland*, (3rd edition), 1785.

—— . 'On the trade in wool and woolens, including an exposition of the commercial situation of the British Empire', *Communications to the Board of Agriculture*, 7 (1811), 376–418.

—— . *Remarks on the bill of the last parliament for the amendment of the poor laws . . .*, 1819.

—— . *Remarks on the deficiency of grain . . .*, 1801.

——— . *Strictures on the necessity of inviolably maintaining the navigation and colonial system of Great Britain*, 1804.

Home, E. *The Hunterian Oration in honour of surgery . . .*, 1822.

Hoppit, J. 'Reforming Britain's weights and measures, 1660–1824', *English Historical Review*, 108 (1993), 82–104.

Houghton, W. E. 'The English virtuoso in the seventeenth century', *Journal of the History of Ideas*, 3 (1942), 51–73, 190–219.

Hunter, M. 'The Crown, the public and the new science, 1689–1702', *Notes and Records of the Royal Society*, 43 (1989), 99–116.

——— . *Science and society in Restoration England*, Cambridge: Cambridge University Press, 1981.

Hyam, R. and Martin, G. *Reappraisals in British imperial history*, Macmillan, 1975.

Innes, J. 'Parliament and the shaping of eighteenth-century social policy', *Transactions of the Royal Historical Society*, fifth ser., 40 (1990), 63–92.

James, L. *The rise and fall of the British Empire*, Abacus, 1995.

Jenkins, B. *Henry Goulburn, 1784–1856*, Montreal: McGill, 1996.

Jenkinson, C. *The coins of the realm*, 1805.

——— . *A collection of all the treaties of peace, alliance and commerce between Great Britain and other powers . . .*, 3 vols, 1785.

Jones, J. R. *Country and court. England 1658–1714*, Edward Arnold, 1978.

Judge, A. 'The idea of a mercantile state', *Transactions of the Royal Historical Society*, fourth series, 21 (1939), 41–69.

Jupp, P. 'Landed elite and political authority in Britain c.1760-1850', *Journal of British Studies*, 29 (1990), 53–79.

Keay, J. *The honourable company. A history of the English East India Company*, Harper Collins, 1991.

Keir, D. 'Economical reform, 1779–1787', *The Law Quarterly Review*, 50 (1934), 368–85.

Kippis, A. *A narrative of the voyages round the world performed by Captain James Cook*, 1883.

Kinnaird, L. 'Creassy's plan for seizing Panama, with an introductory account of British designs on Panama', *Hispanic American Historical Review*, 13 (1933), 46–78.

Kolb, W. 'State' in J. Gould and W. Kolb (eds), *A dictionary of the social sciences*, Tavistock, 1964, pp. 690–91.

Kumar, D. *Science and the Raj 1857–1905*, Delhi: Oxford University Press, 1995.

——— . 'The evolution of colonial science in India: natural history and the East India Company' in J. MacKenzie (ed.), *Imperialism and the natural world*, Manchester: Manchester University Press, 1990, pp. 51–66.

Lambert, S. *House of Commons sessional papers of the eighteenth century*. Vol. 75, *George III Corn and Tobacco Trades 1789 and 1790*, Wilmington, Delaware: Scholarly Resources, 1975.

Langford, P. *Polite and commercial people: England 1727–1783*, Oxford: Clarendon Press, 1989.

——— . *Public life and the propertied Englishman, 1689–1790*, Oxford: Clarendon Press, 1991.

Lloyd, C. *Mr. Barrow of the Admiralty. A life of Sir John Barrow 1764–1848*, Collins, 1970.

Lloyd, T. *The British Empire 1558–1983*, Oxford: Oxford University Press, 1984.

Lodge, E. *Portraits of illustrious personages of Great Britain*, 12 vols, 1835.

Lubbock, C. *The Herschel chronicle*, Cambridge: Cambridge University Press, 1933.

Lyons, H. *The Royal Society 1660–1940. A history of its administration under its charters*, Cambridge: Cambridge University Press, 1944.

Lysaght, A. M. *Joseph Banks in Newfoundland and Labrador, 1766: His diary, manuscripts and collections*, Faber and Faber, 1971.

Lyte, C. *Sir Joseph Banks. Eighteenth century explorer, botanist and entrepreneur*, Sydney and Wellington: Reed, 1980.

McClellan, J. *Science reorganized: Scientific societies in the eighteenth century*, New York: Columbia University Press, 1985.

McGucken, W. 'The central organisation of scientific and technical advice in the UK during World War II', *Minerva*, 17 (1979), 33–69.

McKay, D. 'Great Britain and Iceland', *Mariner's Mirror*, 59 (1973), 85–95.

Mackay, D. 'A presiding genius of exploration. Banks, Cook and empire 1767–1805' in R. Fisher and H. Johnson (eds), *Captain James Cook and his times*, Canberra: Australian National University Press, 1979, pp. 21–40.

——. 'Direction and purpose in British imperial policy 1783-1801', *Historical Journal*, 17 (1974), 487–501.

——. *In the wake of Cook. Exploration, science & empire, 1780–1801*, Croom Helm, 1985.

McLachlan, N. 'Bathurst at the Colonial Office, 1812–27', *Historical Studies*, 13 (1967–9), 477–502.

Madden, A. 'The imperial machinery of the Younger Pitt' in H. R. Trevor-Roper (ed.), *Essays in British history presented to Sir Keith Feiling*, Macmillan, 1964, pp.173–94.

with D. Fieldhouse *Select documents in the constitutional history of the British Empire and Commonwealth. Imperial reconstruction 1763–1840*, Westport, Conn.: Greenwood Press, 1987.

Maiden, J. *Sir Joseph Banks: the 'Father of Australia'*, Sydney: W. A. Gullick, London: Kegan Paul, 1909.

Mann, M. *States, war and capitalism. Studies in political sociology*, Oxford: Basil Blackwell, 1988.

Manning, H. *British colonial government after the American Revolution*, New Haven: Yale University Press, 1933.

Marshall, D. *Eighteenth century England*, Longman, 1963.

Marshall, P. 'The first and second British empires', *History*, 44 (1964), 13–23.

——. *Problems of empire 1757–1813*, Allen and Unwin, 1968.

Martin, J. *Francis Bacon, the state, and the reform of natural philosophy*, Cambridge: Cambridge University Press, 1992.

Mathias, P. and O'Brien, 'Taxation in England and France, 1715–1810', *Journal of European Economic History*, 5 (1976), 601–50.

Miller, D. P. 'Joseph Banks, empire, and "centers of calculation" in late Hanoverian London' in D. P. Miller and P. Reill (eds), *Visions of empire. Voyages, botany, and representations of nature*, Cambridge: Cambridge University Press, 1996, pp. 21–37.

——. 'The revival of the physical sciences in Britain, 1815–40', *Osiris*, 2nd ser., 21(1986), 107–34.

——. 'The Royal Society of London 1800–1835: a study in the cultural politics of scientific organization', unpublished PhD thesis, University of Pennsylvania, 1981.

Mitchison, R. 'The old Board of Agriculture (1793–1822)', *English Historical Review*, 74 (1959), 41–69.

Morton, W. 'The local executive in the British Empire, 1763–1828', *English Historical Review*, 78 (1963), 436–57.

Namier, L. and Brooke, J. *The House of Commons 1754–90*, 3 vols, published for the History of Parliament Trust by HMSO, 1964.

Namier, L. *The structure of politics at the accession of George III*, Macmillan, 1957.

Nelson, R. *The Home Office, 1782–1801*, Durham, NC: Duke University Press, 1969.

Norris, J. 'The policy of the British cabinet in the Nootka crisis', *English Historical Review*, 70 (1955), 562–80.

O'Brian, P. *Joseph Banks. A life*, Collins Harvill, 1987.

O'Brien, P. 'The political economy of British taxation, 1660–1815', *Economic History Review*, 41 (1988), 1–32.

——. *Power with profit. The state and the economy, 1688–1815. An inaugural lecture delivered in the University of London*, 1991.

O'Brien, P. and Hunt, P. 'The rise of a fiscal state in England, 1485-1815', *Historical Research*, 66 (1993), 129–76.

O'Gorman, F. *The rise of party in England: The Rockingham Whigs 1760–1782*, Allen and Unwin, 1975.

Pacey, H. *Considerations upon the present state of the wool trade . . . 1781.*

Paine, T. *Rights of man* (H. Collins, ed.), Harmondsworth: Penguin Books, 1969.

Pares, R. *King George III and the politicians*, Oxford: Oxford University Press, 1973.

Parris, H. *Constitutional bureaucracy. The development of British central administration since the eighteenth century*, Allen and Unwin, 1969.

Parry, J. *Trade and dominion. European overseas empires in the eighteenth century*, Cardinal, 1974.

Percival, R. *An account of the Cape of Good Hope . . .*, 1804.

Perkins, J. *Sheep farming in eighteenth and nineteenth century Lincolnshire*, Sleaford: Society for Lincolnshire History and Archaeology, 1977.

Philips, C. H. *The East India Company 1784–1834*, Manchester: Manchester University Press, 1968.

Phipps, C. *A letter from a member of parliament to one of his constituents on the late proceedings of the House of Commons in the Middlesex elections*, 1769.

——— . *A voyage towards the North Pole . . . 1773*, 1774.

Pinkerton, J. *Literary correspondence*, 2 vols, 1830.

Plumb, J. 'The discovery of western Africa' in his *Men and places*, 1963, pp. 169–92.

Poole, R. '"Give us our eleven days!" Calendar reform in eighteenth-century England', *Past and Present*, no. 149 (1995), pp. 95–139.

Porter, R. S. *Gibbon: Making history*, New York: St Martin's, 1988.

Pritchard, E. 'The instructions of the East India Company to Lord Macartney on his embassy to China and his reports to the Company, 1792–94', *Journal of the Royal Asiatic Society of Great Britain and Ireland*, 1938, 201–30, 375–96, 493–509.

Ragatz, L. J. *The fall of the planter class in the British Caribbean 1763–1833*, New York: Octagon, 1963.

Rappaport, R. 'Government patronage of science in eighteenth-century France', *History of Science*, 8 (1969), 119–36.

Rashid, S. 'Economics, economic historians and mercantilism', *Scandanavian Economic History Review*, 28 (1980), 1–14.

Rauschenberg, R. A. 'The journals of Joseph Banks's voyage up Great Britain's West coast to Iceland and to the Orkney Isles July to October, 1772', *Proceedings of the American Philosophical Society*, 117 (1973), 186–226.

Ritcheson, C., *Aftermath of revolution; British policy towards the United States 1783–1795*, Dallas: Southern Methodist University Press, 1969.

Rodgers, N. *The insatiable earl: A life of John Montagu, fourth Earl of Sandwich, 1718–1792*, Harper Collins, 1993.

Rose, G. *A brief examination into the increases of the revenue, commerce, and manufactures, of Great Britain, from 1792 to 1799*, 2nd ed., 1799.

Rossi, P. *Francis Bacon: From magic to science*, Chicago: University of Chicago Press, 1968.

Roy W. 'An account of the trigonometrical operation, whereby the distance between the meridians of the Royal Observatories of Greenwich and Paris has been determined. Read February 25, 1790, *Philosophical Transactions of the Royal Society of London*, 80 (1790), 111–270.

——— . 'An account of the measurement of a base line on Hounslow Heath. Read April 21 to June 16, 1785, *Philosophical Transactions of the Royal Society of London*, 75 (1785), 385–478.

Rubinstein, W. D. 'The end of "Old Corruption" in Britain, 1778–1860' *Past and Present*, 101 (1986), 55–86.

Rutherforth, H. 'Sir Joseph Banks and the exploration of Africa, 1788 to 1820', unpublished PhD thesis, University of California at Berkeley, 1952.

Salomon, J. *Science and politics*, Cambridge, Mass: Harvard University Press, 1973.

Schaeffer, R. 'The entelechies of mercantilism', *Scandanavian Economic Historical Review*, 29 (1981), 81–96.

Schlereth, T. *The cosmopolitan ideal in Enlightenment thought. Its form and functions in the ideas of Franklin, Hume, and Voltaire, 1694–1790*, Notre Dame: University of Notre Dame Press, 1977.

Schremmer, D. 'Taxation and public finance: Britain, France and Germany' in P. Mathias and S. Pollard (eds), *The Cambridge economic history of Europe*, vol. VIII, *The industrial economies: the development of economic and social policies*, Cambridge: Cambridge University Press, 1989, pp. 315–494.

Sinclair, J. *Address to the landed interest, on the corn bill row depending in parliament*, 1791.

———. *Thoughts on the agriculture and financial state of the country: and on the means of rescuing the landed and farming interests from their present depressed state*, 1815.

Smith, A. *Wealth of nations*, Chicago: Encyclopedia Britannica, 1952.

Sprigge, T. *The correspondence of Jeremy Bentham*, Athlone Press, vol. 2, 1968.

Stafford, R. *Scientist of empire. Sir Roderick Murchison, scientific exploration & Victorian imperialism*, Cambridge: Cambridge University Press, 1989.

Stearn, W. 'The bread crisis in Britain, 1795–96', *Economica*, 31 (1964), 168–187.

Steven, M. *Trade, tactics and territory. Britain in the Pacific 1783–1823*, Melbourne: Melbourne University Press, 1983.

Stewart, L. *The rise of public science. Rhetoric, technology, and natural philosophy in Newtonian Britain, 1660–1750*, Cambridge: Cambridge University Press, 1992.

Stone, L. (ed.) *An imperial state at war. Britain from 1689 to 1815*, Routledge, 1994.

Strauss, W. 'Paradoxical co-operation: Sir Joseph Banks and the London Missionary Society', *Historical Studies, Australia and New Zealand*, 2 (1965), 246–52.

Sutherland, L. *The East India Company in eighteenth century politics*, Oxford: Clarendon Press, 1952.

Suttor, G. *Memoirs, historical and scientific, of the Right Honourable Sir Joseph Banks, Bart.*, Parramatta, 1855.

Teichgraeber, R. F. '"Less abused than I had reason to expect": The reception of *The Wealth of Nations* in Britain 1776–90', *Historical Journal*, 30 (1987), 337–66.

Thiselton-Dyer, W. 'Historical account of Kew to 1841', *Bulletin of miscellaneous information, Royal Botanic Gardens, Kew*, 60 (1891), 279–327.

Thomas, M. 'Creassy's plan for seizing Panama', *Hispanic American Historical Review*, 13 (1942), 82–103.

Thorne, R. (ed.) *The House of Commons, 1790–1820*, 5 vols, published for the History of Parliament Trust by HMSO, 1986.

Tilly, C. 'Reflections on the history of European state-making' in C. Tilly (ed.), *The formation of the nation states in Western Europe*, Princeton: Princeton University Press, 1975, pp. 3–83.

Tomlinson, H. 'Financial and administrative developments in England 1660–1688' in J. R. Jones (ed.), *The restored monarchy 1660–1688*, Macmillan, 1979, pp. 94–117.

Torrance, J. 'Social class and bureaucratic innovation: the commissioners for examining the public accounts, 1780–7', *Past and Present*, 78 (1978), 56–81.

Tuckey, J. *Narrative of an expedition to explore the River Zaire, usually called the Congo, in south Africa, in 1816...*, 1818.

Turner, L. 'Cape of Good Hope and the Anglo-French conflict 1797–1806', *Historical Studies, Australia and New Zealand*, 9 (1961), 368–78.

Venturi, F. *Italy and the Enlightenment. Studies in a cosmopolitan century*, Longman, 1972.

Webster, C. *The Great Instauration: Science, medicine and reform, 1626–1660*, Duckworth, 1975.

Weeks, E. 'The chemical contribution of Charles Hatchett', *Journal of Chemical Education*, 15(1938), 153–38.

Weld, C. R. *A history of the Royal Society, with memoirs of the presidents*, 2 vols, 1848.

Westfall, R. S. *Never at rest. A biography of Isaac Newton*, Cambridge: Cambridge University Press, 1983.

Wheatley, H. B. (ed.) *The historical and posthumous memoirs of Sir N. W. Wraxall, 1772–1784*, 5 vols, 1884.

Wickwire, F. 'King's friends, civil servants, or politicians', *American Historical Review*, 71 (1965–6), 18–42.

Widmalm, S. 'Accuracy, rhetoric, and technology: the Parish–Greenwich triangulation, 1784–88', in T. Frängsmyr, J. L. Heilbron and R. E. Rider (eds), *The quantifying spirit in the eighteenth century*, Canton, MA: Science History Publications, 1990, pp.179-206.

Williams, B. *The Whig supremacy 1714–1760*, Oxford: Clarendon Press, 1974.

Williams, G. *The British search for the northwest passage in the eighteenth century*, Longman, 1962.

Willmoth, F. *Sir Jonas Moore. Practical mathematics and Restoration science*, Woodbridge, Suffolk: Boydell, 1993.

Wilson, K. *The sense of the people. Politics, culture and imperialism in England, 1715–85*, Cambrige: Cambridge University Press, 1995.

Wilson, R. 'Newspapers and industry: the export of wool controversy in the 1780s' in M. Harris and A. Lee (eds), *The press in English society from the seventeenth to the nineteenth centuries*, Associated University Press, 1986, pp. 80–104.

Woods, T. 'Lord Bathurst's policy at the Colonial Office 1812–21, with particular reference to New South Wales and the Cape Colony', unpublished PhD thesis, University of Oxford, 1971.

Woodward, E. L. *The age of reform 1815–1870*, Oxford: Clarendon Press, 1958.

Woolf, H. *The transits of Venus: A study of eighteenth-century science*, Princeton: Princeton University Press, 1959.

Young, A. 'On the necessity of county associations of the landed interest', *Annals of Agriculture*, 10 (1788), 402–18.

Young, D. *The Colonial Office in the early nineteenth century*, Longman, 1961.

[Young, W.] *An examination of certain commercial principles, in their application to agriculture and the corn trade, as laid down in the fourth book of Mr. Adam Smith's treatise* . . ., 1800.

Zupko, R. *Revolution in measurement: Western European weights and measures since the age of science*, Philadelphia: American Philosophical Society, 1990.

Index

Lightning Source UK Ltd.
Milton Keynes UK
177711UK00004B/68/P